MW00488283

WAVs, MIDIs, & RealAudio®

WAVs, MIDIs, & RealAudio®

Enjoying Sound on Your Computer

Judi N. Fernandez

IDG Books Worldwide, Inc.

An International Data Group Company

Foster City, CA ■ Chicago, IL ■ Indianapolis, IN ■ New York, NY

WAVs, MIDIs, & RealAudio®

Published by
MIS: Press, an imprint of IDG Books Worldwide, Inc.
An International Data Group Company
919 E. Hillsdale Blvd., Suite 400
Foster City, CA 94404
www.idgbooks.com (IDG Books Worldwide Web site)

Library of Congress Catalog Card Number: 98-88383

ISBN: 0-7645-7507-4

Printed in the United States of America

10 9 8 7 6 5 4 3 2

1P/RQ/RR/ZY/IN

Distributed in the United States by IDG Books Worldwide, Inc.

Distributed by Macmillan Canada for Canada; by Transworld Publishers Limited in the United Kingdom; by IDG Norge Books for Norway; by IDG Sweden Books for Sweden; by Woodslane Pty. Ltd. for Australia; by Woodslane (NZ) Ltd. for New Zealand; by Addison Wesley Longman Singapore Pte Ltd. for Singapore, Malaysia, Thailand, Indonesia, and Korea; by Norma Comunicaciones S.A. for Colombia; by Intersoft for South Africa; by International Thomson Publishing for Germany, Austria, and Switzerland; by Toppan Company Ltd. for Japan; by Distribuidora Cuspide for Argentina; by Livraria Cultura for Brazil; by Ediciencia S.A. for Ecuador; by Ediciones ZETA S.C.R. Ltda. for Peru; by WS Computer Publishing Corporation, Inc., for the Philippines; by Unalis Corporation for Taiwan; by Contemporanea de Ediciones for Venezuela; by Computer Book & Magazine Store for Puerto Rico; by Express Computer Distributors for the Caribbean and West Indies. Authorized Sales Agent: Anthony Rudkin Associates for the Middle East and North Africa.

For general information on IDG Books Worldwide's books in the U.S., please call our Consumer Customer Service department at 800-762-2974. For reseller information, including discounts and premium sales, please call our Reseller Customer Service department at 800-434-3422.

For information on where to purchase IDG Books Worldwide's books outside the U.S., please contact our International Sales department at 650-655-3200 or fax 650-655-3297.

For information on foreign language translations, please contact our Foreign & Subsidiary Rights department at 650-655-3021 or fax 650-655-3281.

For sales inquiries and special prices for bulk quantities, please contact our Sales department at 650-655-3200 or write to the address above.

For information on using IDG Books Worldwide's books in the classroom or for ordering examination copies, please contact our Educational Sales department at 800-434-2086 or fax 317-596-5499.

For press review copies, author interviews, or other publicity information, please contact our Public Relations department at 650-655-3000 or fax 650-655-3299.

For authorization to photocopy items for corporate, personal, or educational use, please contact Copyright Clearance Center, 222 Rosewood Drive, Danvers, MA 01923, or fax 978-750-4470.

 is a trademark under exclusive license to IDG Books Worldwide, Inc., from International Data Group, Inc.

 is a registered trademark of IDG Books Worldwide, Inc.,

ABOUT IDG BOOKS WORLDWIDE

Welcome to the world of IDG Books Worldwide.

IDG Books Worldwide, Inc., is a subsidiary of International Data Group, the world's largest publisher of computer-related information and the leading global provider of information services on information technology. IDG was founded more than 30 years ago by Patrick J. McGovern and now employs more than 9,000 people worldwide. IDG publishes more than 290 computer publications in over 75 countries. More than 90 million people read one or more IDG publications each month.

Launched in 1990, IDG Books Worldwide is today the #1 publisher of best-selling computer books in the United States. We are proud to have received eight awards from the Computer Press Association in recognition of editorial excellence and three from Computer Currents' First Annual Readers' Choice Awards. Our best-selling ...For Dummies® series has more than 50 million copies in print with translations in 31 languages. IDG Books Worldwide, through a joint venture with IDG's Hi-Tech Beijing, became the first U.S. publisher to publish a computer book in the People's Republic of China. In record time, IDG Books Worldwide has become the first choice for millions of readers around the world who want to learn how to better manage their businesses.

Our mission is simple: Every one of our books is designed to bring extra value and skill-building instructions to the reader. Our books are written by experts who understand and care about our readers. The knowledge base of our editorial staff comes from years of experience in publishing, education, and journalism — experience we use to produce books to carry us into the new millennium. In short, we care about books, so we attract the best people. We devote special attention to details such as audience, interior design, use of icons, and illustrations. And because we use an efficient process of authoring, editing, and desktop publishing our books electronically, we can spend more time ensuring superior content and less time on the technicalities of making books.

You can count on our commitment to deliver high-quality books at competitive prices on topics you want to read about. At IDG Books Worldwide, we continue in the IDG tradition of delivering quality for more than 30 years. You'll find no better book on a subject than one from IDG Books Worldwide.

John Kilcullen
Chairman and CEO
IDG Books Worldwide, Inc.

Steven Berkowitz
President and Publisher
IDG Books Worldwide, Inc.

WINNER

*Eighth Annual
Computer Press
Awards ⪰1992*

WINNER

*Ninth Annual
Computer Press
Awards ⪰1993*

WINNER

*Tenth Annual
Computer Press
Awards ⪰1994*

WINNER

*Eleventh Annual
Computer Press
Awards ⪰1995*

IDG is the world's leading IT media, research and exposition company. Founded, in 1964, IDG had 1997 revenues of $2.05 billion and has more than 9,000 employees worldwide. IDG offers the widest range of media options that reach IT buyers in 75 countries representing 95% of worldwide IT spending. IDG's diverse product and services portfolio spans six key areas including print publishing, online publishing, expositions and conferences, market research, education and training, and global marketing services. More than 90 million people read one or more of IDG's 290 magazines and newspapers, including IDG's leading global brands — Computerworld, PC World, Network World, Macworld and the Channel World family of publications. IDG Books Worldwide is one of the fastest-growing computer book publishers in the world, with more than 700 titles in 36 languages. The "...For Dummies®" series alone has more than 50 million copies in print. IDG offers online users the largest network of technology-specific Web sites around the world through IDG.net (http://www.idg.net), which comprises more than 225 targeted Web sites in 55 countries worldwide. International Data Corporation (IDC) is the world's largest provider of information technology data, analysis and consulting, with research centers in over 41 countries and more than 400 research analysts worldwide. IDG World Expo is a leading producer of more than 168 globally branded conferences and expositions in 35 countries including E3 (Electronic Entertainment Expo), Macworld Expo, ComNet, Windows World Expo, ICE (Internet Commerce Expo), Agenda, DEMO, and Spotlight. IDG's training subsidiary, ExecuTrain, is the world's largest computer training company, with more than 230 locations worldwide and 785 training courses. IDG Marketing Services helps industry-leading IT companies build international brand recognition by developing global integrated marketing programs via IDG's print, online and exposition products worldwide. Further information about the company can be found at www.idg.com.   10/8/98

Credits

Acquisitions Editor
Martine Edwards

Development Editors
Carolyn Welch
Tracy Brown

Technical Editor
Peter D. Hipson

Copy Editor
Timothy J. Borek

Project Coordinator
Regina Snyder

Graphics and Production Specialists
Lou Boudreau, J. Tyler Connor,
Angela F. Hunckler, Brent Savage,
Michael Sullivan

Proofreaders
Christine Berman, Kelli Botta,
Michelle Croninger,
Rachel Garvey,
Nancy Price, Rebecca Senninger,
Janet M. Withers

Indexer
Rachel Rice

About the Author

Judi N. Fernandez is one of the most popular and prolific computer book authors today. She has written more than 40 titles, including a nominee for the Best Introductory Computer Book of the Year.

This book is fondly dedicated to a wonderful group of people who love playing with Internet sound, graphics, and scripts, the Newsplay newsgroup. They often served as both inspiration and motivation as I worked on this book. If you're a member of the Microsoft Network, you'll find the Newsplay newsgroup at `msn.forums.survivors.newsplay` *on the* `msnnews.msn.com` *server.*

Preface

WAVs, MIDIs, & RealAudio helps users identify, access, download, upload, and transmit various sound files (WAVs, MIDIs, and AUs, to name a few) on the Internet. This book shows you how you can share sounds with all your friends, whether they have a PC, a Mac, a UNIX machine, a Sun workstation, or some other kind of computer. It tells you what to do with the sounds they send you that your computer doesn't recognize. Especially important for people who like to chat on the Internet, *WAVs, MIDIs, & RealAudio* shows you how to convert Windows WAV files to Macintosh System 7 files and vice versa. You'll also find lots of references to great sound sites on the Web, where you can learn how to download sound files from a Web page and how to identify sound formats by looking at them with a plain text editor such as Windows Notepad.

"WAVs" in the book's title represents any kind of sampled recordings. "MIDIs" in the title refers to files containing instructions for an electronic synthesizer. You'll also learn about two other emerging synthesizer formats — MOD and Karaoke. The book's CD-ROM includes some advanced players so you can build collections of WAVs, MIDIs, and other sound files and play them like CD albums.

The Audience for This Book

This book is for almost anyone who wants to learn more about sound on his computer and on the Internet. I say *almost* because if you are already an audiophile searching for advanced technical details, this is not the book for you. But if you're wondering why you can't hear the chat room sounds on AOL, or why MIDIs sound better on your friend's computer than on yours, or how to record your own sounds, this is definitely the book for you.

How This Book Is Organized

Each chapter begins with a detailed list of the topics covered, giving you a chance to decide quickly whether you need to read that chapter.

Chapters 1 through 3 explain the differences between WAV and MIDI sound formats and why you can't convert one to the other. Other sampled sound formats you learn about are Macintosh System 7 snd resources, SND, AU, AIFF, MP3, and even a few less common ones.

If you use Windows 95 or 98, **Chapter 4** is stuffed with information on how to use sounds with your system. You learn all about Windows sound events, where you can find them, and how you can change them. You learn to use sound schemes and Microsoft Plus! themes. You even learn how create your own sound events.

Have you ever noticed that speaker icon in your system tray? That's your Windows Volume Control, and Chapter 4 shows you how to use it. It even shows you how to get rid of it to free up some room in your system tray. You also learn other ways to configure your sound devices.

No, I haven't left out Macintosh users. **Chapter 5** is the Mac version of Chapter 4. Here you learn how to select an alert sound, create your own alert sounds, and set up and use talking alerts. You see how to select sound devices and control their volume. If you have installed PlainTalk, you see how to make SimpleText read documents out loud, as well as how to record and play back voice annotations in SimpleText documents. Chapter 5 also shows you how to access and change a program's sound resources. (You too can have spooky Halloween sounds on AOL.) And last but not least, you learn what sound suitcases are and how to create and manage them.

Speaking of America Online (AOL), **Chapter 6** shows you how to use sounds with each of the major online services—AOL, CompuServe, The Microsoft Network (MSN), and mIRC (even though it's not an online service). You see how to change their basic event sounds such as the welcome and new mail sounds. Then you learn how to play and exchange sounds while chatting—including using PowerTools on AOL and WaVGeT on mIRC. And because you'll be needing a lot more sounds, the chapter shows you how to find and use their sound libraries.

The third type of audio mentioned in the title, "RealAudio," refers to streaming sound, whether stored in files or broadcast live. **Chapter 7** explains RealAudio plus several other popular streaming applications, such as Macromedia Shockwave, Xing StreamWorks, and Microsoft NetShow. The book's CD-ROM includes a variety of browser plug-ins and standalone players so you can listen to and enjoy all these sound formats, on the Internet or offline.

Speaking of plug-ins, you learn the difference between plug-in and helper applications in **Chapter 8**. You find out which plug-ins and helper applications you have installed, how to select the ones you actually want to use, and how to get rid of the others. All the major audio plug-ins are reviewed in the chapter, and many of them are included on the book's disk.

Did you ever browse to a MIDI Web site and want to save some of its music for offline listening? **Chapter 9** shows you how to capture music and other sounds from the Internet—Web sites, FTP sites, and newsgroups. You learn how to download sounds with both Netscape Navigator and Microsoft Internet Explorer. For newsgroups, you see how to use Netscape's newsreader, CompuServe's newsreader, and Microsoft Outlook Express. Chapter 9 also explains how to upload sounds to newsgroups, one way of sharing your favorite sound files with your friends.

Another way to share sounds with your friends is e-mail. **Chapter 10** describes how to send and receive sound files in e-mail. Several popular mailers are covered: America Online, CompuServe, Outlook Express, and Netscape. For the last two, you also see how to embed sound in a letter so that it plays as soon as someone opens the letter, as well as how to extract an embedded sound from a letter.

In **Chapters 11 and 12**, you learn how to record and edit your own sound files. I have included a couple of editors on the book's CD-ROM, one for Mac OS and one for Windows. These two chapters show you how to use the editors. And because you may want to add your new recordings to your own Web site, **Appendix D** explains how to do that.

I've mentioned a few of the programs included on the book's CD-ROM. In all, there are more than 20 audio-related programs on the CD-ROM. Most of them are useful, but a few are included just for fun. You find the complete list in **Appendix A**.

In **Appendix B** you find two tables showing 128 instruments of the General MIDI patch map and 48 percussion instruments of the General MIDI percussion key map. Chapter 3 explains these tables.

I have coached many beginning PC users who didn't know that they could listen to audio CDs on their computers. I couldn't write a book on computer sound without spending a chapter on how to play and control audio CDs. **Appendix C** shows you how to use the players that come with Windows and Mac OS.

Conventions Used in This Book

To help you identify recommended, noteworthy, or cautionary text, look for the following margin icons:

Tip

The Tip icon offers basic tips and recommended settings to save you time and help you work more efficiently.

Note

The Note icon indicates a special point or offers supplementary information that is not crucial for understanding the concepts covered in the book.

 Caution

The Caution icon signals things or procedures you need to know to discourage you from "messing up" your system.

The following formatting conventions are used throughout the book:

Menu commands are shown in chronological order by using this command arrow: File ➪ Open.

URLs and code appear in monospace font.

Who I Am and How to Reach Me

When I was in college, my dorm mates hung a sign on my door that said, "Judi is in love with an IBM 650 with curly blond control wires and baby blue panel lights." It was true. My love affair with computers and technology continues unabated. Nowadays, I'm in love with, first and foremost, my husband Paul, whom I met in an online chat room. He shares my love of computers, and since you can never completely catch up with all there is to know about computers and "cyberia," I'm sure we'll have plenty to talk about and to work towards for the rest of our days.

When I entered the world of computers, I quickly discovered that my niche was writing manuals, online help, self-study guides, multimedia courses, and other learning materials to help people use these wonderful tools. I have now published more than 40 how-to books like this one. Some have won awards for technical communication; a few have even hit the computer best-seller list — which isn't the same as *The New York Times* best-seller list, but it makes me (and my publisher) happy. My specialty is explaining complex topics in language that my 12-year-old daughter can understand. (She's a grown-up now, and a computer professional herself, but I still try to explain things to that 12-year-old she used to be.)

By the way, that sign was hung on my door in 1959, when I was 18 years old. I first fell in love with computers when I was 16 and took a programming course at IBM. I've been working with and studying computers ever since. I used to claim that I was the first teenage computer nerd, but I recently received a letter from a reader who started working with computer-operated radar systems right after World War II, when he was 19 years old. I'm not sure that counts as a computer nerd by today's standards, but I'll change my claim to this: I believe I was the first *high school* computer nerd. If you know of a high school teenager who fell in love with and started working with computers earlier than 1957, please let me know. I'll be glad to revise my claim once again.

My Web site

I maintain a Web site just for my readers. You'll find it at http://members.aol.com/jnfbooks. It includes a page for each of my books, with corrections and errata if necessary (sigh), color versions of some of the images in this book, additional information on certain topics, Internet links, and any other information I find useful. The pages grow as I hear from my readers, so be sure to check it often.

My e-mail address

Just because we haven't met doesn't mean I don't want to hear from you. I'm on America Online much of the time as *JudiNorth*. If you're on AOL, too, and want to say hi or ask a question, please feel free to send me an Instant Message (IM). I've become good friends with some readers who caught up with me that way. But if you can't catch me online, write me. I love getting letters from my readers! My Internet address is judinorth@aol.com.

Acknowledgments

So many people helped me write this book, it's impossible to thank them all individually. But I would like to say thank you to my family and all my friends who provided so much support. They put up with me and encouraged me even when I didn't have the time or energy to be a good wife, mother, sister, friend, and online buddy. There are times when I wish I were a poet instead of a technical writer, so I could put into words how much I appreciate their love and friendship.

I also want to thank several people who contributed directly to this book. Peter D. Hipson reviewed the entire manuscript and provided many witty and wise technical comments and corrections. Gus Hallgren made some extremely helpful suggestions for the sections on Outlook Express. But most of all, I'd like to thank Carolyn Welch, my development editor, for all her editorial accomplishments, organization, encouragement, prodding, understanding, and laughter.

Contents at a Glance

Contents

Chapter 1

Sound and Your Computer

If you've ever taken an introductory physics course, you've learned that sounds travels through the air in waves. You may even have debated the age-old conundrum, "If a tree falls in the forest . . . ." But just to make sure we're all speaking the same language, this chapter begins by describing the elementary characteristics of sound. Most of the chapter, however, deals with sound in personal computers and on the Internet.

What you'll learn:

- Some basic sound concepts: what it is and how we measure it

- How to digitize sound for computers and the Internet

- How to encode files using some popular audio codecs: PCM, MACE, ADPCM, μ-law, A-law, TrueSpeech, and MPEG

- What audio hardware and software you need to play and record sound on your computer

A Few Sound Concepts

Sound happens when some motion disturbs the air to create waves of compressed air that spread outward like ripples in a pond (see Figure 1-1). The source of sound is always a vibrating object, such as vocal chords, a musical instrument, or an audio speaker membrane. Figure 1-1 shows just a few waves, but in reality the waves are generated as fast as the source vibrates, so the horn in the drawing is likely to be producing hundreds or thousands of waves per second, depending on what note it is playing. The waves radiate outward from the source until they strike our eardrums and make them vibrate. The vibrations are converted by the structure of the ear into signals that our brains interpret as sound.

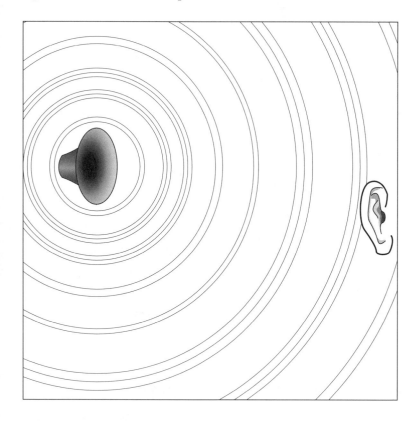

Figure 1-1 *Sound ripples outward from a source as waves of air.*

The characteristics of a sound are determined by the amplitude, frequency, and shape of the waves. Figure 1-2 shows what the cross-section of three different sound waves might look like. Each drawing represents one hundredth of a second. That's a short period of time; if you could hear these waves played by themselves, each would sound like a tiny blip.

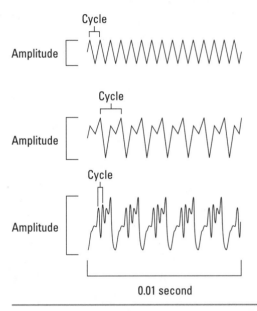

Figure 1-2 *Sound waves are characterized by amplitude, frequency, and shape.*

Amplitude refers to the height of the waves, which determine their volume. The higher a wave is, the louder it sounds. In Figure 1-2, the top wave is soft, the middle one is a little louder, and the bottom is quite a bit louder in general, although it has some soft moments.

Frequency refers to how close together the waves are, measured in *hertz* (Hz). One hertz is one cycle per second. A cycle goes from a peak to a valley and up to the next peak. In Figure 1-2, I have marked one cycle in each wave. High-frequency waves are close together and produce high-pitched sounds. Low-frequency waves are further apart, producing low-pitched sounds. The top wave in Figure 1-2 represents a moderately high tone—you can see 14 cycles in one hundredth of a second, so the frequency is 1,400 Hz or 1.4 *kilohertz* (kHz). The middle is a lower note. You can see only seven cycles in one hundredth of a second, so the frequency is 700 Hz. The bottom wave varies in frequency because it is not a simple note but a recording of me singing. (Don't worry, you don't have to listen to it.)

Note

The hertz is named after German physicist Heinrich Rudolf Hertz, who first described the properties of electromagnetic waves.

The air is filled with waves that you can't hear because they are not in the audible frequency range. Young human ears respond to waves from about 20 to 20,000 Hz. But as you get older, your lose the ability to hear the extreme frequencies, especially the high frequencies.

The *shape* of the wave determines the quality or *timbre* of the sound. In Figure 1-2, the top wave has a simple and regular shape. It would be a pure but relatively uninteresting tone, perhaps produced by a tuning fork or an electronic oscillator. The middle wave has more character, with a few peaks and valleys within the cycle. It might be produced by a flute or chime. The bottom wave demonstrates the highly complex and colorful timbre of the human voice in full song.

The shape of the wave, and thus the timbre it produces, are influenced by *harmonics*—the overtones that accompany a root tone. When someone blows the note A on clarinet, it's the harmonics added to the note by the material and shape of the instrument that tells us its a clarinet, not a flute or a saxophone. Each instrument has its own pattern of harmonics. In the middle wave in Figure 1-2, that slight dip near the peak of each cycle is caused by a simple harmonic added to the root tone. The bottom wave is full of harmonics pulling the wave into interesting little nooks and crannies. Harmonics is a fascinating study where not all the answers are known, as you'll see in Chapter 3, where we talk about synthesizing musical instruments on your computer.

Digitizing Sound

When we use a microphone to record sound, the microphone converts the sound waves into an electromagnetic waveform much like those illustrated in Figure 1-2. We use the term *analog* to describe this type of signal because it continuously varies. In an analog recording system, the signal is processed, stored, and played back in analog form. The most common analog recording media for sound are phonograph records and audiotape.

. The pros and cons of analog recordings are argued endlessly by audiophiles, but for our purposes in this book, one disadvantage outweighs everything else. Today's personal computers are *digital* devices. They process and store numeric data only. Everything that you input to a personal computer — including text, images, and sound — must be converted into digital form. Everything you transmit or receive via the Internet must be digital. Your computer cannot process analog waveforms, nor can they be transmitted on the Internet.

Sampling

We convert analog sound waves into digital data by a process called *sampling*, illustrated in Figure 1-3. The wave in Figure 1-3 is from the same sound clip as the bottom wave in Figure 1-2, but this time I spread it out to .001 second (a thousandth of a second) so you could clearly see the samples. Each dot represents a point where the wave was measured and a number recorded. The number scale on the right side shows the numbering system that was used, from -128 to 127. I marked a few numbers in the wave to show you how they are generated. The scale along the bottom identifies the frequency of the samples. You can see 22 samples in the drawing.

The result of sampling is a series of numbers. The wave in Figure 1-3, for example, yields the numbers -70, -70, -70, -65, -54, -40, and so on. Now we have data that a digital computer can sink its teeth into. It could be stored in a file, copied to a disk, e-mailed to our friends, and posted on a Web page. And eventually, it could be turned back into an analog waveform again. When we play back the recording, the player uses the sampled numbers to re-create the original waveform — more or less, as you'll see in the next section.

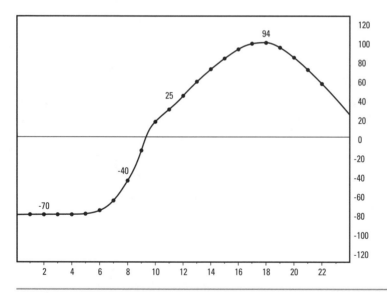

Figure 1-3 *Analog waveforms are digitized by sampling the waveform at regular intervals.*

Sampling rate

Two factors control how well the digital data reproduces the original analog waveform: the sampling rate and the sample size. The *sampling rate* describes the number of samples that are taken per second, expressed in kilohertz (kHz). The example in Figure 1-3 uses a sampling rate of 22,050 samples per second. The higher the sampling rate, the closer we approximate the original waveform. Compare the wave in Figure 1-3 to the one in Figure 1-4. Both were taken from the same original waveform, but the wave in Figure 1-4 was sampled at only 4 kHz, producing only a rough similarity to the original wave. The most common sampling rates used today are 8, 11.025, 22.050, and 44.1 kHz. The lowest rate of 8 kHz should be used for speech only. Audio CDs are recorded at 44.1 kHz, with superb results.

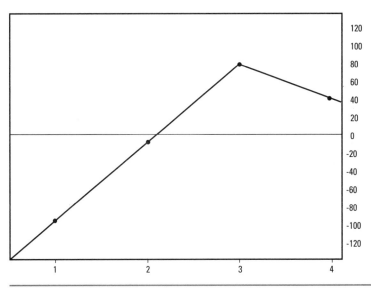

Figure 1-4 *Slower sampling rates produce significantly lower-quality sound.*

Note

For convenience throughout this book, I round off the sampling rates to 11, 22, and 44 kHz.

When talking about sound samples, the term *bandwidth* refers to the range of frequencies of the recording. You could say that the human bandwidth is 19,980 Hz, since we could hear from about 20

Hz to about 20,000 Hz when we were young. But we usually ignore the low end of the range and simply say that the bandwidth is 20 kHz. Similarly, if a recording includes frequencies up to 10 kHz, its bandwidth is 10 kHz. An important rule called the *Nyquist Theorem* says that a sound clip's sampling rate must be twice its bandwidth. Or, to put it backwards, the bandwidth of a recording will be half the sampling rate you used. Thus, to adequately sample a clip with a 10 kHz bandwidth, you need a sampling rate of at least 20 kHz. Plain old telephone service provides a bandwidth of about 3.5 kHz, so a sampling rate of 8 kHz is more than adequate for a telephone-quality recording. A sampling rate of 44 kHz easily covers the entire human bandwidth of 20 kHz.

Note

The term *bandwidth* is bandied about a lot on the Internet. Most often, you'll hear it used to express connection speeds in *kilobits per second* (Kbps). Don't confuse that with sampling bandwidth, which is expressed in *kilohertz*.

Sample size

The *sample size* describes the numeric accuracy of each sample. The sound clip in Figure 1-2 uses a scale from -128 to 127. But since analog waveforms are continuous, many sampled values actually fall between two numbers. For example, a sample value may be part way between 2 and 3. We have to round the value either up to 3 or down to 2. This introduces a *quantization error* into the data that results in noise (an audible hiss) when the sampled recording is played back.

Suppose instead that we use a scale from -32,768 to 32,767. Fewer samples will fall between the numbers on our scale. And when they do, the quantization errors are smaller and result in less noise. The general rule of thumb is, larger sample sizes produce less noise and more accurate sound.

Note

Sample size is also known as *bit depth* or *sample resolution*.

Why do we use such strange ranges of numbers? Why not use -200 to 199 or -10,000 to 9,999? The answer lies in the way that computers represent numbers. Because computers have to represent numbers with electrical voltages, and switches, and magnetic spots, they use the binary number system to represent values. A binary digit, known as a bit, can have only two values, 0 or 1. We have to combine bits into bytes to be able to represent meaningful data. In a personal computer, eight bits make a byte, which is capable of storing 256 values, from 0 to 255 for unsigned numbers or from -128 to 127 for signed numbers. Some audio clips use an 8-bit sample size, resulting in a low-quality recording. It's fine for speech, but music sounds pretty bad. Higher quality recordings use 12 or 16 bits to reduce the amount of noise and more accurately represent the waveform. With 16 bits, you can represent 65,535 values, -32,768 to 32,767 for signed numbers, which is more than adequate for CD-quality sound.

The sample size also determines the *dynamic range* of the recording—the range of volume from the softest to the loudest sound. Each bit that you add to the sample size adds 6 decibels (dB) to the dynamic range, which effectively doubles the dynamic range. Sixteen-bit samples allow a dynamic range of 96 dB, which is just about the dynamic range of the human ear. By comparison, audio-tape achieves a dynamic range of only 65 dB.

So we just use a 44 kHz sampling rate and a 16-bit sample size for fantastic recordings. Right? Well yes . . . but. Consider a three-minute song. That's 180 seconds times 44,100 samples per second times 2 bytes per sample equals 15,876,000 bytes! Do you want to download a 15MB file just to hear your nephew sing "Old MacDonald"? Neither do I. The highest-quality sampling rate and sample size are perfect for recording audio CDs. But for files that we share over the Internet, we have to find a trade-off that produces reasonable file sizes with acceptable—not perfect—quality. Most often, we record at 11 or 22 kHz with an 8-bit sample size for speech and a 12-bit or 16-bit sample size for music.

Channels

My calculations for that three-minute, 15MB song assume that it is a monaural (mono) recording. If it's recorded in stereo, as most audio CDs are, it takes up 30MB. Stereo requires two recorded channels — one for the left track and one for the right — so a stereo recording is twice as large as a mono recording.

Some recordings have more than two channels. 3D sound, for example, uses four channels: front left and right, and rear left and right. Surround Sound uses six channels. Other forms of spatial sound use anywhere from three to 16 channels — used mostly in games and simlations. Just think how much RAM and disk space you'd need to record 16 channels!

Using Audio Codecs to Encode Files

A software module that encodes and decodes audio data is known as a *codec*, for *co*der/*dec*oder. In other words, it does the sampling when you record an audio file, and interprets the samples when you play back the file. Sound recorders such as Windows Sound Recorder or Macintosh Sound Manager make use of a variety of codecs so you can choose the sampling rate, sample size, and number of channels you want.

Many codecs also compress the sampled data to keep file sizes as small as possible. Compression reduces a file's size by removing unnecessary data. Compression methodologies fall into two general categories: lossless and lossy. A *lossless* compression method removes data in such a way that it can be restored completely by decompression. Lossless techniques are crucial for compressing text files, drawings, databases, and other documents where missing data damages the document. Programs such as PKZip and StuffIt provide lossless compression.

But lossless compression is not nearly as effective as *lossy* compression techniques, in which some data is permanently lost. Sound clips, videos, and photographs lose some quality when data is permanently removed, but they are still usable. The trick is to lose the least noticeable data, and that's what audio codecs strive to do.

Pulse Code Modulation

Pulse Code Modulation (PCM) is the simplest codec, as it just samples the sound at whatever rate, size, and number of channels you specify. It does not attempt to compress the sampled data. It's the most commonly used codec, especially in Windows systems, even though it offers no compression.

ADPCM

When encoding human speech, *Adaptive Differential PCM* (ADPCM) manages to get near 16-bit accuracy using only 4-bit samples by storing not the samples themselves but the differences from one sample to the next. Rather than store -70, -70, -70, -65, for example, it stores -70, 0, 0, 5. To keep the numbers small, it also takes advantage of the fact that human speech waveforms are highly predictable. After sampling the beginning of a section, ADPCM can predict what the next samples will be. This isn't quite the same as when your mother finishes your sentences for you — ADPCM works at the microsecond level. Take a look at the bottom waveform in Figure 1-2 and you can see how repetitive the human voice is at that level. The inaccuracy of the predictions introduce distortion in the higher frequencies of the recording. The higher the sampling rate, the less distortion you get. At 11 kHz, for example, distortion is noticeable, but at 44 kHz it almost disappears.

Since it can reduce a 12-bit or 16-bit sample size to four bits, ADPCM codecs reduce a file's size to one third to one fourth compared to PCM encoding. But it works only on files consisting of human speech. Music is much more unpredictable, and ADPCM shows no noticeable savings and a considerable reduction in quality when applied to music clips.

μ-law and A-law

μ-law encoding was originally developed for telephone systems, but it is popular for Internet audio. It reduces 16-bit samples to 8-bit samples, yielding 50 percent compression. A variation of *μ*-law called A-law is popular in Europe, where it was developed for European telephone systems.

Note

> The Greek letter μ is pronounced "mu," and you will often see *μ*-law written as mu-law or u-law in situations where printing a *μ* is difficult or impossible.

μ-law uses a method called *companding* (*com*pressing/ex*panding*) to get 16-bit accuracy in eight bits, thus saving 50 percent of the file size. Companding uses a logarithmic sampling scale instead of the usual linear scale. Figure 1-5 shows how this works. Notice that the numbers are close together near the zero point, where the volume is soft, and farther apart at the extremes, where the volume is loud. The widely spaced numbers introduce more noise than the closely spaced numbers, but you won't hear it because of the loudness of the sound.

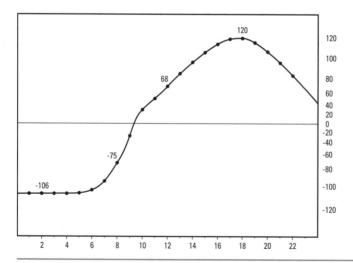

Figure 1-5 μ-*law's companding technique spaces the sampling scale to allow noise at volume extremes, where you won't hear it.*

MACE

The *Macintosh Audio Compression and Expansion* (MACE) codec was developed by Apple specifically for Macintosh. It supports an 8-bit sample size only, and you can select either 3:1 or 6:1 compression. That is, you can compress the file to one third or one sixth of its PCM size. As with all lossy compression techniques, some sound quality is lost by the compression/decompression process. As you might expect, you lose more fidelity with 6:1 compression than with 3:1 compression. The 6:1 compression ratio, which cuts the sampling rate in half to double the compression ratio, is recommended for speech only.

TrueSpeech

TrueSpeech was developed by DSP Group, Inc., for its telephony applications. But since Windows 95, 98, and NT include the TrueSpeech codec with Sound Recorder and Media Player, it is being used to compress many types of speech-only files. It achieves a whopping 93 percent compression, so it reduces a 15MB file to just 1MB. That's considerably more compression than ADPCM or μ-law can achieve.

TrueSpeech takes a completely different approach to recording sound data. It does not record sound samples, but analyzes the vocal characteristics of the talker and records information on how to recreate what was said and how it was said. This takes significantly less space than recording sound samples, but the quality suffers.

MPEG

The Motion Picture Experts Group (MPEG) was commissioned to develop video compression standards, but since video includes audio, they ended up developing audio compression standards, too. MPEG so far has created three general standards, known as MPEG-1, MPEG-2, and MPEG-3. (A fourth is on the way.) MPEG-1 defines three audio standards known as Layer 1, 2, and 3, representing increasing levels of compression (and also complexity). The MPEG-1 Layer 3 standard provides the highest compression and audio quality available on the Internet, but at a cost that some users aren't able to pay — encoding a file takes so much computation that many personal computers simply can't handle the job. But if all you want to do is listen to MPEG-encoded files, not encode them yourself, your computer should be able to handle the decoding, which isn't nearly as difficult.

MPEG examined much psychological research in acoustics — known as psychoacoustics — to determine which parts of a sampled sound are most important to human hearing, and which parts can be thrown away. But the answers weren't conclusive, and MPEG made its final decisions by simply trying out different techniques. The results are impressive.

The MPEG codec works by taking a second look at the problem of quantization noise. As I said earlier, you need larger sample sizes to avoid noise from the encoding process. But psychoacoustics reveals that louder tones mask nearby softer tones. In other words, if you play a loud note at 440 Hz and a softer note at 445 Hz, the human ear hears only the 440 Hz tone. MPEG takes advantage of this fact to permit noise where it will be masked by legitimate sounds. It turns out that a large proportion of an audio file can have its sample size reduced with little or no audible effect. And as you know, reducing the sample size produces less data and results in smaller files.

Your Sound Hardware and Software

If you read the Introduction, you know that this book is not about hardware. But you should be aware of what hardware you need to record and play back sound on your computer. Without getting into a lot of details, brand names, and specifications, I'll just briefly overview the bare minimum. Most of these items are built into a

Macintosh, although they can be supplemented or replaced with higher-quality ones. If you have a PC, these may have been installed at the factory, or you may need to buy and install them yourself.

- A sound board, the newer the better. The capabilities of your sound board determine how mch you can do in recording and playing back. If you have an older 8-bit sound board, for example, you won't be able to record 16-bit files, and you can only play back 16-bit files with 8 bits.

- An onboard synthesizer for playing MIDI, MOD, and karaoke files. It's probably on your sound board, but it might be directly on your motherboard.

- A CD-ROM drive if you want to play and record from audio CDs. If you want to record your own audio CDs, you need a CD-R or CD-RW (CD rewritable) drive.

- Speakers or headphones. Speakers may either be built into your monitor, or plugged into your sound board. If you have a PC, the tinny little speaker that beeps when you start up is not good enough. Many CD-ROM drives include a headphone jack.

- A microphone for recording voice messages. You don't need a microphone to record from your CD player, though.

In terms of software, you need at least one recorder and enough players to handle the various types of sounds you want to play, such as sampled sounds, MIDIs, and audio CDs. You may already have several recorders and players. Windows comes with Sound Recorder, CD Player, and Media Player. Macintosh includes Sound Manager, which both records and plays back. It's built into System 7.5.3 and higher, and can be added as an extension to earlier versions of Mac OS. Macintosh OS 7 and higher also includes AppleCD Audio Player.

Your sound board might also come with its own software, including a recorder and one or more players. Be sure to check any disks that came with the player to see what software they contain. If your sound board was installed at the factory, look for a folder on your hard drive that contains its files.

If you plan to do any serious recording, you'll also need a sound editor. Windows Sound Recorder can do some basic editing tasks. Macintosh Sound Manager's recorder does not. In either case, you'll probably want to get a better sound editor.

Now here's the good news. You're holding a great collection of recorders, players, and editors in your hand right now. The CD-ROM at the back of this book includes some of my favorite audio software for Windows and Macintosh. And the rest of this book shows you, chapter by chapter, how to use them. I hope you'll install them and try them out as you read the chapters that describe them.

What's Next?

Chapter 2 explores the popular audio file formats for storing sampled sounds on the Internet: WAV, SND, AU, and several other formats.

Chapter 2

WAVs and Other Sampled Sound Files

Have you ever sent your buddies a favorite sound file only to find that they couldn't play it on their computers? Have you ever downloaded a sound file that your computer couldn't play? Windows, Mac OS, and UNIX all speak different languages when it comes to sound. A Macintosh can't play a Windows WAV file; Windows can't play a Mac SND file; and neither of them can handle a UNIX AU file. Not to mention the Internet flavor of the month, MP3 files, which only the newer operating systems recognize. This chapter explains all of these sound files, along with a few others that you'll bump into on the Net. It also introduces software to play all the popular types, including MP3, and to convert them to formats your buddies can use.

What you'll learn:

- What we mean by the term *file format*
- What these file formats are and how they differ: WAV, RIFF, Macintosh SND, AIFF, AIFC, AU (and NeXT SND), MP3, plus a few others
- How to use Windows Media Player to play sounds
- How to use DirectShow (ActiveMovie) to play sounds
- How to use Jet-Audio for Windows to play sounds
- How to use SoundApp for Macintosh to play and convert sounds

17

Understanding Audio File Formats

You can't just dump audio information helter-skelter into a file and expect various playback programs to be able to correctly interpret it. It must be *formatted* in a way that players know how to read it. Each audio file format represents one specific layout that computer programs use to read and write audio information. A WAV file and an AIFF file could record the same sound, but if you compared their bits and bytes, they would look quite different. For that reason, a WAV player can't interpret or play an AIFF file, and vice versa. Most of today's players, however, are sophisticated enough to handle both formats, and many more.

The following sections describe *sampled* sound formats — that is, sound files containing digital samples taken from analog recordings. All these formats can store the same types of sound, and you can convert sound data from one format to another.

WAV Files

The WAV format was developed by Microsoft and IBM as the Windows native audio format. It's the file format that Windows uses for its own sounds, such as the musical startup or the error message ding. Windows plays those sounds without starting a separate playback program; the WAV player is built into the main program. But WAV popularity has grown way beyond Windows itself; it's the most popular type of audio file on bulletin board systems, online services, and the Internet, especially the Web.

Note

The name WAV comes from a WAV file's usual extension, .wav, which stands for *waveform*.

WAV and RIFF formats

The WAV format is a form of RIFF—the Resource Interchange File Format—which was developed as a generic data format and can be used for audio, video, and other types of data. In fact, you can mix several types of data in one file, although most WAV files usually contain only WAV data. The format accommodates any sampling rate, sample sizes up to 32 bits, any number of channels, and a wide variety of encoding schemes, including PCM, A-law, μ-law, and many others. Low-end players might not be able to interpret all these variations, though. A simple player might handle only 8- or 16-bit samples, a few sampling rates, a single channel, and PCM encoding.

A RIFF file is made up of *chunks*. Each chunk starts with a four-character identifier. What the rest of the chunk contains depends on the type of chunk. Many chunks in turn contain chunks, called *subchunks*, as you'll see shortly.

Figure 2-1 diagrams the layout of a WAV file. The RIFF file itself is considered to be the highest level chunk, identified by the word RIFF. The next four bytes contain the length of the remainder of the chunk. The RIFF chunk contains one subchunk, the WAVE chunk, beginning with the identifier WAVE.

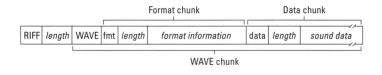

Figure 2-1 *A WAV file is really a RIFF file containing a WAVE chunk.*

A WAVE chunk can contain several subchunks, but most only have two: a format chunk that indicates the format of the audio data, and a data chunk that actually contains the data. The format chunk is identified by "fmt" followed by a space. Next comes its length. The format information includes, among other things, the type of encoding, the number of channels, and the samples per second. A WAV player needs this information to successfully interpret the data in the data chunk.

Finally comes the data chunk. It starts with the identifier "data" followed by its length. Sampled data is stored in frames, where each frame represents one sample for all the channels. Sixteen-bit stereo PCM data, for example, needs four bytes per frame: two bytes for the first channel's sample, followed by two bytes for the second channel's sample.

If you're ever stuck with an unidentified file—whether it's audio or some other kind—try opening it as a text file in your word processor or text editor. Many file formats have an identifier somewhere near the beginning that tells you what type of file it is. Figure 2-2 shows the contents of a WAV called `mywebwel.wav`, displayed in WordPad. Even though most of the "text" is unreadable—the binary data displays as extended characters such as θ and ÿ—you can clearly see "RIFF" in columns 1 through 4 and "WAVEfmt" in columns 9 through 16. Now that you're familiar with the WAV format, you know that this must be a WAV file. (By the end of this chapter, you'll be able to identify several more types of sound files.)

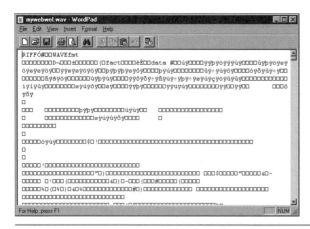

Figure 2-2 *You can tell this is a WAV file by examining its contents in a text editor.*

Macintosh Files

The two audio file formats closely associated with a Macintosh are SND and AIFF. I'll talk about SND here and AIFF in the "AIFF and AIFC formats" section later in the chapter.

The Macintosh SND format

SND is the native Mac format and is used for the OS alert sounds, game sounds, and other application sounds. Mac users have also created thousands of SND files for sharing with each other. You'll find Mac SND forums on most of the major online services and hundreds of SND FTP and Web sites.

Tip

Chapter 5 shows you how to play SND files as well as create standalone files out of SND resources, and vice versa. You'll learn how to record your own SND files in Chapter 11.

Sounds built into a Mac program are not SND files but *snd resources* stored in the program's resource fork. The Mac OS alert sounds, for example, are stored in the resource fork of the System file. A SND file is simply a Finder file with a single snd resource. Even though everyone calls them SND files, their actual file type is SFIL.

Note

For my PC friends: A Macintosh file has two parts called *forks* – resource and data. The resource fork contains items referenced by the data fork, such as icons, sounds, color palettes, and fonts. A PC file would be similar to the data fork of a Mac file.

An snd resource consists of header information followed by the sound data. (None of it is readable by humans, so I won't try to show it to you here.) The sound data could be a set of commands and/or a sampled sound or wavetable data. Sound commands tell Sound Manager how to create the desired sound. For example, they might say to play a tone at 440 cycles per second for two seconds at a certain amplitude (volume) with a certain timbre. (That would result in a rather ugly beep using the note A.) If a sampled sound is also included in the resource, the sound commands tell Sound Manager how to play it. Sampled sounds include a second header providing necessary information such as the sample size, the sampling rate, and the type of encoding.

Figure 2-3 shows the contents of a SND file displayed as text. The sound's name, `TKTempleBells`, appears starting in column 50, the SFIL type in columns 67 through 70 and again in columns 83 through 86, and the creator in columns 71 through 74 and 87 through 90. Everything else is binary data.

Figure 2-3 *The expression "sfil" in columns 67 through 70 tells you that this is a Macintosh SND file.*

Sounds are played by the Mac OS Sound Manager, which can handle 8- or 16-bit samples with one or two channels and any sampling rate up to 64 kHz. It will automatically convert 16-bit samples into 8-bit samples if your system does not have the necessary 16-bit sound hardware.

AIFF and AIFC formats

Apple developed the Audio Interchange File Format (AIFF) as an interchange format for Macintosh sounds. (Silicon Graphics, Inc. (SGI), codeveloped AIFF and AIFC formats, which are used on its

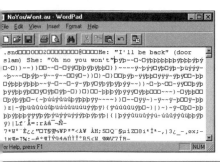

Figure 2-7 *The .snd at the beginning of the file tells you this is an AU file (or a NeXT SND file).*

MP3 Files

MP3 is the file format for MPEG-1 Layer 3 compression — not MPEG-3 compression as some people think. It's worth repeating here that this format provides the best compression and quality that you will find on the Internet today. As you'll see if you visit a few MP3 sites, its advocates tend to be somewhat fanatical about it. An MP3 file simply contains MPEG-1 Layer 3-encoded sound data, as Chapter 1 describes. There aren't any text IDs or headers, so I can't show you how to identify one.

If I wrote this book two or three years from now, it would probably be called *MP3s, MIDIs, & RealAudio*. The popularity of MP3 format for sampled sound is growing by leaps and bounds, and I believe that it will soon displace WAV, SND, and the other sampled formats on the Internet. But WAV and SND won't disappear as the Windows and Mac native formats — at least not soon. As I write this, MP3 players and plug-ins are not yet common, but you will probably have at least one player by the time you read this. Windows Media Player has already been upgraded to handle MP3. Other players and plug-ins will soon add MP3 capabilities.

workstations.) Although SND is the Mac's native format, it isn't used much for interchange across platforms because most other systems can't interpret files with two forks. AIFF fills in the gap. As you can see in Figure 2-4, its format is similar to RIFF. (There's a reason for this similarity — they're both based on an earlier format called IFF that was developed for the Amiga.) The file is identified by the word *FORM*, and the AIFF chunk by the word *AIFF*. The common chunk serves the same purpose as the format chunk in the RIFF format and contains the same type of information. It gives the number of channels, the sample rate, and the bits per sample (up to 32), but does not specify the type of encoding because only PCM coding is permitted.

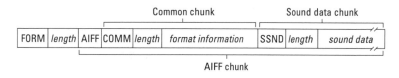

Figure 2-4 *The AIFF file format is similar to RIFF.*

The sound data chunk contains the sound information stored in sequential frames just like WAV format. Also like WAV format, AIFF permits any number of channels, any sampling rate, and sample sizes up to 32 bits. Not every player can handle all these variations, however. Other types of chunks are possible but are not often used.

Figure 2-5 shows the contents of a file named monkey. You can tell that it's an AIFF file by the FORM in columns 1 through 4, AIFF in columns 9 through 12, COMM in columns 13 through 16, and SSND in columns 39 through 42.

Figure 2-5 *The FORM and AIFF identifiers provide the clues that this is an AIFF file.*

A revision to the original AIFF standard allows for data compression. It is known as the AIFF-C or AIFC format, and its identifier is AIFC. The common chunk has been expanded to indicate the type of compression. A new format version chunk specifies the version number of the AIFC format. This was included to permit future updates without having to create another new identifier. A sound accelerator chunk helps to eliminate problems in decompressing when a sound loop doesn't return to the first frame.

UNIX and Sun AU Files

The Internet was originally created on UNIX machines, and even though there are now millions of PCs and Macs accessing it, UNIX still has a huge presence on the Net, especially among college users. In fact, the majority of the computers that host today's Internet are UNIX computers. And since UNIX uses the AU format, developed by Sun Microsystems, many FTP and Web sites offer AU sounds.

Note

The AU format seems to have about half a dozen comm names. It's also known as Sun Audio, NeXT audio (beca it's also used by NeXT computers), and μ-law or mu-law o law (because it uses μ-law compression). And just to m sure you're paying attention, on NeXT machines it's called the SND format, not to be confused with Mac's S format, which isn't the same at all.

AU format

AU files are known around the Net for being small but poor. Th because they have a history of recording 8-bit, 8 kHz mona samples, compatible with the sound hardware on many UNIX UNIX-like systems such as Sun and Linux. Today's AU forn however, supports up to two channels, up to 32-bit samples, and sampling rate up to 44 kHz. While high-quality samples are no common as the "small but poor" ones, they're not completely either.

The AU format, shown in Figure 2-6, is much plainer than other formats explored in this chapter. It starts with the iden .snd, which explains why it is sometimes called SND instead of The formatting information specifies sample size, sampling number of channels, and other essential information. Next com optional text description of the sound. And last is the sound using μ-law compression.

.snd	*format information*	*text description*	*sound data*

Figure 2-6 *This is a typical AU file layout.*

Figure 2-7 shows the contents of an AU sound file, which can spot by the ".snd" in the first four columns. This one also description starting in column 25, but you can't always count or because the description is optional.

Note

The AU format seems to have about half a dozen common names. It's also known as Sun Audio, NeXT audio (because it's also used by NeXT computers), and μ-law or mu-law or u-law (because it uses μ-law compression). And just to make sure you're paying attention, on NeXT machines it's also called the SND format, not to be confused with Mac's SND format, which isn't the same at all.

AU format

AU files are known around the Net for being small but poor. That's because they have a history of recording 8-bit, 8 kHz monaural samples, compatible with the sound hardware on many UNIX and UNIX-like systems such as Sun and Linux. Today's AU format, however, supports up to two channels, up to 32-bit samples, and any sampling rate up to 44 kHz. While high-quality samples are not as common as the "small but poor" ones, they're not completely rare either.

The AU format, shown in Figure 2-6, is much plainer than the other formats explored in this chapter. It starts with the identifier .snd, which explains why it is sometimes called SND instead of AU. The formatting information specifies sample size, sampling rate, number of channels, and other essential information. Next comes an optional text description of the sound. And last is the sound data, using μ-law compression.

.snd	format information	text description	sound data

Figure 2-6 *This is a typical AU file layout.*

Figure 2-7 shows the contents of an AU sound file, which you can spot by the ".snd" in the first four columns. This one also has a description starting in column 25, but you can't always count on that because the description is optional.

Figure 2-7 *The .snd at the beginning of the file tells you this is an AU file (or a NeXT SND file).*

MP3 Files

MP3 is the file format for MPEG-1 Layer 3 compression—not MPEG-3 compression as some people think. It's worth repeating here that this format provides the best compression and quality that you will find on the Internet today. As you'll see if you visit a few MP3 sites, its advocates tend to be somewhat fanatical about it. An MP3 file simply contains MPEG-1 Layer 3-encoded sound data, as Chapter 1 describes. There aren't any text IDs or headers, so I can't show you how to identify one.

If I wrote this book two or three years from now, it would probably be called *MP3s, MIDIs, & RealAudio*. The popularity of MP3 format for sampled sound is growing by leaps and bounds, and I believe that it will soon displace WAV, SND, and the other sampled formats on the Internet. But WAV and SND won't disappear as the Windows and Mac native formats—at least not soon. As I write this, MP3 players and plug-ins are not yet common, but you will probably have at least one player by the time you read this. Windows Media Player has already been upgraded to handle MP3. Other players and plug-ins will soon add MP3 capabilities.

Note

Yes, there are also MP1 and MP2 files, but you'll seldom run into them.

Other Sampled Formats

There are dozens of other sampled sound formats, but most of them are used by specific applications or hardware. You might occasionally find files in these formats:

- SVX — This is similar to the WAV format and is used on the Commodore Amiga.
- VOC — This is the native format for Creative Labs Sound Blaster cards.
- PCM — This file type often refers to raw PCM sound data.

Playing Your Sampled Sounds

You probably have a lot of sampled sounds on your computer, supplied by your operating system and multimedia applications. And it doesn't take too long to build up quite a collection of sound files downloaded from various online resources. (Some of my online buddies have gone a little whacko in this department. A couple of them even had to buy Zip disks for extra storage space. This section is fondly dedicated to them.)

Which player you use depends on what type of file you want to hear. Your operating system probably includes a player for its own sound format. Your sound board may also provide some players, which may be installed on your hard drive or on a CD-ROM or floppy disk that came with the board. As an example, my Creative Labs sound board came with players for audio CDs, MIDIs, and WAVs, with a lot more features than the ones provided by Windows. If you don't have the players you want, you can find several good shareware ones. I have included two in this chapter: Jet-Audio for Windows and SoundApp for Macintosh.

Note

Be sure to search around for any software that came with your sound board. My sound board was installed at the factory when I bought my computer, so I didn't realize at first all the goodies that came with it. One day I looked in the board's folder on my hard drive and found ten programs that I didn't know I had. Imagine my surprise.

In the following sections, I show you how to use the players that come with your systems: Media Player for Windows and Sound Manager for Macintosh. And because those players are a bit short on features, I'll also show introduce you to some shareware players with great bells and whistles. I looked for players for both Windows and Mac that have at least these features:

- Plays at least WAV, AU, AIFF, AIFC, Macintosh SND, and MP3 formats

- Also plays MIDIs and MODs (coming up in Chapter 3)

- Enables you to build a playlist of files to listen to while you work

- Can also play CDs (See Appendix C on the CD-ROM.)

- Does not cost a fortune (to me, less than $50)

As you'll soon see, I found a couple of programs that have all these features and a lot more. But first, the free stuff.

Media Player for Windows

Media Player is Windows' player for both sound and video. Windows 95 and 98 each provide a version of Media Player. They both use the same interface, shown in Figure 2-8. The Windows 98 version is a slight improvement over the Windows 95 version, handling a few more file formats.

Figure 2-8 *The Windows 95 and 98 versions of Media Player use the same interface.*

But as I write this, Microsoft is testing a greatly expanded Media Player 5.2. Figure 2-9 shows what it looks like when playing an audio file. It is both a standalone player and an Internet Explorer plug-in. It is planned to handle all major audio and video formats, including the all-important MP3, so it can be your only audio and video player. Some people will like the convenience of having just one player for everything. Others may prefer to have a selection of players. When you install Media Player 5.2, it replaces your former standalone Media Player and any plug-ins you have installed for Internet Explorer. By the time you read this, Media Player 5.2 has probably been released and you can download it free of charge from Microsoft's Web site at this address:

    http:\\www.microsoft.com

Figure 2-9 *Media Player 5.2 sports an entirely new interface, shown here without the video window.*

This section assumes that you will want to upgrade to Media Player 5.2 when it becomes available. It shows you how to play sampled files and create playlists using the standalone player.

Media Player 5.2 basics

When you start Media Player 5.2 for a sound file, the window shown in Figure 2-9 opens. If you have not yet opened a file, choose File ⇨ Open to open a common browse box where you can select the file you want. The bar in the middle, called the *Seek Bar*, shows where you are in the current file. The bar represents the entire file, and the slider represents your current position. In the example in Figure 2-9, roughly one quarter of the sound has been played so far. The status bar in the lower-right corner confirms that the slider is currently located 3 seconds from the beginning of the 12-second audio.

The buttons on the control panel are designed to look like those on a standard tape or CD player, and they work the same way.

▶ Choose the Play button to listen to the audio. As it plays, the slider moves along the Seek Bar and the status bar shows the elapsed time.

❙❙ The Play button becomes a Pause button. To interrupt the audio before it finishes, choose either Pause or Stop (the next button in the margin).

■ The Stop button resets the slider to the beginning of the file, while the Pause button leaves it where it is. You can also drag the slider around as desired to move forward or backward.

The speaker icon mutes the player. Click it a second time to restore sound. The slider next to the speaker adjusts the volume.

Note

The other Media Player 5.2 controls work with Microsoft NetShow, explained in Chapter 8.

Keeping track of your favorites

Media Player helps you locate and open your favorite media files using the Favorites menu, shown in Figure 2-10. You can create your own folders on this menu, add files to the folders or to the menu itself, and open files for playing. The bottom part of the menu shows you whatever files and folders are located in the C:\Windows\Favorites\Media folder. Although you can tailor the menu using the Organize Favorites option, I think it's a heck of a lot easier to just use Windows Explorer to make changes to the Media folder. The changes show up the next time you open Media Player. To play a favorite song, simply select it from the Favorites menu.

Figure 2-10 *Media Player's Favorites menu gives you quick access to your favorite media files and sites.*

Tip

When you first install Media Player, the Favorites menu is loaded with links to Internet multimedia sites. To cut the menu down to a reasonable size, I suggest that you move them all into a folder like the Multimedia Links folder shown in Figure 2-10.

DirectShow (ActiveMovie)

If you have installed Microsoft Internet Explorer, you also have an ActiveX control called ActiveMovie that can play audio and video files. Although ActiveX is meant to be run by another program, such as Internet Explorer, you can use a Windows program called Rundll32 to run it. Rundll32's entire purpose is to enable you to run modules that you couldn't ordinarily run because they are not stand-alone programs, such as ActiveMovie. (Windows also provides a sister program called Rundll for running 16-bit modules.) I don't want to get too deeply into Rundll32, as it's quite complex and doesn't pertain to the main topic of this book. But I think you should be aware of it because you're likely to see it pop up in some dialog boxes associated with ActiveMovie.

If ActiveMovie is installed on your system, you should be able to start it up by choosing Start ➪ Programs ➪ Accessories ➪ Multimedia ➪ ActiveMovie Control. Unlike a standalone program, you must choose a file to open immediately. The ActiveMovie window is a lot simpler than even the Media Player window. Play, stop, and pause are its only functions. The reason I bring up ActiveMovie is because Internet Explorer may have installed it as your default WAV and MIDI player. If so, when you open an audio file by double-clicking it, you'll see the ActiveMovie control instead of one of your other players.

Jet-Audio for Windows

Now let's have some fun! Jet-Audio for Windows is a 32-bit media component system from COWON that has just about every feature they could think of. It includes six independent components and a "remote control," all designed to look like a high-end stereo rack system. Figure 2-11 shows the components discussed later in this chapter: Digital Audio player, Sound Effector, and Mixer, along with the main control panel.

Note

The other components are MIDI Player (covered in Chapter 3), CD Player (Appendix C), Digital Video Player (not covered), and Remocon (remote control – not covered).

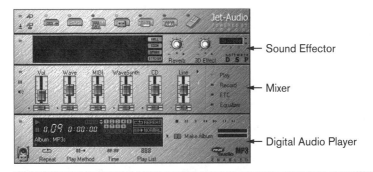

Figure 2-11 *Jet-Audio's components for playing sampled sounds include Digital Audio Player, Sound Effector (Digital Signal Processor or DSP), and Mixer.*

The fine print

Jet-Audio's shareware registration fee is $29, but you can try it for 30 days before you pay the fee. It works with Windows 95, 98, and NT. It requires a 486-DX2/66 or better CPU, but needs a Pentium 90 or higher for playing MP3 and RA files. Sixteen megabytes of RAM is recommended, along with at least 4MB of disk space.

Installing and starting Jet-Audio

To install Jet-Audio, insert the book's CD-ROM into your CD-ROM drive and open the Windows Software/Jet-Audio folder. Double-click the file named Jet-Audio and follow the directions on your screen. After it's installed, choose Jet-Audio from your Start menu to start it.

At the top of the Jet-Audio window is the main control panel, where you select the components with which you want to work. You open and close a component by clicking its image in the control panel. If you find the images a bit difficult to identify — me too — you can pause your mouse pointer over each one to pop up its name.

For this chapter, please open Sound Effector, Mixer, and Digital Audio Player, and close MIDI Player, CD Player, Digital Video Player, and Remocon.

Digital Audio Player

Digital Audio Player, shown in Figure 2-12, can play WAVs, MP1s, MP2s, MP3s, AIFFs, AUs, and SNDs. (It can also play RealAudio files, as you'll learn in Chapter 7.) In a sense, it enables you to create virtual CDs out of your sound files. You group them into albums and then open and play the albums. You could create albums of quiet classics, patriotic music, sound effects, and Holiday music, to suggest a few. Since your albums are stored on your hard drive, their sizes are not as limited as real CDs — you can have hundreds of files per album.

 — Make Album

Figure 2-12 *Digital Audio Player gives you an interface for managing and playing sampled files.*

How to create an album:

1. Choose the Make Album button, shown in Figure 2-12, to open the Make Album window (see Figure 2-13).

2. Click the New Album button.

3. Type a title in the Album Title box.

4. Choose Add Files to Album to pop up a list of three choices: Add File(s), Add File(s) in Folder, or Add File(s) in Folder (Including Sub-Folders).

5. If you want to select individual files for the album, follow these steps:

    a. Choose Add File(s) to open a dialog box where you can browse for files.

b. Drop down the Files of Type list and choose the type of sound files for this album.

c. Select one or more files and choose Add to List. The selected songs are added to the list at the bottom of the dialog box.

d. Repeat steps a through c until you have added all the desired files.

e. Choose Close to close the dialog box and return to the Make Album window, where you'll see the added songs in the playlist at the bottom of the window.

6. If you want to add all the sound files from a folder, or from a folder and its subfolders, follow these steps:

a. Choose Add File(s) in Folder or Add File(s) in Folder (Including Sub-Folders). In either case, a dialog box opens where you can locate and select a folder.

b. Select the desired folder and then choose OK. The dialog box closes and you return to the Make Album window, where the new files appear in the playlist at the bottom of the window.

7. Repeat steps 3 through 6 until you have added all the desired files to the album.

8. You can change the order of the files in the album by dragging them up or down.

9. To describe a file, select it and then type a description in the Description box.

10. When your playlist is finished, choose OK to close the Make Album window.

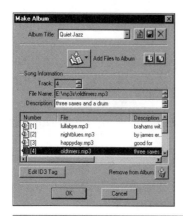

Figure 2-13 *You create and edit albums in the Make Album window.*

 When you're ready to open an album, choose the Select Album button, shown here. This pops up a list of your albums so you can select one. Use the controls on the right to start, pause, stop, advance to the next track, return to the previous track, and so on.

> ### Tip
>
> Pause your mouse pointer over any control on the player to pop up a tool tip telling you what that control does.

The status window includes a play mode indicator that you can click to toggle among these three modes:

⏸⏩ NORMAL	*Normal mode* plays straight through the album in sequential order.
↻ RANDOM	*Random mode* selects songs from the entire album at random.
⏭ PROGRAM	*Program mode* plays songs from a programmed playlist in sequential order.

Choose the Playlist icon, shown here, to open a window where you can create a playlist. In the window, select one or more files and choose Add to Program List. You can drag the files around in the playlist to change their order. When you choose OK to return to the main window, be sure to choose Program mode to play just the playlist.

The numbered squares, shown in the margin, are file indicators. Yellow squares indicate files on the current playlist, if there is one. Pausing your mouse pointer over a square pops up the name of the file. Click a square to start that file. When an album contains more than 15 files, you can scroll the numbered squares up and down with the arrows. If there are scores of files in the album and you don't want to be bothered scrolling through them, click the track number indicator to pop up a complete list of the album where you can select the one you want to start with.

The status window also shows the current repeat mode, which you click to toggle among these three modes:

No repeat

Repeat the current file

Repeat the entire playlist or album

Sound Effector

Sound Effector, shown in Figure 2-14 is a digital signal processor (DSP) that creates the effect of four different environments: room, stage, hall, and stadium. Select an environment by clicking the appropriate button. Hall mode is selected in Figure 2-14. You adjust the effect with the Reverb and 3D knobs. Click the small red button under each knob to turn the effect on and off. Then click the + and - signs to adjust it.

Spectrum Analyzer

On/Off

Figure 2-14 *Sound Effector is a DSP with a twist.*

The spectrum analyzer window — which works with MPEG files, MIDIs, and CDs — graphically displays the audio spectrum as the file plays. It is a display tool only; you can't adjust it or use it to adjust the sound.

Sound Effector also includes a sleep timer. It turns off whatever is playing after the designated time interval. The sleep timer shown in the margin has 58 minutes and 42 seconds to go. To set the sleep timer, click the red button to turn it on with the default time of one hour. Then click the up and down arrows to adjust the time. Click the blue arrow to start it.

Mixer

Use Mixer to adjust the volume and balance of the various players to which you're listening. If your system is capable of playing or recording multiple sounds — perhaps you can listen to sampled sounds, MIDIs, and CDs at the same time — you can adjust the mix with this device. Suppose you're listening to a favorite MP3 album while you surf the Web, and you don't want any MIDI background files on Web pages to disturb your music. You can turn down or mute the MIDI controls to suppress any MIDI music.

To adjust the volume of a device, drag the vertical slider up and down. To adjust the balance between speakers, drag the horizontal slider left and right. To mute a device, click the tiny red button next to the balance button. It glows bright red when it is muted. To adjust all the sound at once, use the Vol control on the left. Muting a device is different from pausing or stopping it in that the file continues to play, even though you can't hear it.

> **Tip**
>
> The small speaker icon to the left of the Vol control is an attenuation (ATT) switch, which turns all sound down but not off, so you can make a phone call or talk to someone. Click it again to restore the former volume.

For MPEG files, choose Equalizer to change the main display from a volume mixer to a six-band graphic equalizer, as shown in Figure 2-15. Here also you drag the sliders to adjust the balance between the six ranges, boosting low tones, perhaps, or damping the mid-to-high range. The ATT switch is available in this view too so you don't have to switch back to the mixer to hush the volume.

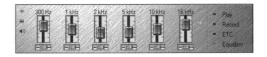

Figure 2-15 *Equalizer works on MPEG files just like the equalizer on a stereo system.*

SoundApp for Macintosh

SoundApp 2.5 by Norman Franke is a Macintosh sound player and converter. You can use it to listen to many different sound types and to convert sound resources to other types of files for sharing with others. You can also convert other types of files into sound resources. It enables you to work with individual sound files as well as playlists. It provides extensive AppleScript support so that you can incorporate SoundApp into your AppleScript solutions.

SoundApp can play System 7 snd resources and SND files, AU, WAV, AIFF, AIFC, MIDI, MOD, and several other formats. It can convert to System 7, sound suitcase, AIFF, AU, and other formats. (The Readme file that comes with SoundApp lists all the formats it can handle.) It can also change the sample rate, compression mode, channels, and sample size of a sound file without changing its format.

The fine print

SoundApp 2.5 is freeware. Feel free to use it and share it with your friends. It requires Mac OS 7.0 or higher and Sound Manager 3.1 or higher. It also needs QuickTime 2.0 or higher if you want to be able to play QuickTime movies and to convert to and from QuickTime formats. SoundApp is located in the SoundApp folder in the Macintosh Software folder on the book's CD-ROM. Copy it to your hard drive and double-click it to install it.

Playing files with SoundApp

Playing a sound is as easy as dropping the sound file on the SoundApp icon. You can drop several files at once to queue them up for playing. You can continue to drop more files on the icon while a sound is playing. If you drop a folder on the icon, SoundApp plays all the sound files in the folder and its subfolders.

SoundApp's status window, shown in Figure 2-16, shows you which sound is playing, how far along it is, and technical info about the file. You control the player with these keys:

. (period)	Stop all files and close list
→	Skip to the next sound
←	Return to the previous sound
spacebar	Pause and resume
;	Stop playing after current file finishes
+	Increase volume
-	Decrease volume

Tip

If you have trouble remembering the control keys, choose Options ⇨ Show Controls to display a CD player-style control panel. To view technical information about a file without actually playing it, select the file and choose File ⇨ Get Info.

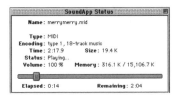

Figure 2-16 *SoundApp's status window provides information about the sound currently being played.*

How to convert a sound file:

1. Use the options on the Convert menu to select the format, encoding, sampling rate, channels, and bit depth for the converted file.

Tip

To create a sound suitcase, choose Convert ⇨ Format ⇨ Sound Suitcase. Sound suitcases are explained in Chapter 5.

2. To convert files using the selected settings, hold down the Shift key while you drop one or more files on the SoundApp icon. A dialog box opens so you can indicate where you want to save the converted files.

3. Select or create a folder and choose Save.

Tip

Use Convert ⇨ Save Settings to save your current settings with a name such as "AIFF settings" or "For Windows users." The name you assign appears at the bottom of the Convert menu where you can click it to restore those settings.

How to create a playlist:

1. Choose File ⇨ New Play List to open the playlist dialog box, shown in Figure 2-17.

2. Drag as many files as you wish into the playlist dialog box. (Or choose File ⇨ Add to add them to the playlist.)

3. Drag the files around in the playlist to change their order.

4. Choose File ⇨ Save to give the playlist a name and save it in a folder (or on the desktop).

Figure 2-17 *You create and access a playlist with this window.*

Choose File ⇨ Open to open a playlist. In the playlist window, choose Play All or Convert All to play or convert the entire list. (Enable Shuffle and/or Repeat as desired.) Or you can select one or more individual files and choose Play, Convert, or Info.

 Tip

Check out the Options ⇨ Preferences and SoundApp Help for other things you can do with SoundApp.

What's on the CD-ROM

In the Windows Software folder you'll find these programs:

> CD/Spectrum Pro is a rack system similar to Jet-Audio but with fewer features. I included it because it has one fun feature that Jet-Audio doesn't have: It includes two amazingly good screen savers that dance in time to whatever music you're playing. I love it!

> Digital Peace (Light version) plays soft environmental WAVs (rain forest, forest stream, and ocean continuously while you work. It's a nice change of pace.

> Media Blaze 98 helps you manage your sound files when they're starting to overwhelm you.

What's Next?

MIDIs don't record sampled sounds, they create music from scratch via your computer's sound board. Chapter 3 describes MIDIs and other synthesized music formats.

Chapter 3

MIDIs and Other Synthesized Music Files

Did you know that your computer's sound board includes a complete synthesizer, just like rock stars play? True, it doesn't have a keyboard, but all the internal circuitry is there. And you don't have to be a rock star to play it. All you need do is start a MIDI file, which generates music on your synthesizer. Many multimedia games use MIDI files for background music while WAVs provide action sounds in the foreground. You have probably visited Web sites that play MIDIs on your synthesizer while you browse. You can also build your own collection of MIDIs on your hard drive. Tens of thousands of MIDIs are on the Internet for you to download and enjoy — rock, pop, jazz, country, classical, ethnic, almost any category you can think of. In this chapter, I'll show you how to play and enjoy MIDIs and related files — karaoke, anyone?

What you'll learn:

- How your synthesizer works
- What the General MIDI standard is and how it affects you
- Important extensions to the MIDI standard: GS, XG, and DLS
- What a MIDI file is
- How to play MIDI files in Windows and Mac OS

- How MOD files are different from MIDI files (and why some people like them better)
- How adding lyrics to MIDI files creates karaoke (KAR) files
- Where to find tons of MIDI, MOD, and KAR files on the Internet

Synth I Met You, Baby

As I said at the outset, this book is not about hardware. But because synthesizers and MIDIs go together like computers and programs, I find it impossible to explain MIDIs without talking a bit about synthesizers. In fact, I'm going to take you on a brief historical tour of synthesizers and electronic music. Stop that moaning . . . it won't be too painful.

The first synthesizers, developed in the 1960s by Robert Moog and others, were meant to help composers try out their compositions without going to the expense and bother of hiring an orchestra by simulating, or *synthesizing,* the needed instruments in their studios. Moog was an electronics engineer, not a musician, and from an electronics standpoint, the synthesizer was a relatively simple device. An ordinary oscillator generated an electronic waveform, which was modulated for characteristics such as pitch (the note or tone), volume, reverberation, and *timbre*—the complex of overtones that give each instrument its unique voice. Add a keyboard and some buttons and wheels so the user can play notes and adjust the aforementioned characteristics, and voilá—instant orchestra.

But the synthesizer was not so simple from a musician's standpoint. It was child's play to reproduce the sound of an electronic organ, but not too many people wanted to compose tunes for solo electronic organ. No one knew, or could discover, how to adjust a synthesizer to recreate the rich timbre of a cello, guitar, kettle drum, or just about any other instrument. We still don't know. So, in a sense, that early synthesizer was a failure. But before it got dumped on the trash heap, musicians — primarily rock musicians — began experimenting with the "synth" as an instrument in its own right. The world has never been the same since.

Nowadays, a synthesizer doesn't necessarily come wrapped in a keyboard. It might have strings, valves, drum pads, or some other human interface. Or — the reason we're all here — it could be built into a computer sound board and be driven solely by software. And we've come full circle, because with the exploding popularity of MIDIs on the Internet, people once again want synthesizers to realistically synthesize orchestral instruments.

Today's sound board synthesizers employ two common technologies. At the low end, *FM synthesis* comes closest to the original technology, although today's device is digital rather than analog. Unfortunately, because we still don't know how to analyze or recreate timbre, most FM synthesis sounds pretty artificial. Only the cheapest sound boards these days employ FM synthesis. More expensive boards use *wavetable sampling,* which bypasses the timbre problem by using the real thing. A *wavetable* is a collection of recorded sound samples of real pianos, guitars, bassoons, kettle drums, violins, harmonicas, flutes, ukuleles, piccolos, accordions . . . well, you get the idea. The synthesizer pulls samples as needed from the wavetable and modulates them for pitch, reverberation, and other characteristics. The result is a lot closer to the real thing.

Don't expect your computer to sound exactly like the New York Philharmonic or the Glenn Miller Band just yet. It's close, but even a tin ear can tell the difference. Many synthesizer instruments are near perfect — listen to a piano piece played on your synthesizer and you'll think it's a recording. But string and wind instruments still have an artificial quality to them. Of course, a lot depends on the quality of the sound samples in the wavetable. We'll come back to that point a bit later in this chapter.

The General MIDI Standard

Let's go back for a minute to those hip musicians of the 1970s exploring their new electronic synths. It seems only natural that someone would eventually patch two of them together and control both from one console. And once you figure out how to connect two, why not four . . . eight . . . twenty? You might call this the pre-MIDI era, when synthesizers began sprouting ports and patch cords, but no standard dictated how they communicated. Each manufacturer developed its own interface, so you couldn't connect a Roland to a Yamaha, nor a Casio to an E-mu. To bring some order to the chaos, the *Musical Instrument Digital Interface* (MIDI) standard was developed to define the way digital musical instruments (now called MIDI instruments when they adhere to the standard) could communicate. The original standard, which was released in the early 1980s, was upgraded in 1991 to the *General MIDI* (GM) standard, which remains the current standard. The GM standard calls for the following requirements:

- A five-pin connector for devices that have ports. Your computer's sound board probably doesn't have a MIDI port, by the way. If you want to connect it to an external MIDI instrument, you would use a cable designed to connect the MIDI port on the instrument to a serial or game port on your computer.

- A bank of 128 instruments. The original standard did not define the instruments but merely allowed for 128 of them. Instruments are selected by number, not name. So a trio using instrument numbers 3, 17, and 25 sounded like piano, sax, and drums on one synthesizer but ukulele, bassoon, and piccolo on another. General MIDI solved this problem by standardizing the *patch map* (think of it as a wavetable) shown in Table B-1 in Appendix B on this books CD-ROM.

Note

On early synthesizers, you had to connect modules together via patch cables to create the sound you wanted. The word *patch* came to represent a particular timbre, or instrument, and is still used in that sense today by MIDI composers and musicians. Hence the term *patch map*.

- Sixteen output channels. Each channel represents one instrument, so you can have a maximum of 16 instruments playing at once. You can change a channel's instrument at will. Channel 1 may start as grand piano but change to flute, then acoustic guitar, then back to piano, and wind up playing alto sax.

- Channel 10 is reserved for percussion instruments. The note number, which identifies the pitch in any other channel, indicates the percussion instrument on channel 10. Table B-2 on the companion CD-ROM Appendix B shows the GM percussion map.

- At least 24 voices. Multiple voices permit some channels to play more than one note simultaneously, as in guitar and piano chords. Many modern synthesizers exceed this standard, providing 32 or even 64 voices.

- *MIDI messages* to control the sequence of MIDI events. A typical message might turn on note number 100 in channel 7. The sequence of events — note 16 on in channel 3, note 65 off in channel 1, patch instrument 105 to channel 14 — is so crucial that a recorded MIDI song is called a *sequence,* the software you use to record it is called a *sequencer,* and we say the song was *sequenced by,* rather than performed by, Jasper Doohingle. (Jasper might not be a traditional instrumental performer but someone who enters events into the sequencer via computer keyboard and mouse. Just think — you, too, could become a MIDI musician if you have the patience to enter thousands of events to create a single song.)

How GM became GS and XG (with a dash of DLS)

The GM standard does not go far enough for some people. They want more channels, voices, controls, effects, and instruments. To meet their demands, both Roland and Yamaha have devised their own extensions to GM — Roland GS and Yamaha XG. Both extensions provide for many additional instruments plus other extra features. Each company has recorded extensive banks of instrument samples for use with their standards. If you want to start an argument, ask a room full of MIDI enthusiasts which extension is better — GS or XG. In general, Roland's GS seems to be winning out. Microsoft has licensed the Roland instrument samples for inclusion with the GS-compliant software synthesizer that comes with Windows 98. Apple also has licensed the Roland samples for its GS-compliant software synthesizer included with QuickTime 3.0. I have the feeling that XG will eventually join the ranks of electronics also-rans, along with Betamax VCRs.

You'll often see the notation GM, XG, or GS next to a MIDI filename on an Internet site, indicating the standard for which the sequence was created. You don't necessarily need to avoid MIDIs that use a different standard than your synthesizer. A GS or XG synthesizer can play a GM sequence with no problems simply by using the GM instrument bank. On the other hand, a sequence that takes advantage of the GS or XG extras will still sound pretty good on your plain vanilla GM synthesizer. The additional GS and XG sound banks have been carefully designed to complement the GM bank so that a GS sequence will sound okay, but not enhanced, on a GM synthesizer. Other additional features, such as extra effects, are simply ignored. The sequence will sound a lot better on a GS or XG synthesizer, though.

In 1996, the MIDI Manufacturer's Association (MMA) extended the GM standard to include DLS — downloadable sounds. Rather than storing wavetables permanently in the sound board's ROM, with DLS a wavetable is stored in RAM and is easily replaceable. Thus you could change your wavetable whenever you wish. Or, as you'll see when we talk about MODs later in this chapter, a sequence could come with its own wavetable, giving the composer/sequencer total control over the way the music sounds. Games developers in particular take advantage of downloadable sounds to add their game sounds to your basic set. Downloadable sounds have long been used on Creative Labs boards, which incorporate E-mu synthesizers along with E-mu's SoundFonts downloadable sounds.

Are you now wondering whether your sound board's synthesizer is GM, GS, or XG compatible? What sound banks you're currently using and how to change them? Whether you can use SoundFonts or other types of downloadable fonts? And if so, how you download and install them? Here are some suggestions on how to find out:

- Read its manual.

- Read the box it came in.

- Locate its folder on your hard drive and read all the documentation files (.txt, .doc, .hlp, and so on).

- Check the manufacturer's Web site. (Use a search tool to find it, or just try http://www.*companyname*.com, as in http://www.creative.com.)

- Contact its manufacturer. (You can find contact information on the company's Web site.)

- Look for newsgroups about MIDI, synthesizers, electronic music, sound boards, and so on.

- If it was installed at the factory when you bought your computer:

  - Look for a folder on your hard drive containing information about your computer; read all the documentation files there.

  - Contact your computer's manufacturer.

  - Contact the dealer where you bought the computer.

Mighty Mini MIDIs

It took us a while to get here, but we have finally arrived at the main topic of this chapter, MIDIs—more correctly called MIDI files. They are even more correctly called Standard MIDI Files, or SMF, but you'll see that phrase just about as often as you'll see the president referred to as William Clinton or WJC.

Note

Most MIDI files today have the extension .mid. You will find some with the extension .rmi, from Microsoft's RMID format.

It's important to understand that a MIDI file is not a sampled recording, nor any other kind of recording. It can't capture your acceptance speech, Elmer Fudd singing Wagner's "I killed the wabbit," or the sound of an egg frying on the sidewalk. That's the job of the sampled file formats we talked about in Chapter 2. MIDI files store only MIDI messages, which a MIDI player can interpret on a MIDI instrument such as your sound board's synthesizer.

The big advantage of MIDI files over sampled files—I should say *humongous* advantage—is their tiny size. A 15K MIDI might produce more than three minutes of music. By contrast, a 15K WAV using low-quality settings (8-bit, 11 Kbps, one channel) lasts less than two seconds. Is it any wonder that people prefer MIDIs to sampled sounds on the Internet?

MIDI files come in three flavors:

- *Format 0* assembles all MIDI data on a single track, so even the simplest player can play it.

- *Format 1* provides multiple tracks for sequencers that can record and playback separate tracks, an important feature for people who create sequences. This is the most popular format.

- *Format 2* permits multiple tracks and multiple sequence patterns and is rarely used.

Most of the MIDI files you'll encounter on the Internet use format 1. A few use format 0. Your player should be able to handle both formats. You probably won't even be aware of the file format when you download and play a MIDI.

Interpreting a MIDI sequence requires a lot of processing power, and it has to be done quickly or the music doesn't come out right. A slower processor — even an early Pentium — would not have time to decompress the file as well. Hence MIDI files are not compressed. Fortunately, they're small files and compression is not important.

Playing back MIDI files

Once a MIDI file is stored on one of your local drives, you play it back just like any of the sound files discussed in Chapter 2. Windows Media Player, ActiveMovie, QuickTime, Jet-Audio, Mac's Sound Manager, SoundApp, and many other players all play MIDI files. Be sure to check whether a MIDI player is included with your sound board, too.

For Windows, I prefer the Jet-Audio MIDI player, shown in Figure 3-1, because it enables you to make albums out of your MIDIs. When you collect a group of MIDIs into an album, you can play them much like a CD, with repeat mode, random mode, and a programmed playlist. An album on the MIDI player can contain many types of sequenced files, not just MIDIs. For example, it can also contain MOD and karaoke files, which are explained later in this chapter. To make or play an album, see the "Digital Audio Player" section in Chapter 2.

ATT →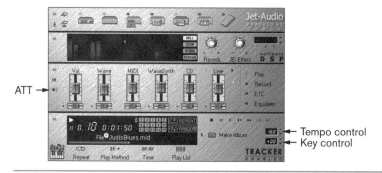

Tempo control
Key control

Figure 3-1 *Jet-Audio's MIDI player plays many formats of MIDI, MOD, and karaoke files.*

Want to sing along with the music? You may need the two controls at the right side of the player. The top control, called the Tempo control, changes the speed of the playback. Click the up arrow to make it faster or the down arrow to make it slower. The bottom control, called the Key control, transposes the music to other keys. Click the up arrow for a higher key or the down arrow for a lower one.

I included Mixer and Sound Effector in Figure 3-1 because they interact with MIDI Player. Mixer can be used to control the volume of the MIDI music in relationship to any other devices that are currently playing, such as WAVs from an application that you are using. You can use the attenuation (ATT) button, shown in Figure 3-1, to lower the volume while you talk to someone and then raise it again. Mixer's graphic equalizer has no effect on MIDIs. Sound Effector's spectrum analysis display responds to music played by MIDI Player. The sleep timer works with MIDI Player, but the DSP effects do not.

Other file types that contain MIDI sequences

The MIDI file format (or SMF) is not the only file format that contains MIDI sequences. MOD files, which have a wavetable built into the file, are gaining a near-cult following. And you can imagine how popular karaoke files have become.

MOD files

One way for a composer to make sure a MIDI sequence sounds exactly the same on everyone's system is to include the desired wavetable right in the file. The player uses the included sound samples instead of those provided by the sound board, and the music sounds right on everyone's computer. You can't include a wavetable in a MIDI file, but you can in a MOD file. In fact, that's the major difference between MIDI and MOD.

Note

MOD is short for modules.

While the included wavetable makes a MOD much larger than a MIDI, it is still significantly smaller than a WAV or other sampled recording. So why isn't MOD more popular? For one, because MODs are so much larger than MIDIs. For two, because MOD editors — which are called *trackers* not sequencers — tend to be hard to use, so many composers don't bother to learn them. And for three, because the several forms of MOD files aren't necessarily compatible with each other. A MOD player often can't play all the different types of MODs. You may run into the following MOD variations:

- .mod — Files tracked by ProTracker, FastTracker 1, StarTrekker, Noise Tracker, and others
- .669 — Files tracked by Composer 669
- .mtm — Files tracked by Multi Module Edit
- .s3m — Files tracked by ScreamTracker

- .stm — Files tracked by ScreamTracker 2.*xx*
- .it — Files tracked by Impulse Tracker
- .xm — Files tracked by various trackers

Tip

Notice the phrase *Tracker Enabled* on the Jet-Audio MIDI Player in Figure 3-1. That means it can play MODs as well as MIDIs.

Karaoke files

Add lyrics to a MIDI file and what do you get? Karaoke! KAR files are played on a karaoke player that shows the lyrics while playing the music. A good player uses some method to mark off the lyrics so you know where you are in the music. Some display a bouncing object, while others simply change the color of the words. As I write this, a few shareware karaoke players and editors are available, but I couldn't find one I liked well enough to include with the book. Internet karaoke is an up-and-coming field, so some excellent players/editors may be available by the time you read this. Check this book's Web site for recommendations:

```
http://members.aol.com/jnfbooks
```

In the meantime, you can play karaoke files with QuickTime, which is included on this book's CD-ROM. Both Windows and Macintosh versions of QuickTime 3 are on the CD-ROM. When you open a KAR file, QuickTime converts a KAR file to its own MOV format and then displays it as a movie with a sound track and a text track. This is not the ideal solution, but if you're a karaoke fan, it's better than no player at all. QuickTime marks off the lyrics by changing colors, as shown in Figure 3-2. Unfortunately, QuickTime doesn't enable you to change the speed or key of the music, so you have to sing along with the music as is.

Figure 3-2 *QuickTime times the karaoke lyrics to the music by changing the color of the text.*

Note

Jet-Audio's MIDI player plays KAR files and enables you to adjust the key and the speed of the music, but it does not display lyrics.

The fine print

(Please try to read this in a fast voice.) There is no charge for the basic version of QuickTime. The Windows version works with Windows 95, 98, and NT 4.0. It requires a 486-DX2/66 or higher, 16MB RAM, and a Sound Blaster-compatible card. Also, the following are recommended for better performance: DirectX 3.0, DirectDraw, and DirectSound. (These can all be downloaded from Microsoft's Web site.) The Macintosh version works with System 7.1 or higher. It requires 16MB RAM for PowerPC or 8MB RAM for 68K machines; 68K-based computers must also support Color QuickDraw.

How to play karaoke files with QuickTime:

1. With QuickTime active, choose File ⇨ Open to open a browse box.

2. Locate and select the KAR file and then choose Convert. QuickTime displays a dialog box so you can save the converted file.

3. Change the name of the new movie file, if desired, select a folder for it, and choose Save. QuickTime opens the new movie file but does not play it.

Now you can control the song with these buttons:

▶	Play
‖	Pause
▐▶	Jump forward to next verse
◀▌	Jump backward to preceding verse
◀⧉	Volume control

You can also move around in the song by dragging the slider. If a group of people are trying to read the lyrics, click Movie ⇨ Double Size from the menu bar to double the size of the display. Choose Movie ⇨ Normal Size to return it to its regular size.

When you convert a KAR file to a movie file, QuickTime enables you to choose such things as font, size, and color for the text. If you don't want to use the default settings, choose the Options button in the dialog box. This opens a MIDI import options dialog box, where you choose the Text Options button to open the Text Import Settings dialog box. Figure 3-3 shows the Windows version of this dialog box, but the Macintosh version is nearly identical.

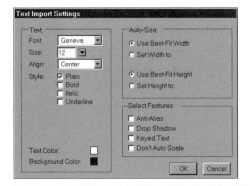

Figure 3-3 *When you convert a karaoke file with QuickTime, you can select text properties in this dialog box.*

In the Text group, you choose the font, point size, style, alignment, and the foreground and background colors. To change a color, click the colored box to open a color panel where you can select the desired color. The Auto-Size group affects the size of the text display window, not the size of the font. If you select the Auto-Size options, QuickTime selects the best size to display the text of the song. If you enter specific width and/or height, in pixels, text lines might have to be wrapped to fit the window.

By default, if the designated font size is so large that lines must be wrapped in the window, QuickTime adapts the font size to fit the window. Also, if you enlarge or shrink the window, QuickTime automatically adapts the font size to fit. But if you enable Don't Autoscale, then QuickTime is forced to use the designated font size, no matter what size the window is.

The Keyed Text option displays the lyrics on a white background. If the text is also white, it's invisible until its color changes. So instead of the lyrics appearing all at once and changing color, they pop onto the screen in time with the music.

You can download karaoke files from several sites on the Internet. To get you started, I have included a karaoke Webring in Appendix A on the CD-ROM. If you have a karaoke editor, you can create your own by typing in the lyrics for MIDI files that you already have. Plain-old vanilla QuickTime 3 plays karaoke movie files but cannot edit the text. Upgrading to QuickTime 3 Pro ($29.95) gives you the ability to create and edit text tracks in any MOV file, including karaoke movies.

What's Next?

We've touched a bit on the Windows sound features. Chapter 4 explores in greater detail what you can do with sound in Windows 95 and 98, including some hints on how to configure your MIDI synthesizer.

Chapter 4

Using Sound Files with Windows 95, 98, and NT

Now that you have some sound files, what are you going to do with them? Windows 95, 98, or NT give you lots of sound facilities. You can configure your sound properties, assign sounds to your Windows events, and of course, listen to all those sounds offline.

What you'll learn:

- How to assign sounds to sound events in Windows and in your applications

- How to use Volume Control to control the volume and mix of your sound devices

- How to use the Multimedia applet to set properties for your sound devices

Most of the explanations in this chapter are the same for all three versions of Windows. Whenever there's a difference, I included separate explanations for each operating system.

Dressing Up Your Windows Sounds

You're probably used to Windows dinging, beeping, and chiming as you work. But did you know that it could chirp, bark, and hiss instead? Or perhaps you'd like it to cough, hiccup, and belch, especially on days when you feel like annoying your co-workers. Any kinds of sounds are possible, as you can assign any WAV file to a *sound event* — a program event that triggers a sound. You could even set up Windows so that, when it starts up, your voice says, "Keep your scabby hands off my computer, you verminous cretin!"

Windows sound events

Windows provides over 20 general sound events, such as the Question event that happens whenever a question box pops up. Other sound events occur when Windows starts or ends, a warning message pops up, an error is detected, and on several other occasions. Figure 4-1 shows the Sounds Properties window, where you can scroll through a list of all the sound events in your system. You'll learn how to use the Sounds Properties window to review and change your sound assignments in this section.

Figure 4-1 *The Sounds Properties window shows the sound events registered with Windows.*

How to open the Sounds Properties window:

1. Choose Start⇨Settings⇨Control Panel to open the Control Panel.

2. Start the Sounds applet to open the Sounds Properties window.

Some sound events have no WAVs assigned to them by default. For example, sound events occur when you open a menu, choose a menu item, maximize or minimize a window, restore the window's former size, and open or close a program. If you actually assigned sounds to all these events, your computer would keep up a constant racket. Not only that, but playing all those WAVs would noticeably slow down your system. Notice in Figure 4-1 that the Close Program event has no speaker icon, meaning that file is assigned to no sound assignment, the default setting for this particular event.

Tip

Most sound events should have the shortest possible WAVs. Trust me, you don't want to wait for your favorite tenor to sing all of "O Sole Mio" each time you pull down a menu.

Application sound events

Many sound-enabled applications add their own events to your list. You can see an example in Figure 4-2, where I have scrolled down in Sounds Properties to show the Microsoft NetMeeting group. You can also see the beginning of the America Online group. The events in these groups are unique to their applications, whereas the Windows events pertain to all applications. Nonetheless, you can change the sound assignments for these application events just as you can for the Windows events.

Figure 4-2 *Application sound events also show up in the Sounds Properties window.*

WAVs to use with sound events

You probably have more WAV files on your hard drive than you realize. Windows offers several collections of sounds, your sound-enabled applications add more, and of course, you may have added quite a few yourself. All these WAV files are candidates for assignment to sound events.

WAVs provided by Windows

Windows provides a sample set of WAVs that you might call the "starter set:" Chimes, Ding, Chord, Tada, and the Microsoft Sound that plays by default when you start Windows. (The sample set includes several MIDIs, but only WAVs can be assigned to sound events.) Windows also offers an extensive library of alternative sounds in four collections. The Jungle collection provides birds chirping, frogs croaking, and animals growling. The Musica collection includes guitar chords, drum taps, horn toots, and other musical sounds. (One Musica WAV sounds to me like someone yelping, but then, so does some music.) The Robotz collection are high-tech electronic sounds. The Utopia collection are modernistic clicks, pops, thweeps, psssts, and several sounds that I can't describe. These additional WAVs are named for the sound events they were designed for — names like Musica Asterisk, Jungle Error, and Robotz Maximize — but they're not limited to those events. You could, if you wish, assign Utopia Maximize to the Asterisk event and Robotz Critical Stop to the Open Program event.

The sample sounds and the four additional collections are located in your Windows\Media folder. If yours are missing and you want to try them out, you can install them from your Windows CD-ROM as long as you have 6.8MB of space available on your hard drive.

How to install the additional windows sounds collections in Windows 95 and 98:

1. Choose Start ⇨ Settings ⇨ Control Panel to open the Control Panel.

2. Open Add/Remove Programs.

3. Choose the Windows Setup tab (see Figure 4-3).

4. Open Multimedia by double-clicking it. Figure 4-4 shows the Multimedia dialog box.

5. Select Multimedia Sound Schemes.

Caution

Be careful not to select or deselect any other item. If you add a check mark to another item, Windows installs that item. Worse, if you accidentally remove an existing check mark, Windows uninstalls that item.

6. Choose OK to close the Details dialog box. Then choose OK to close the Add/Remove Programs Properties dialog box.

7. At this point, Windows installs the items you selected. Follow the onscreen directions, which tell you when to insert the Windows disc into the CD-ROM drive.

Figure 4-3 *The Windows Setup page lets you add and remove Windows features.*

Figure 4-4 *Use the Multimedia dialog box to add the Multimedia Sound Schemes.*

How to install the additional windows sounds collections in Windows NT:

1. Choose Start ➪ Settings ➪ Control Panel to open the Control Panel.

2. Open Add/Remove Programs.

3. Choose the Windows NT Setup tab.

4. Open Multimedia by double-clicking it.

5. Select the schemes you want to add, such as Robotz Sound Scheme and Utopia Sound Scheme.

Caution

Be careful not to select or deselect any other item. If you add a check mark to another item, Windows installs that item. Worse, if you accidentally remove an existing check mark, Windows uninstalls that item.

6. Choose OK to close the Details dialog box. Then choose OK to close the Add/Remove Programs Properties dialog box.

7. At this point, Windows installs the items you selected. Follow the directions on the screen, which tell you when to insert the Windows disc into the CD-ROM drive.

Tip

The Windows floppy disks do not have the additional sound files. But all is not lost, as you can download the WAVs free from Microsoft's Web site:

http://www.microsoft.com/windows95/info
In case that address no longer works, don't forget to check this book's Web site for an updated address:

http://members.aol.com/jnfbooks

All the other sounds on your hard drive

You may have a lot of WAVs that weren't provided by Windows. You may have hundreds of WAVs here and there on your hard drive that were installed by various programs, or that you created or downloaded. Since they can all be used with sound events, it's good to know everything available to you. The Windows Find feature helps you locate every WAV file on your hard drive.

How to find all the WAVs on your hard drive:

1. Choose Start ➪ Find ➪ Files or Folders to open the Find window, shown in Figure 4-5.

2. In the Named box, type *.**wav**.

3. Drop down the Look In list and choose your hard drive. If you have multiple hard drives, choose them one at a time in Windows 95, or choose Local Hard Drives in Windows 98 or NT.

4. Make sure that "Include subfolders" is checked.

5. Choose Find Now.

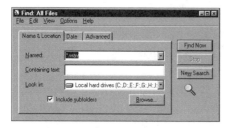

Figure 4-5 *Windows Find function can locate all the WAV files on your drives.*

Windows adds a new area to the bottom of the Find window (see Figure 4-6), where it lists the files it finds. In the figure, I have chosen View ➪ Details so that you can see the file locations, sizes, and dates. The other views don't include this information, and you need it when you're trying to organize your WAVs.

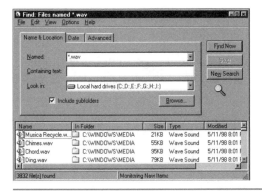

Figure 4-6 *Find builds a list of found files in the bottom part of its window.*

Tip

Resize or maximize the window to see as much of the list as possible.

You use the Find list just like an Explorer window. You can play sounds by double-clicking them; sort the list by name, folder, size, and date; and move, copy, rename, and delete files. You can even save the list if you think you'll want to come back to it later. First, choose Options ⇨ Save Results to enable this option. (If it already has a check mark next to it, don't select it or you'll disable it.) Then choose File ⇨ Save Search. Windows places an icon on your desktop labeled Files named *.wav. Double-click this icon to reopen the list of found files.

Tip

You can use these same search techniques to find other types of files too. For example, you could search for ***.mid** or ***.rmi** to find MIDI files.

How to assign WAVs to sound events

You have already seen a couple of examples of the Sounds Properties window, where you can review and change sound event assignments. In the example in Figure 4-7, I have selected the Asterisk event. (Applications generally use the Asterisk event to add emphasis to a message.) The Name box shows the name of the WAV assigned to this event, in this case Chord.wav. You can hear the sound by clicking the preview icon (shown here in the margin).

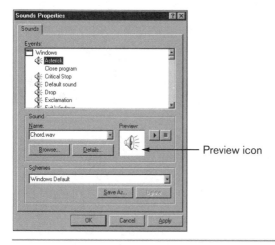

Preview icon

Figure 4-7 *When you select an event, Sounds Properties displays the sound assigned to it.*

Displaying your filename extensions

Tip #41 to avoid premature aging: Notice that the filename shown in Figure 4-7 includes the .wav extension. Windows normally suppresses registered extensions, driving this old DOS user batty. I force Windows to show all filename extensions, registered or not.

How to display filename extensions in Windows 95 and NT:

1. Open My Computer or Explorer. (Either one will do.)

2. Choose View ➪ Options to open the Options dialog box.

3. For Windows 95, disable "Hide MS-DOS file extensions for file types that are registered." For Windows NT, disable "Hide file extensions for known file types." (By *disable*, I mean click it to remove the check mark from the check box.)

4. Choose OK to close the dialog box.

How to display filename extensions in Windows 98:

1. Open My Computer or Explorer. (Either one will do.)

2. Choose View ⇨ Folder Options to open the Options dialog box.

3. Choose the View tab to open the View options page.

4. Disable "Hide file extensions for known file types." (By disable, I mean click it to remove the check mark from the check box.)

5. Choose OK to close the dialog box.

This affects every dialog box that lists filenames, including My Computer, Explorer, and Open and Save As dialog boxes in applications such as Word and Lotus 1-2-3.

The Name box is a drop-down list showing all the WAVs in the Windows\Media folder. You can select a WAV from this list or click the Browse button to view other folders. When you browse another folder, that folder's WAVs replace the default list until you close the dialog box. The next time you open the dialog box, the Windows\Media folder once again appears in the drop-down list.

Tip

Store all the WAVs that you use for sound events in the Windows\Media folder. (Copy them to the Media folder if they're also needed elsewhere.) It's easier to find them in the Media folder when you're assigning sounds, Windows doesn't have to change folders to play them, and it's less likely that you'll delete them when weeding out your hard drive.

How to change the WAV assigned to a sound event:

1. Open the Sounds Properties window.

2. Scroll through the Events list and select the event you want to change.

3. Drop down the Name list and select a file, or click the Browse button to locate and select the desired file.

4. Listen to the selected file by clicking the preview icon.

5. If you decide that you don't want to use this sound, repeat steps 3 and 4 until you find the sound you want to assign.

6. Repeat steps 2 through 5 for all the events you want to change.

7. Click OK to close the window and put your new sounds into effect.

The Browse dialog box (see Figure 4-8) has a couple of features that make your life a little easier. First, it has its own preview icon so you can listen to sounds while browsing—a real time-saver. Second, after you play around long enough in various folders, you might forget what event you were trying to assign. Fortunately, the title of the dialog box includes the name of the event, as in Browse for Asterisk Sound or Browse for Critical Stop Sound.

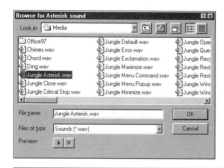

Figure 4-8 *Use the Browse for Sound dialog box to locate a sound to assign to an event.*

Note

The first item in the drop-down list is always (None). Choose (None) to unassign an event.

Sometimes when you're cleaning up your hard drive, you accidentally delete, rename, or move a WAV that is assigned to a sound event. The next time that event occurs, Windows won't be able to find the file. It does not display an error message (thank goodness) nor play a default sound. If you go to the Sounds Properties window and select that event, however, you'll see this error message: `Windows cannot find the file` *xxxxxxx*. `Do you want to use the file for this event anyway?` Click No to clear the message and then reassign or unassign the sound event, if you wish.

Sound schemes

So far you have seen how to assign sounds one at a time. With a sound scheme, you assign all your events at once. Windows gives you a few sound schemes to start with, and it's a simple task to create your own. Read on.

Creating and installing sound schemes

A *sound scheme* is a named set of sound assignments stored in your system so that you can go back to it at any time. For example, suppose you want some spooky Halloween sounds in October but your usual sounds again in November. First you save your current setup as a scheme, perhaps naming it Normal. Then you assign the new sounds. You also might save the new sounds as a scheme named Halloween. It takes just one step to return to your Normal scheme after the holiday. And it's just as easy to reinstate the Halloween scheme next October.

How to save a sound scheme:

1. In the Sounds Properties dialog box, set up all the events the way you want them.

2. In the Schemes group, choose Save As to open the Save Scheme As dialog box (see Figure 4-9). Windows provides the current scheme's name as the default in this dialog box.

3. Type a name for your scheme, which can be a new name or an existing one. If you use an existing name, Windows replaces the existing scheme with the new one.

Tip

You can't replace or modify the two basic schemes provided by Windows, No Sounds and Windows Default. These two schemes are described in the next section. (In Windows NT, the default theme is called Windows NT Default.)

4. Choose OK.

5. If you used an existing name, you must confirm that you want to replace the scheme.

Your new scheme now appears in the Schemes drop-down list.

Figure 4-9 *You provide a name for your sound scheme in the Save Scheme As dialog box.*

A sound scheme stores the status for *all* sound events, those with sounds and those with none. When you recall the sound scheme, it restores the status of all events, not just the ones with assignments. Suppose, for example, that you currently have sounds assigned to the Maximize and Minimize events. If you install the Windows Default scheme, Minimize and Maximize will be cleared.
How to install a sound scheme:

1. Open the Sounds Properties window.

2. Select the desired scheme from the Schemes drop-down list.

Tip

You modify a sound scheme by installing it, making whatever changes you want, and then saving it with the same name.

How to delete a sound scheme:

1. Select the scheme in the Schemes drop-down list and choose Delete.

2. A dialog box asks if you're sure you want to delete the scheme. You must choose Yes to delete it.

   Because you have just deleted the current sound scheme, Windows automatically returns to the No Sounds scheme.

Windows sound schemes

Windows provides a few schemes to get you started. The default sound assignments appear in a scheme called Windows Default. Returning to this scheme is like wiping the slate clean and starting over—you go back to the five sample sounds. The No Sounds scheme clears all sound assignments, which comes in handy in settings where quiet is essential. You cannot modify or delete either of these schemes.

If you have installed the additional sound collections, you also have Jungle, Musica, Robotz, and Utopia sound schemes. Each scheme uses many, but not all, of the sounds from the collection with the same name. They don't assign sounds to the Open Program and Close Program events, for example, even though the collections include WAVs designed for those events. These four schemes are not protected by Windows; you can modify and delete them as you wish.

Microsoft Plus! themes

If you have the Microsoft Plus! pack, you have another way to set sounds—themes. A *theme* is a collection of related sounds, desktop icons, wallpaper, mouse pointers, fonts, screen saver, and colors.

Themes make it easy to coordinate your entire Windows environment with just a few clicks. Figure 4-10 shows the Dangerous Creatures desktop, but I have no way to show you the other elements in the theme. Plus! 95 provides more than a dozen themes, including Science, Nature, Travel, Sports, The 60s USA, and Mystery. Plus! 98 gives you 18 themes, including Architecture, Jazz, Science Fiction, and several based on popular comic strips (Doonesbury, Cathy, and Garfield, for starters) with animated wallpaper.

Tip

Don't worry – Plus! 98 does not remove your Plus! 95 desktop themes. Adding Plus! 98's themes to Plus 95's themes, gives you nearly three dozen themes from which to choose.

Figure 4-10 *The Dangerous Creatures theme features the cougar wallpaper and various creature icons for the standard Windows objects on your desktop.*

To use themes, you must first install them from the Plus! CD-ROM. If you haven't already done that, the following procedure will guide you.

How to install desktop themes:

1. Insert the Plus! CD-ROM into your CD-ROM drive. If Plus! doesn't start automatically, use Windows Explorer to view the contents of your CD-ROM drive and double-click `autorun`.

2. If you have already installed Plus! and just need to add Desktop Themes, follow these steps:

    a. Choose Add/Remove Programs to open the Setup Maintenance wizard.

    b. Select the Add/Remove option and click Next.

    c. In the list of Plus! components, enable Desktop Themes and click Next.

    d. Follow the directions on your screen while Plus! installs your themes.

3. If you have not yet installed Plus!, choose Install Plus! and follow the directions on your screen. Be sure to include Desktop Themes when you select components to install.

Tip

Actually, you don't need Plus! to get the Dangerous Creatures theme. You can download it for free from Microsoft's Web site as a demo of the Plus! package. Here's the URL:

`http://www.microsoft.com/windows95/info`

Now you can select whichever theme you're in the mood for. How to select a theme:

1. Open the Control Panel.

2. Open the Desktop Themes applet to open the Desktop Themes window shown in Figure 4-11.

3. Select a theme from the Theme drop-down list. The sample desktop in the window shows the new theme. Keep trying out themes until you find one you like.

4. Choose OK to close the window and put the new theme into effect.

Figure 4-11 *The Desktop Themes window lets you preview and select from all the installed schemes.*

While you're in the Desktop Themes window, you can preview the sounds and other elements by clicking the buttons in the Previews section in the upper-right corner of the window.

The Wave Events editor

For people like me, the sound event features built into Windows aren't quite enough. Wave Events is a shareware program by Gregory Jones that gives you the ability to add and remove sound events for specific applications.

What Wave Events does

Wave Events can't create sound events that would be unique to an application, such as opening a file or recalculating a worksheet. It assigns only general Windows events: Open Program, Maximize, Menu Command, and so on. What makes Wave Events different from the basic Windows facility is that it can assign different sounds for each application. So you could set up WordPad, for example, with sounds for Minimize, Maximize, Question, and Asterisk, that are different from Calculator's sounds for those same events. With Wave Events, you can assign sound events to applications (EXE files), screen savers (SCR files), and links to applications and screen savers (LNK files).

Here's what you can do with Wave Events:

- Add new sound events for specific applications
- Remove existing sound events (except for the standard Windows events)
- Assign and unassign sounds
- Randomize sound assignments

The Wave Events interface

Starting Wave Events opens the window shown in Figure 4-12. As with many Windows applications, Wave Events gives you several ways to accomplish a task, including menus, shortcut keys, toolbar buttons, drag-and-drop, and context menus. If I showed you all these methods, this chapter would be twice as long. I personally prefer toolbar buttons, which are always right there when you need them, so I use those in this section.

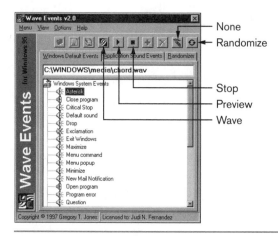

None
Randomize
Stop
Preview
Wave

Figure 4-12 *The Wave Events window shows your current sound assignments and lets you change them.*

The speaker icons in the events list are slightly different from those in the Sounds Properties window. A yellow icon indicates an assigned event, a gray icon indicates an unassigned event, and a red X over a yellow icon (see Exclamation in Figure 4-12) indicates an assigned event where the sound file is missing.

Windows system events

Figure 4-12 shows the Windows Default Events page, where you can see the Windows System Events group. You can do only two things with these events: you can change or remove sound assignments. Changes you make on this page affect all applications that don't have specific sound assignments, just like making the changes in the Sounds Properties window.

Adding your own application events

Choosing the Application Sound Events tab takes you to the page shown in Figure 4-13, where you can see all the currently installed application events. I have expanded the Quicken group so you can see the events I installed for that application.

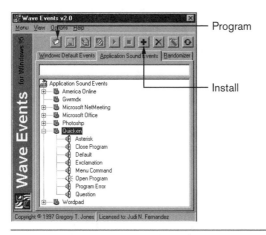

Program

Install

Figure 4-13 *You create new sound events for your applications on the Application Sound Events page.*

How to add an application to the Application Sound Events page:

1. Choose the Application Sound Events tab.

2. Choose the Program button, shown in Figure 4-13. A common Open dialog box appears. (If you have not registered Wave Events, you must respond to a nag screen before the dialog box appears.)

3. Locate and select the program for which you want to create sound events. The Install Events dialog box appears (see Figure 4-14), showing 13 possible sound events divided into two categories: Basic and Other.

4. Choose one of the four buttons depending on whether you want to install All 13 events, the Basic events, the Other events, or just the events you have Selected from the list. The dialog box closes and the new events appear in the Wave Events window.

Figure 4-14 *The Install Events dialog box lets you create new sound events for an application.*

If the application already has a group, you don't need to go through the above steps. All you have to do is add more sounds to the existing group.

How to add more sound events to an application:

1. In the Wave Events window, choose the Application Sound Events tab.

2. Select the desired program.

3. Choose the Install button, shown in Figure 4-13. The Install Events dialog box appears (see Figure 4-14).

4. Choose one of the four buttons depending on whether you want to install all 13 events, the basic events, the other events, or just the events you have selected from the list. The dialog box closes and the new events appear in the Wave Events window.

Note

The only events that make sense for screen savers are Open Program and Close Program. Even though Wave Events lets you assign other events, they could never be triggered.

Assigning sounds to events

So far, your new events are unassigned. You use the following procedure to assign sounds to any events, Windows or applications, new or old, assigned or not.

How to assign sounds to events:

1. Select the desired event.

2. If the event currently has a sound, you can listen to it by choosing the Preview icon (shown in Figure 4-12).

3. Choose the Wave button to open the Event Sound dialog box (see Figure 4-15).

4. Locate and select the desired WAV. (You can preview WAVs by clicking the Preview icon. If you start one that goes on forever, use the Stop button, to interrupt it.)

   To unassign the selected event, choose the None button.

5. Choose OK to close the dialog box and assign the selected WAV (or none) to the event.

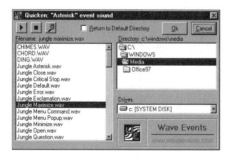

Figure 4-15 *The Event Sound dialog box lets you assign a WAV to an event.*

Removing application events

The thing I like best about Wave Events is that it lets you *remove* sound events, which you can't do via Sounds Properties. At last you can get rid of events that some long-dead application orphaned in your system. Simply select an event (or an entire application) and press Delete.

Currently you can't remove Windows system events, just application events. Gregory Jones tells me that some day he might add a capability for advanced users to remove Windows system events. But you would be wise to exercise extreme caution with such a feature; once you've removed a Windows system event, you have to reinstall Windows to get it back.

Randomizing event assignments

If you have a strong need for constant change, try playing musical chairs with your Windows system event assignments via Wave Events' randomizer. It gives you two ways to randomize:

- A single time when you choose the randomize button
- Each time you boot

Choosing the Randomizer tab opens the page shown in Figure 4-16. On this page, you select the events that you want to randomize. For each event, you build a list of WAVs for the randomizer to choose from. The example in Figure 4-16 shows the list I have created for the Start Windows event. Each time I randomize, Wave Events assigns one of the sounds in this list to the Start Windows event.

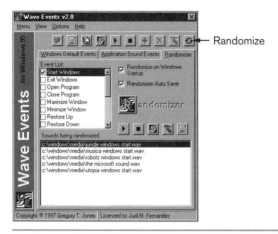

Randomize

Figure 4-16 *Use the Randomizer page if you want to randomize some of your sound assignments.*

How to set up randomization:

1. Choose the Randomizer tab.

2. Select an event that you want to randomize.

3. Click the Wave button to open the dialog box called Select a WAVe File for the *xxx* Event (see Figure 4-17).

Tip

Drag the dialog box to the side so you can also see your list of WAVs in the Randomizer page. It's easier to recall what WAVs you have already selected when you can see the list.

4. Select a WAV file for the event. As always, the Preview and Stop buttons help in finding WAVs.

5. Choose the Add button to add the currently selected WAV to the event's WAV list.

6. Repeat steps 4 and 5 until you have selected all the WAVs for the event. (You can come back later and add more, if you wish.)

7. Choose Exit to close the dialog box.

8. Repeat steps 2 through 7 for each event you want to randomize.

Figure 4-17 *You build a list of WAVs for an event in this dialog box.*

Now that you have set up the randomization list, choose the Randomize button (shown in Figure 4-16) to randomize your sounds immediately. Or enable Randomize on Windows Startup if you want Wave Events to randomize your sounds each time you start up Windows.

Note

To remove a sound from an event's randomization list, select the sound and press Delete.

Volume Control

Suppose you're listening to some music when the phone rings. How do you mute the sound while you answer the phone? If your speakers have a volume knob, the answer is simple — just turn it down. But even if you don't have a volume knob, it's still fairly simple: pop up Volume Control and select Mute.

Or suppose you're listening to a CD while you work, but your word processor's WAVs interfere with your enjoyment of the music. In many systems, Volume Control acts as a mixer, so you can turn down the WAVs and turn up the CD in relationship to each other while keeping the overall volume the same.

Note

If your sound board doesn't provide a volume control, you probably want to skip this section.

What Volume Control does

Volume Control gives you the ability to adjust or mute the volume of your various sound devices. It also gives you a master volume control to adjust all the devices at once. But that's not all it does. You can also use it for these features:

- Adjust the balance between your speakers for each device and for the master control.
- Select the devices to use in cases where you have more than one.
- Configure advanced features for your devices.

And of course, you can tailor the Volume Control window.

The Volume Control window

Volume Control is a Windows program, but its contents are determined by your sound hardware and software. I wish I could show you exactly what yours looks like, but unless you have the same sound hardware and software I do, yours will be different from what you see here. All I can do is show you my Volume Control, based on Creative's AWE64 with some Yamaha enhancements. Yours should be similar, but it might not be identical.

Your system might be set up to display the Volume Control icon, a tiny yellow speaker, in your system tray. If so, you can open Volume Control by double-clicking the icon. In any case, you can open it by choosing Start ⇨ Programs ⇨ Accessories ⇨ Multimedia ⇨ Volume Control. Figure 4-18 shows my Volume Control window, which acts as a mixer, letting me adjust the master volume as well as each individual device. The master control affects all sound, whereas the individual controls affect just the indicated devices.

Tip

To pop up just the master control without the entire mixer, single-click the Volume Control icon in the system tray.

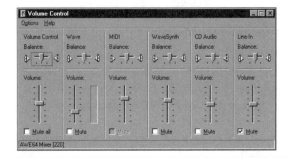

Figure 4-18 *The Volume Control window acts as a mixer.*

Using Volume control is fairly simple. Drag a vertical slider up and down to adjust a device's volume. Drag a Balance slider left and right to adjust a device's balance. Enable Mute to silence a device.

Note

For all sampled and streaming media, use the Wave control.

Volume Control properties

The Options menu provides commands to configure the Volume Control window. In my system, choosing Options ⇨ Properties opens the Properties dialog box shown in Figure 4-19. Again, yours might be different from the one shown in the figure. At the top, you can select a mixer device if you have more than one. In the middle group ("Adjust volume for"), you can select which type of devices you want to display. The Playback option displays your playback devices: WAV device, MIDI device, CD-ROM drive, and so on. When you want to record something, change to the Recording option so that the mixer includes devices such as the microphone. Several devices appear on both lists since you might both listen to and record from the CD-ROM drive, a MIDI instrument, or the line-in port. The Other option makes room for other types of sound features you may have, such as voice commands.

Figure 4-19 *Use the Volume Control Properties dialog box to configure your Volume Control window.*

Once you have selected the category of devices for the Volume Control, you can enable and disable specific devices in the list box at the bottom of the dialog box. I usually leave them all enabled — Why not? — but some people may prefer to see just the devices they're actually using. When you choose OK to close the dialog box, you'll see the controls for the selected devices in your Volume Control window.

Advanced settings

Some of your devices might have advanced options. To find out, choose Options ➪ Advanced Controls, which adds Advanced buttons to your Volume Control window for those devices that have such options. Figure 4-20 shows my Volume Control window with two Advanced buttons: one for the master volume control and the other for the WaveSynth control. As always in this section, your system may offer different advanced options, or none at all.

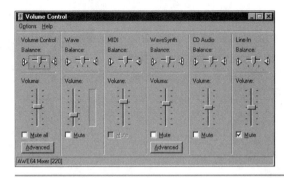

Figure 4-20 *The Advanced Control option adds Advanced buttons to your Volume Control window.*

 Tip

Look for Advanced Controls for all three categories of devices from the Properties dialog box: Playback, Recording, and Other. You may find advanced options for any of these types of devices.

Clicking an Advanced button opens a dialog box where you review and set the advanced options for the indicated device. Figure 4-21 shows my Advanced Controls for Volume Control dialog box, which opens when I choose the Advanced button for my master volume control. As you can see, I can control tone (bass and treble) and 3D Stereo Enhancement.

Figure 4-21 *Choose an Advanced button to open a dialog box showing your advanced controls.*

Tip

Don't forget that media players such as Jet-Audio and CD/Spectrum Pro also provide mixers. Since they all affect the same sound board, the settings on one mixer are reflected on all the others.

The Multimedia Properties

The Multimedia Properties window, shown in Figure 4-22, configures your multimedia devices, including your sound devices. Some features overlap with Volume Control, but others are unique to this window. Start the Multimedia applet on your Control Panel to open the Multimedia Properties window. Figure 4-12 shows the Windows 98 version of the window. The Windows 95 and NT dialog boxes are similar, but not exactly the same.

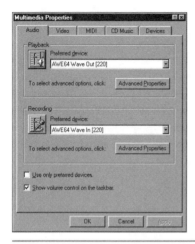

Figure 4-22 *Use the Audio Multimedia Properties to configure your multimedia devices.*

Audio (WAV) properties

The Audio page shown in Figure 4-26 sets the properties for your WAV devices — playback and recording. Here you can select your preferred devices if you have more than one of each. In Windows 98, the button in each box opens the playback or recording version of Volume Control. In Windows 95 and NT, the dialog box includes volume sliders.

The Volume Control taskbar icon

It's nice to have program icons in your system tray where you can reach them easily and start your favorite programs with a simple double-click. But if your system is like mine, so many programs want to put their icons in your system tray that it threatens to take over your taskbar. I eliminate the programs that just as easily can be started from the Start menu. I like having Volume Control in my system tray, though, because I like to be able to mute the volume quickly when I get a phone call.

Notice in the Figure 4-22 a check box labeled "Show volume control on the taskbar." This option refers not just to your WAV playback device but to the Volume Control taskbar icon. The option is selected by default, giving the icon residence in your taskbar. Disable this option to get rid of the icon.

MIDI properties

Figure 4-23 shows the MIDI properties. Here you can select your MIDI device. If you have more than one possibility and don't know which one you prefer, it's fairly easy to try them out.

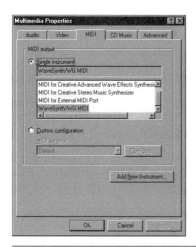

Figure 4-23 *You configure your MIDI devices in the MIDI Multimedia Properties window.*

How to try out your MIDI devices:

1. Open a MIDI file but don't play it yet.
2. Open the MIDI page in your Multimedia Properties window.
3. Select a device.

4. Choose Apply to put the new device into effect without closing the window.

5. Play the MIDI file.

6. Stop the MIDI file so you can select another device. (You can't change instruments while a MIDI is playing.)

7. Repeat steps 3 through 6 until you find the device you want.

8. Choose OK to close the window and continue using the chosen device.

CD Music properties

Figure 4-24 shows the Windows 98 version of the CD Music properties. If you have only one CD-ROM drive, the CD-ROM drop-down list should show only that drive. For multiple drives, the drive you select here becomes the default drive for Media Player and CD Player. You can also set the volume for each CD-ROM drive here. This control is somewhat different than Volume Control's. It affects the volume of the CD-ROM drive, while Volume Control affects the volume of the sound board. When playing music through your speakers, it doesn't matter which control you use — the effect is the same. But if you want to adjust the volume of the CD-ROM drive's headphone jack, assuming your CD-ROM drive doesn't provide a manual volume knob, you must use this control. (In Windows 95 and NT, this volume control is labeled "Headphone.")

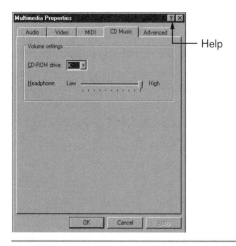

Figure 4-24 *You configure your CD player in the CD Music Multimedia Properties window.*

What else can you do in Multimedia Properties?

I have explained here the basic options in the Multimedia Properties window. Since so many multimedia configurations are possible, you might have additional features that other people don't. Notice in Figure 4-24, for example, that the whole bottom section of my CD Music page is dimmed. On my system, I cannot choose between analog and digital CD audio. Can you?

I encourage you to completely explore all the pages in your Multimedia Properties window. Click any Advanced buttons to see what other options you have. (Some "advanced" options aren't really advanced at all. They're just labeled "advanced" because they don't appear on the main page.)

If you're not sure what an option does, you can get pop-up help in Windows 95 and 98. A Help icon, shown in Figure 4-24, appears in the window's title bar. To pop up a brief explanation of an option, first click the Help icon and then click the option. Click the pop-up box to close it again. Finally, if you're still not sure what the option does, why not try it to see what happens? Just remember (or write down) the former setting so you can restore it if need be.

What's Next?

This chapter has concentrated on using sounds with Windows. But I haven't left the out Macintosh users. Chapter 5 explains the sound facilities on the Mac OS.

The fine print

Wave Events is a shareware program. Its registration fee is $10. You can try it out for 30 days free of charge, but some of the functions are disabled in the unregistered version. It also nags you to register until you pay the fee. Wave Events works by editing the Windows Registry, where sound events are stored. It works with Windows 95 and 98 but not with NT, whose registry is structured differently.

Chapter 5

Sound with Mac OS

As any Macintosh owner will tell you, sometimes loudly and proudly, a Mac comes with sound. It plays music, alerts, and sound effects using the built-in hardware and software. It can even talk to you, and in some models you can talk back to it. This chapter shows you how to control sound on your Mac with Sound Manager (the Mac OS basic sound software) and PlainTalk, the speech extension. And since Mac OS doesn't quite do everything people want, you'll also learn how to use Agent Audio and SoundApp to manage snd resources and sound suitcases.

What you'll learn:

- How to manage your system alert sound: selecting one, adding new ones to the list, removing old ones from the list, recording your own, and setting the volume

- How to manage your sound input and output devices: setting the volume, configuring them, and selecting them

- How to use Text-to-Speech: selecting a voice, reading documents out loud in SimpleText, adding voice annotations to SimpleText documents, and using talking alerts

- How to use Agent Audio to manage a program's snd resources: viewing and playing sounds, extracting sounds, and replacing sounds

- How to use SoundApp to create and manage sound suitcases

System Alert Sounds

Mac OS uses one sound as the *system alert* or system beep. It plays the alert sound to call your attention to error messages and other events. It gives you several sounds to choose from, and you can add more sounds to the list if you wish.

Selecting an alert sound

You use the Monitors & Sound control panel to change your alert sound. Figure 5-1 shows an example of the control panel, with the Alerts section selected. The figure shows the five basic sounds provided by Mac OS. You'll see how to add more sounds in the next section.

Figure 5-1 *You change your system alert sound in the Monitors & Sound control panel.*

How to change the alert sound:

1. Choose Apple menu Control Panels Monitors & Sound to open the control panel.

2. Choose the Alerts button to display the Alerts panel. This panel lists all the sounds that can be alert sounds. The current one is highlighted.

3. Click each sound to hear what it sounds like.

4. When you find the sound you want to use, drag the System Alert Volume slider to adjust its volume. Keep playing it and adjusting the volume until you're satisfied with the way it sounds.

5. Close the panel when you're done.

Locating more sound files

You aren't limited to the few alert sounds that Mac OS gives you. You can add as many sounds to the list as you'd like. Before I show you how to do that, let's look at how you can find some sounds to use. The following procedure uses Find File to build a list of sound files. It doesn't find all possible sounds on your system because it doesn't locate snd resources. You'll see how to access snd resources in the "Managing snd Resources with Agent Audio" section later in this chapter.

How to find all your sound files:

1. Choose Apple menu ⇨ Find File to open the Find File window, shown in Figure 5-2.

2. Set the five pop-up menus so that the window reads, "Find items *on all disks* whose *kind is sound*," as shown in the figure.

3. Choose Find to begin the search.

Figure 5-2 *File Find helps you locate all the sound files on your computer.*

Find File opens a new Items Found window to list the files it finds, as you can see in Figure 5-3. The top panel lists the files. When you select a file in the top panel, the bottom panel shows the location of the file. In the example, the Droplet sound is selected in the top panel, and the bottom panel shows that it is in the SoundApp68K folder. You can resize the bottom panel by dragging the bar between the two panels. You can access a file directly from the top panel. Double-click a sound to listen to it, or drag it from the window to move it to the desktop or some other folder.

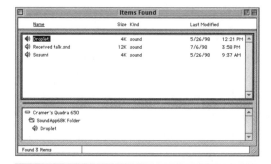

Figure 5-3 *The Items Found window displays the results of a File Find search.*

Adding more system alert sounds

The Alerts panel lists all the snd resources in the System file (also called the System suitcase). You can add any sound to the list by moving or copying it into the System file. The following procedure shows you how.

Tip

Tip #51 to avoid premature aging: Keep your system alert sound short and pleasant. You have to listen to it a lot.

How to add more system alert sounds:

1. Quit all programs (except Finder). You can't change the System file if any program is running.

2. Open your startup disk by double-clicking its icon on your desktop.

3. Open the System Folder and locate the System file. (Don't open it, just find it.)

4. Locate the sound file that you want to add.

5. Drag the sound file to the closed System file. The next time you open the Alerts panel, you'll see the new sound in the list.

Tip

If you're having trouble dragging the sound from its current folder to the System file, try dropping it to the desktop. Then drag it from the desktop to the System file.

To remove an unwanted sound from the alert sounds list, drag it out of the System file. If you want to keep it, drop it on the desktop or in another folder. Or drop it in the Trash to delete it. Another way to delete it is to choose the Delete button in the Alerts panel (refer back to Figure 5-1). The Delete button completely eliminates the snd resource; it does not put it in the Trash.

Working with Your Sound Devices

Your Macintosh comes with a variety of sound devices. It probably includes a built-in microphone and speaker. Your monitor might include better speakers. Perhaps you also have added some external sound devices. The Monitors & Sound control panel gives you a way to select the devices you want to work with and adjust their volumes.

Adjusting volume

You use the Sound panel, shown in Figure 5-4, to adjust the volume of all your sound devices. It displays the sound devices attached to your system, so yours might show different devices than those in the figure. Each device can be adjusted independently, and each can be muted without affecting the others.

Figure 5-4 *The Sound panel lets you adjust the volume of your sound devices.*

How to adjust the volume of a sound device:

1. Choose Apple menu ➪ Control Panels ➪ Monitors & Sound to open the control panel.

2. Choose the Sound button to display the Sound panel.

3. Drag the volume slider to adjust the volume of all your devices. The system plays your alert sound so you can hear the new volume.

4. To mute the device, click the Mute box to place an *X* in it. To unmute it, click it again to remove the *X*.

Note

A device cannot be muted if its Mute check box is dimmed (light gray).

Selecting sound devices

Even if you have several sound devices, you can use only one input (or source) device and one output (or playback) device at a time. You select and configure the devices you want to use in the Sounds control panel.

The sound source

The sound source determines which of your input devices you are currently listening to or recording. If you have not added any input devices to your system, your built-in device is your only sound source. By the way, your built-in CD-ROM drive counts as part of the built-in device. If you have added external sound sources — perhaps a CD player or a tape player — you can select and configure them in the Sound control panel.

When you select an external sound source, you have the option of playing it through the current output device. Suppose, for example, that you have added an external tape player to the sound input port. To listen to a tape on your built-in speakers, you would select the tape player as your sound source and enable the Playthrough option. If you don't enable Playthrough, the tape will play but you won't hear it.

Note

Playthrough should be disabled when recording from an external source.

How to select a sound source:

1. Choose Apple menu ⌘ ⇨ Control Panels ⇨ Monitors & Sound to open the Sound control panel.

2. Choose the Sound button to display the Sound panel.

3. Select the device you want from the Sound Monitoring Source pop-up menu. If you select the microphone and start getting feedback (a loud howl), click Mute immediately. Shield the microphone from the speakers to prevent feedback.

4. If the Playthrough option is available, enable it to play the sound through your output device.

The playback device

When you play a sound, where do you hear it? If you have added devices to your system, you probably want to use them instead of the built-in devices. The Sound Out panel lets you choose your playback device.

How to select a playback device:

1. Choose Apple menu ➪ Control Panels ➪ Monitors & Sound to open the Sound control panel.

2. Choose the Sound button to open the Sound panel.

3. In the Sound Output section, select the device you want to use.

4. Depending on your hardware, you may see some device options in the panel. Set the Rate, Size, and Use options for the device, if necessary.

Recording your own alert sounds

The Mac OS alert sounds are a little on the dull side, don't you think? Of course, you can download more interesting sounds from many places on the Internet. (Chapter 9 shows you how.) But it's also fun to record yourself saying "Oops" or "huh?" or your favorite companion barking, meowing, or chirping.

How to record your own alert sound:

1. Following the above procedures, choose and configure the microphone that you want to use as your sound source. Make sure that Playthrough is disabled if you have that option.

2. In the Monitors & Sound control panel, choose the Alerts button to open the Alerts page.

3. Choose Add to open the recorder controls, shown in Figure 5-5.

4. Choose Record to start recording. As you record, the speaker icon displays the volume and the fill bar displays the elapsed time. (Reminder: Keep it short.)

5. Choose Stop to complete the recording.

6. Choose Play to listen to your new recording.

7. Repeat steps 4 through 6 until you have a recording that you want to use.

8. Choose Save and give your new recording a name. The recorder controls disappear and the new sound appears in your Alert Sounds list.

Figure 5-5 *The recorder controls let you make your own voice recordings.*

Note

Chapter 11 explains a lot more about how to record sounds.

Text-to-Speech

PlainTalk gives your Macintosh the ability to talk with you. It can speak to you and recognize what you say, to a limited extent. The technologies of computer speech and voice recognition are still in development, so don't expect too much from your Mac. It can do a lot more than most PCs, but it's still not like talking with your next-door neighbor, unless you live next to Robbie the Robot.

The quality of your text-to-speech depends in large part on which version of the speech software you install. The text-to-speech portion of PlainTalk, called MacinTalk, comes in several levels.

MacinTalk Pro, which sounds fairly natural but strangely Swedish, requires at least a 68040 processor and System 7.0. MacinTalk 3, which sounds more mechanical, can run on the 68030 and higher processors with at least 300K of RAM. MacinTalk 2, which uses wavetable synthesis techniques, runs on any Macintosh with System 6.0.7 or higher and at least 150K of RAM.

All Macintosh processors support English text-to-speech. The 68020 and higher processors also support Mexican Spanish text-to-speech. If your system does not have PlainTalk installed, you can download the English and Mexican Spanish versions at no charge from the following site. You'll also find the latest PlainTalk news, additional voices, applications, and browser plug-ins here:

```
http://www.speech.apple.com/
```

Selecting a voice

MacinTalk provides a variety of voices, and you can download more from Apple's PlainTalk site. A few voices, such as Junior and Fred, are fairly clear. Others are just for fun — Cellos sings everything to the tune of "In the Hall of the Mountain King," and Bahh bleats like a goat.

How to select a voice:

1. Choose Apple menu ⬤ ⇨ Control Panels ⇨ Speech to open the Speech control panel (see Figure 5-6).

2. Select Voice in the Options pop-up menu.

3. Select a voice in the Voice pop-up menu.

4. Click the speaker icon to hear what the voice sounds like. (Hint: You can change the speed of the voice with the Rate slider.)

5. Repeat steps 3 and 4 until you find the voice you want to use.

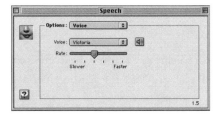

Figure 5-6 *The Speech control panel lets you select a voice for text-to-speech.*

Most likely, both MacinTalk 3 and MacinTalk Pro are installed on your system. MacinTalk 3 provides nearly 20 voices, including Junior, Fred, Cellos, and Bahh. MacinTalk Pro provides three higher quality voices: Agnes, Bruce, and Victoria. All three need a lot more RAM, so if they sound choppy to you, or if they produce error messages, you might need to choose one of the MacinTalk 3 voices until you can install more RAM.

SimpleText speech

SimpleText is the Mac OS document editor with text-to-speech capabilities. It can read aloud all of a document or any selected part. You can also add a recorded message, called a voice annotation, to any document. This section shows you how to use SimpleText's speech features.

Reading documents aloud

SimpleText's Sound menu controls the text-to-speech features. The commands on this menu let you start and stop speech as well as change voices.

How to listen to a document:

1. Open the document in SimpleText.

2. Select the text that you want to hear. (If you don't make a selection, SimpleText reads the entire document.)

3. Choose Sound ➪ Speak Selection (or Speak All if nothing is selected).

Now you can work in other applications while your computer reads the document to you, if you wish. To stop the reading, choose Sound ➪ Stop Speaking. You can change voices via Sound ➪ Voices.

Voice annotations

SimpleText also includes a voice annotation feature. This feature actually has nothing to do with PlainTalk or text-to-speech. It simply records a snd resource. You can then play it back whenever you'd like. Each document can have only one voice annotation.
How to record a voice annotation:

1. Open the document to be annotated in SimpleText.

2. Choose Sound ➪ Record to open the recorder controls. (Refer back to Figure 5-5 to see the recorder controls.)

3. Choose Record to begin the recording.

4. Record your annotation as desired.

5. Choose Stop to end the recording. The recorder controls disappear, and the recording becomes a snd resource in the current document.

6. Choose Sound ➪ Play to listen to the recording. If you decide you don't like it, choose Sound ➪ Erase to get rid of it. Then you try it again, if you wish.

Tip

You can also hear a recorded annotation by dropping the document on the SoundApp icon.

You can't see any indication of the voice annotation in the text itself, but if you pull down the Sound menu, you'll see that the Play and Erase options are available, while Record is not. You might want to add a written note in the document to tell people (including yourself) that a voice annotation is attached and how to play it.

Talking alerts

With PlainTalk 1.5, you can also use talking alerts, where your Mac reads alert messages out loud as well as displaying them. To set up talking alerts, open the Speech control panel and choose Talking Alerts from the pop up menu. Figure 5-7 shows the Talking Alerts control panel.

Figure 5-7 *You set up talking alerts in the Speech control panel.*

The first option, labeled "Speak the phrase," determines what you hear when an alert message first appears. When this option is disabled, each alert is signaled by your standard alert sound. But if you enable this option by clicking it so that an X appears in the check box, the alert sound is replaced by your current PlainTalk voice speaking the selected phrase. The second Talking Alert option, labeled "Speak the alert text," determines whether PlainTalk reads aloud the text of the alert message. PlainTalk pauses the number of seconds indicated by "Wait before speaking" to give you a chance to clear the message before it starts talking.

You can designate a specific alert phrase or choose "Random from the list" to let PlainTalk select a different phrase (or the system beep) each time. "Alert," "Excuse me," "Whoa," and "Rats" are some of the dozen phrases that PlainTalk provides. You can add your own phrases to the list by choosing "Edit phrase list" from the pop-up menu. Then choose Add to add your own, Remove to remove the highlighted phrase, or Edit to change the highlighted phrase.

Tip

You can try out your current talking alerts setup by clicking the speaker icon to the right of the slider.

Managing snd Resources with Agent Audio

It's a little frustrating not to be able to access the snd resources in a file. Sometimes you want to borrow a cool game sound to use as an online chat sound. Or maybe you want to replace an annoying sound with one you like better. Or perhaps you just like to change sounds with the seasons. This book's CD-ROM includes an excellent shareware program called Agent Audio that lets you manage snd resources. With Agent Audio, you can

- View and play sound resources from programs and other files
- Convert sound resources to stand-alone sound files
- Replace snd resources
- Archive snd resources

The fine print

Agent Audio is located in the Macintosh folder on this book's CD-ROM. The registration fee is $12, but you can try it out for one week free of charge. The package includes an electronic manual, where you'll find registration information and a form to print and send.

Viewing and playing sound resources

Figure 5-8 shows the CompuServe sound list displayed in the Agent Audio window. To display any program or file's list of sound resources, simply drop it in either of Agent Audio's two panels. Agent Audio's left-hand panel is known as the Destination and the right-hand panel is known as the Source. To display the CompuServe sound resources, for example, I dropped the CompuServe program icon into Agent Audio's Destination panel. If drag and drop doesn't work for you, use the options on the File menu to open a program or file. Choose File ➪ Open Destination File to open a program or document into the Destination panel. Choose File ➪ Add Source Sounds to open a program or document into the Source panel.

Once the list is displayed, you can listen to any sound by double-clicking it. When you're done with the file, choose Close to remove it from the window again.

Note

Balloon help does not work with Agent Audio. Instead, help appears in the small window near the bottom center as you move your mouse around the Agent Audio window.

Create Sound
Archive

Figure 5-8 *Agent Audio displays the sound resources embedded in any file's resource fork.*

In Figure 5-8, the numbers after the names are not sizes but resource IDs — Button click is resource 15088, Host message is resource 14151 and so on. Programs use the IDs, not names, to access their sound resources. CompuServe activates resource 15088 when you click a button, for example. Every snd resource must have a resource ID, but names are optional.

Extracting sound resources

Suppose one of your game programs has some really cool sounds and you want to "liberate" them to use elsewhere. You use Agent Audio's Create Sound Archive feature to copy snd resources as independent SND files. The original snd resource remains where it is; it is not damaged or deleted when you copy it.

How to copy a snd resource as a separate SND file:

1. Open the program or file containing the snd resource in the Destination panel of Agent Audio.

2. Select the sound that you want to extract from the program.

3. Choose the Create Sound Archive button (see Figure 5-8) to open the window shown in Figure 5-9.

4. Choose System 7 Sound File.

5. Select a location for it. (You can also change its name if you wish.)

6. Choose Save to complete the task.

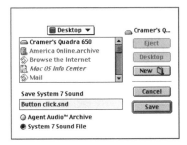

Figure 5-9 *When you extract an snd resource, Agent Audio displays this window so you can assign a name and location to the file.*

Replacing sound resources

Suppose you want to replace one or more of a program's resources. For example, lots of AOL members like to change their standard sound files — Welcome, You've Got Mail, and so on — for holidays or just for fun. Agent Audio gives you the ability to change the sounds in any program or file.

 Before you change anything, you should archive the current sounds so you can restore them later, if you wish. Just follow the above procedure, except in step 4 keep the default option of Agent Audio Archive. When you choose Save, Agent Audio copies all the Destination snd resources into an archive file, using the file icon shown in the margin. You can reopen this archive in Agent Audio at any time by dragging it into either panel.

After you have archived the program's current resources, you're ready to replace them. For the next step, you drop some replacement sounds into the Source panel. You can build the Source list from many different places. You could drop a couple of program icons into the Source panel, add a few independent SND files, and throw in an Agent Audio archive or two. The Destination list can contain resources from only one file or program at a time, but the Source list can receive sounds from a variety of sources. Once you have set up your Source list, the Agent Audio window looks something like Figure 5-10.

Figure 5-10 *Agent Audio lets you copy sounds from the Source list to replace Destination sounds.*

Now all you have to do is select a Destination sound to be replaced, select a Source sound, and choose the Replace/Copy Sound button, shown in Figure 5-10. A black dot appears next to the Destination sound to show that it has been replaced. The Destination sound's name and ID do not change. You can check the new sound by double-clicking it to make sure the change took place. When you're satisfied with all your changes, choose the Save button to save the file with its new snd resources.

Tip

Choose Edit ⇨ Undo to undo your most recent replacement. Choose Revert to undo all your changes since the last time you saved the file.

Using SoundApp to Create Sound Suitcases

A *suitcase* is a special type of Macintosh file that holds system resources such as sounds. It's similar to a folder except that it contains resources instead of files and all the resources are of the same type. It's an efficient and easy way to store and access your sounds.

Chapter 2 introduces SoundApp as a way to play back and convert many types of sound files on your Mac. You also use SoundApp to create a new sound suitcase. First, you need to configure a few options. Start SoundApp and choose Convert⇨File Format⇨Sound Suitcase. This tells SoundApp to convert sounds into the sound suitcase format. It also configures the other submenus of the Convert menu so that only options appropriate for sound suitcases are shown. Next, choose Convert⇨Encoding and select the desired encoding method. Choose Convert⇨Sampling Rate and select the desired sampling rate. Or if you want each converted sound to retain its current sampling rate, choose No Change. Likewise, choose Convert⇨Channels and choose Mono, Stereo, or No Change. You don't need to choose anything on the Convert⇨Bit Depth submenu because the only available option for sound suitcase is 16-bit.

Now you're ready to create a suitcase. Select one or more sounds to start with. Hold down Shift (SoundApp's conversion key) while you drag and drop them on the SoundApp icon. SoundApp displays a window where you can select the location for the new suitcase and give it a name.

Once the suitcase is created, you can add more sounds to it simply by dropping them on the suitcase. You open a sound suitcase just like any folder or file, by double-clicking it. Remove sounds by dragging them out of the suitcase. Double-click a sound to play it.

What's Next?

AOL, CompuServe, and The Microsoft Network all have extensive sound features. Not only do they use sound themselves, but they also provide a treasure trove of sound files for downloading. Chapter 6 shows you how to work with sound on all three of these popular online services.

Chapter 6

Using Sound Files with Online Services

Back in the Dark Ages, online services had no graphics or sound. That was fine because our computers didn't either. But now—wow! Most online services use graphics as their primary interface. Sound often acts as an enhancement rather than playing a major role in the interface.

This chapter deals with sound as it exists today on the three most popular online services—America Online (AOL), CompuServe, and the Microsoft Network (MSN). I am also including a service that is not strictly an online service but where you can chat and share sound files—Internet Relay Chat (IRC) using the mIRC interface for Windows.

What you'll learn:

- How to configure and use America Online's sound events, buddy sounds, and chat room sounds (also, how to use PowerTools to manage chat room sounds)

- How to use configure CompuServe's sound events

- How to use configure, play, and trade sounds in mIRC channels (also, how to use WaVGeT to manage sound files)

- How to configure and use Microsoft Network's sound events and chat room sounds

Sounds on America Online

AOL provides a few sound events, which you can reassign, but the major use of sound here is in the chat rooms, where you can play sounds for the people you're chatting with. In the following sections, you'll learn where to find the AOL sound events, how to play sounds in chat rooms, and where to find lots of sound files to download.

Basic AOL sound events

When you sign on to AOL, a man's voice says, "Welcome," perhaps followed by a delighted "You've got mail." He also bids you "Goodbye" when you leave. (Silly me — I used to think the voice belonged to Steve Case, the founder and CEO of AOL. It's really an actor named Elwood Edwards.) These audio messages are triggered by sound events, of course. Table 6-1 lists the six basic sound events on AOL, along with their Windows filenames. The Mac snd resource names are the same as the sound event names, except that the system alert sound is used in place of Drop. Two more events, associated with AOL's Buddy Lists, are discussed in the next section.

Table 6-1 *AOL Basic Sound Events*

Event Name	Default Windows File	Default Sound
Drop	`drop.wav`	water drop (for PC)
File's Done	`filedone.wav`	"File's done"
Goodbye	`goodbye.wav`	"Goodbye"
IM	`im.wav`	chimes
Welcome	`welcome.wav`	"Welcome"
You've Got Mail	`gotmail.wav`	"You've got mail"

If you're using Windows, you'll find the AOL sound events in your Sounds Properties window, shown in Figure 6-1. You can assign any WAV files to them, just like any other sound events. To change their assignments, use the Sounds Properties window, Wave Events, or another sound editor, as explained in Chapter 4.

Figure 6-1 *The AOL sound events appear in the Windows 95 Sounds Properties window.*

There's another way to change the AOL event sounds — replace the default files. For example, you might record yourself saying, "Welcome," "Is your homework done?" or "Look out cyberworld, I'm online again!" In Windows, name the new file `welcome.wav`. Replace the default file with your new one, and that's the sound you'll hear every time you or anyone else using your computer signs on. Be sure to save the old file in case you ever want to go back to it. You'll find lots of replacement files named `welcome`, `im`, `gotmail`, and so on, in AOL's sound libraries. With a Mac, use Agent Audio (or a similar program) to replace the sound resource in the AOL program file, as explained in Chapter 5.

Note

The event sounds are specific to each computer. If you sign on to your account from someone else's computer, you'll hear their Welcome sound, not yours.

AOL's Buddy List sounds

AOL's Buddy Lists have their own sound events — BuddyIn occurs when someone on your Buddy List signs on, and BuddyOut when someone on your list exits. For Windows, AOL provides two sound themes to start with. The Door theme plays a door opening for BuddyIn and a door slam for BuddyOut. The SDW theme says, "You've got company" for BuddyIn and "Later" for BuddyOut.

Where to find sounds on AOL

The AOL sound libraries are full of WAVs and SNDs for you to use with AOL events and elsewhere. Most of them were created by AOL members and range from amateur to professional. AOL provides some collections too. You've already seen the sound library for Buddy sounds. But there are several more.

PC users should head for keyword: PCSOUND, while Mac users use keyword: MMS to find their Music and Sound forum. The Music and Sound Forum includes message boards, special interest groups such as the Guitar SIG, and a huge software library that offers not only software (players, converters, recorders, and the like) but also lots and lots of sound files. Also try keyword: FILESEARCH to access all of AOL's software libraries. Then search for phrases such as SND, WAV, Christmas, train, welcome, and so on.

Note

The files you download might be compressed by programs such as PKZip (ZIP files) or StuffIt (SIT files). AOL should automatically decompress them when you sign off. If not, you can decompress them yourself with a program such as PKUnzip, WinZip, or StuffIt Expander. See my book *MIME, UUENCODE & ZIP: Decompressing and Decoding Internet Files,* for complete instructions on how to decompress files.

Try keyword: CELEBRITY VOICES to visit AOL's Gallery of Celebrities, where you can download famous voices such as Reba McEntire and Dennis Rodman to replace your Welcome, You've Got Mail, and Goodbye sounds. You'll also find downloadable sounds scattered around various forums, such as Nickelodeon and MuchMusic. Of course, some of the best places to get new sounds are chat rooms. That's the subject of the next section.

Playing chat room sounds

You play a sound file in a chat room by typing a sound command in this format, where *filename* indicates the name of the sound file (without the extension):

```
{S filename}
```

If you want to play a file named ohno, for example, you would type the following command on the chat line and press Enter:

```
{S ohno}
```

Everyone in the room who has a file named ohno on their system will hear it. (They might hear different sounds from yours — they'll hear whatever ohno files reside on their disk.) Windows users must have files named ohno.wav, while Mac users must have snd resources named ohno.

You can leave out the closing brace if the sound command is at the end of a line:

```
Hiya TJ! {S siddown
```

But you must use the closing brace if any chat text follows the command:

```
Hey Bugs {S sploot} to you too!
```

Can't make chat sounds work? Here are the most common reasons:

- Chat sounds are not enabled.

  You must enable chat sounds before you can hear them. Go to keyword: PREFERENCES, open the Chat Preferences, and enable "Enable chat room sounds" (Windows) or "Play chat sounds sent by other members" (Macintosh).

- You don't have the sound files or resources.

  You must download the desired files from somewhere — a sound library or a Web site, perhaps — or get a friend to send them to you.

- You have the sound files, but not in the right place.

  For Windows, the files must be located in the main AOL folder. For Mac OS, snd resources must be in the System suitcase (also known as the System file).

  Many people download sound files to their standard download folder and then try to use them in chat rooms without moving them to the necessary folder. Then they age ten years trying to figure out why other people can hear sounds and they can't. The secret is to move sound files from the download folder to the correct place.

- You didn't spell the name of the file correctly.

- You didn't type the {S *filename*} command correctly.

  There must be a space after the *S*.

Note

Sounds don't work in the AOL auditoriums even though you can chat there.

Managing sounds with PowerTools

Suppose a buddy just played a "boo!" sound and you want to come back quickly with "eek!" You try {S eek}, {S eeek}, {S Eke}, {S EEK} . . . nothing works. By the time you finally get the right filename, you're lagging three miles behind everyone else in the room. It might be time for you to get an AOL add-on to manage your sound files.

An *add-on* is a program that runs in conjunction with AOL to extend AOL's features. The most popular Windows add-on is PowerTools from BPS Software (keyword: BPS). It offers plenty of features for enhancing e-mail, IMs, and chatting. Figure 6-2 shows an AOL window with PowerTools added on. As you can see, it pretty much replaces the standard AOL interface with its own. Notice PowerTool's WavMan window, where you can create groups of WAVs for your different chat environments. Perhaps you might create Trivia WAVs, Romance WAVs, and Just Us Girls WAVs. Open the right WAV group for the chat room you're in — you want the same WAVs as everyone else in the room — and leave the window open while you chat. When you want to play a WAV, you simply select it and choose Send. You can preview it by choosing Play or by double-clicking it.

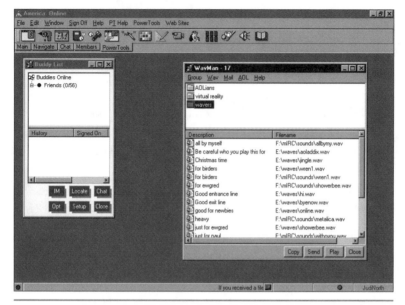

Figure 6-2 *BPS Power Tools includes WavMan to make it easier to handle WAVs while chatting.*

I have not included PowerTools on the CD-ROM that accompanies this book. Its integration with the AOL software is so intensive that even a minor AOL revision forces BPS to upgrade PowerTools. If I put it on the CD-ROM, it would be out of date by the time you get it. You can download the latest version from keyword: BPS.

Note

PowerTools is shareware. You can try it out for 20 days. If you decide to keep it, the shareware registration fee is $29.95 ($24.95 if you register it before the 20 days are up). Some features are disabled in the unregistered version as an incentive to register. It also nags you to register.

How to create a WAV group:

1. Choose PowerTools ⇨ General ⇨ Wav Manager to open the WavMan window. (You can do this offline or online.)

2. In the WavMan window, choose Group ⇨ New to pop up a dialog box where you can name the new group.

3. Type a name for the group and press Enter. The new group appears in the top box in the WavMan window, where your WAV groups are listed.

How to add individual WAVs to a group:

1. Select the group in the top box in the WavMan window.

2. Choose Group ⇨ Add Wav to open a common browse dialog box.

3. Locate and double-click the desired WAV. WavMan asks if you want to enter a brief description.

4. Choose Yes to open the dialog box where you can enter the description.

5. Type a description and then press Enter. The dialog box closes and the new WAV file and description appear in the bottom box in the WavMan window.

How to add all the WAVs in a folder to a group:

1. Select the group in the top box in the WavMan window.

2. Choose Group ⇨ Add all from directory to open a common browse dialog box.

3. Locate and select the desired folder, and then choose Open. WavMan asks if you want to enter a brief description for each WAV.

4. If you choose Yes, WavMan shows you one WAV at a time so that you can enter a description for it.

5. When you're done entering descriptions and the last dialog box closes, all the WAVs in the selected folder are added to the group and appear in the bottom box of the WavMan window.

To remove one or more WAVs, select them and then right-click any one of them to pop up a context menu where you can *Delete from group* (to remove them from the group only) or *Delete from system* (to delete them from your hard drive). In either case you must confirm that you want to delete them. To add or change a description, select the WAV and choose Wav ⇨ Edit description. To move one or more WAVs to a different group, select them and choose Wav ⇨ Move to pop up a dialog box where you can select the destination group.

PowerTools also lets you send WAVs in IMs, but only to other PowerTools users. Select the IM window and then select the WAV in the WavMan window and choose Send.

Tip

Even if you don't have PowerTools, you can use the {S *filename*}. Play a WAV in an IM for someone who does – you won't hear it but they will. Just be sure to include the closing brace in the {S *filename*} command.

You can also use WavMan to reassign your AOL sound events. WavMan's AOL menu provides options to assign the selected WAV to any of the sound events, including the buddy sounds. The Mail menu lets you send one or more WAV files to someone else via e-mail.

Tip

Check out BPS's WavMan site for lots of links to sound files:
http://members.aol.com/bpscowav/wavman/index.html

Sounds on CompuServe

CompuServe 3.0.4 greets you audibly when you arrive ("Welcome to CompuServe") and when you leave ("Thank you for using CompuServe"). In between, sounds provide audio clues as you click buttons and receive various types of messages.

CompuServe's sound events

Table 6-2 shows CompuServe's nine sound events. The Start event occurs when you open the CompuServe program, not when you sign on. Likewise, the Exit event occurs when you close the program, not when you sign off. ButtonDown occurs when you click one of the CompuServe buttons. Some buttons pop back up immediately, triggering the ButtonUp event. The Invitation event occurs when someone invites you to a private chat. After you accept the invitation, you hear Received Talk each time the person you're chatting with sends you a message.

Table 6-2 *The CompuServe Sound Events*

Event	Default Windows File	Default Sound
Start	Wcstart.wav	"Welcome to CompuServe"
Button Down	Wcclick.wav	Slight click
Button Up	Wcclick.wav	Slight click
Host Message	Wcasyn.wav	Tinny beep
Invitation	Wcinvite.wav	"You're invited"
New Forum Messages	Wcformes.wav	Ding
New Mail	Wcgetmai.wav	"You have mail"
Received Talk	Wcinact.wav	Three beeps
Exit	Wcexit.wav	"Thank you for using CompuServe"

With Windows, the sound events are registered with and appear in the Sounds Properties window where you can reassign them as desired. As always, any WAVs will do. For the Macintosh, the sound resources are located in the CompuServe program file and you can change them with the SoundMover program (or a similar program) as explained in Chapter 5.

Where to find sounds on CompuServe

CompuServe's best-known feature is its treasury of forums, and you'll find several devoted to music and sound. Here are a few to get you started:

- MIDI forums group (MIDI)
- Mac Multimedia (MACMULTI)
- Music Hall (music forums group) (MUSIC)
- Sight and Sound (SSFORUM)

But don't just look in the sound forums. Lots of other areas include sound files in their libraries. Forums like Nostalgia (NOSTALGIA), Mac Entertainment (MACFUN), the Beatles Fab Forum (BANDS), and dozens of others include large collections of sound files in their libraries. Try searching for areas pertaining to the types of sounds you want. Choose the Search tool on CompuServe's main toolbar to open the general search page, shown in Figure 6-3. Then try out these search facilities:

- **Forums.** To search for forums by topics such as cartoons, sound effects, and holiday
- **Search by Topic.** To search for forums, communities, online magazines, and more
- **Search for downloadable files.** To search CompuServe's extensive download libraries for WAVs, SNDs, and so on

Figure 6-3 *You can locate lots of sound files via CompuServe's extensive search capability.*

In a forum, the File Libraries button opens a list of all the files in that forum's libraries, much like the one in Figure 6-4. (Some libraries are organized into sections and you must open a section to see the file list.)

When someone uploads a file to a library, they provide a description and a set of keywords to help you decide if you want the file. Select a file and choose Description to read the description, which also shows you the keywords and who uploaded the file. If you decide you want the file, choose Retrieve (to download it immediately) or Retrieve Later (to add it to your to-do list to be downloaded at some later time).

Column head   Search button

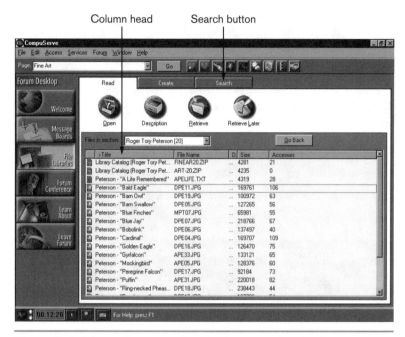

Figure 6-4 *A forum library contains files for you to download.*

Unfortunately, there's no way to sort the list by type of file. The list might contain programs, photos, text documents, and other types of files mixed in with the sound files you're looking for. But you can search the library by choosing the Search button, which opens the search page shown in Figure 6-5. At first, the page contains only two controls, but you can click the More button to add more search controls to it, as shown in Figure 6-5. The More button becomes a Less button, which you can click to return to the original set of two controls. CompuServe builds a list of files that match the search. You use the list just like the library list.

More/less button

Figure 6-5 *You use this page to search a forum's libraries for files.*

Sounds on mIRC

You don't have to forgo sound just because you prefer chatting on Internet Relay Chat (IRC) instead of an online service. IRC clients such as mIRC by Khaled Mardam-Bey make chat sounds fun and (almost) easy. You'll find a copy of mIRC on the CD-ROM at the back of the book. It's a Windows-only shareware program — you can try it out for 30 days. If you decide to keep it, the shareware registration fee is $20. This book's CD-ROM contains the 32-bit version of mIRC. If you use the 16-bit version of Windows, you can download your version of mIRC from the Web site at:

```
http://www.mirc.co.uk
```

The mIRC client cannot access the Internet by itself. You must first sign on to the Internet via whatever access software you usually use. If you use the 32-bit version of mIRC provided on this book's CD-ROM, your Internet access must also be a 32-bit program.

Note

You'll find a link to an excellent IRC client for Macintosh in Appendix E, "Some Handy Internet Sites," on the CD-ROM.

Configuring sounds on mIRC

Before you try to use sounds, take a minute to check your sounds options. Choose the General Options icon, shown here, to open the mIRC Options window. Then select the Sounds tab to open the dialog box shown in Figure 6-6. The most important option is right at the center top of the box. "Accept sound requests" controls whether your computer responds to the sounds that other people play. When it's disabled, only your own sound requests work on your computer. Enable it to hear the sounds that other people play, too.

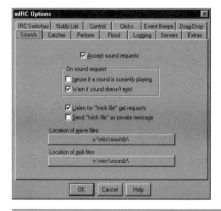

Figure 6-6 Use this mIRC Options dialog box to configure your mIRC sound options.

Assuming that "Accept sound requests" is enabled, the other options determine what happens when someone sends a sound request. If you have a file with the same name in your sounds folder or its subfolders, and if no other sound file is currently playing, your file plays on your computer. It may not be the same sound file that other people hear—only the name must be the same. mIRC looks on your computer for the sound file in the folder identified by "Location of wave files" or "Location of midi files." It also searches all subfolders of the specified folder. In the Sounds dialog box, the current pathname appears on a button that you click to browse for another folder. In the example in Figure 6-6, both buttons contain `c:\mirc\sounds\`.

If a sound is already playing when you receive (or send) another sound request, the option called "Ignore if a sound is currently playing" controls what happens. When this option is enabled, mIRC ignores the new sound request. When it's disabled, mIRC kills the old sound to play the new one. If you don't have the sound file, and "Warn if sound doesn't exist" is enabled, you'll see a message like this:

```
* Sound request: can't find 'amigos.wav'
```

You can ask someone to send you a sound file with a special message that this dialog box refers to as a !*nick file* request. (!*nick file* requests are explained in the next section.) If the option called "Send '!nick file' as private message" is enabled, your request will be sent as a private message. Otherwise it appears in the channel chat, which others may find distracting, especially if several people are collecting files so that the chat screen clutters up with !*nick file* requests.

Of course, people can ask you for sound files, too. Here's some good news: You don't have to waste your chat time responding to all those requests. Enable "Listen for '!nick file' get requests," and mIRC handles all requests automatically. It searches your sound folders for the indicated file and then sends it to the requester.

Enjoying mIRC sounds

Use the /sound command to send a sound request, as in the following examples:

```
/sound hiya.wav
/sound mytheme.mid
```

You can direct the sound to a specific person, instead of the channel at large, by including their nickname in the command:

```
/sound jazzman mytheme.mid
```

You can even direct it to someone in a different channel by adding the name of the channel to their nickname, separated by a slash. For example, to play grandslam.wav for twohearts in the #bridgeplayers channel, you would enter:

```
/sound twohearts/#bridgeplayers grandslam.wav
```

You can also add a message to the command, whether it's directed to the entire channel or an individual:

```
/sound mytheme.mid ::: Judi's theme plays as she glides
smoothly into the room :::
/sound jazzman coolblues.wav Did you record this?
```

Use the /splay command to preview a sound file. /splay plays it on your system only:

```
/splay mytheme.mid
```

The /sound command can also be used to turn sound requests off and on. This is the same as disabling and enabling the "Accept sound requests" option:

```
/sound off
/sound on
```

Trading sound files

When someone else sends a sound request, you see the message [nick SOUND] in the chat screen, where *nick* is the name of the person who sent the sound request. You don't see the name of the sound file, just the word "sound." If you don't have the sound file, you still see the message even though you don't hear the sound. It follows the can't find filename message shown earlier. If you want the file, you can request that the sender send you the file by sending a message in this format:

!nick file

where *nick* is the sender's nickname and *file* is the name of the file. (This is the famous !*nick file* request mentioned earlier.) For example, you can ask wavemaven to send you newtopic.wav like this:

!wavmaven newtopic.wav

You can add a chat text to your request, like this:

Hey !BeatNick parsnips.wav <— I hope you don't mind my asking

Unless the sender ignores your request, you should soon receive an mIRC DCC Get message such as the one shown in Figure 6-7. Choose Get! to download the file to the folder indicated in Save As.

Figure 6-7 *The mIRC DCC Get dialog box appears when someone sends you a file via mIRC's DCC commands.*

 Caution

Never accept candy from strangers. Sound files cannot contain viruses, but program files and some documents can.

When someone asks you for a file, mIRC sends it automatically if you have enabled the "Listen for '!nick file' get requests" option. You'll see a DCC Send request dialog box on your screen—just minimize it for a while. You can close it when the file has been sent or the request canceled.

Using WaVGeT to manage sound files

If you become addicted to sounds on mIRC, you'll probably want a program to help with sounds. I have included a popular mIRC add-on called WaVGeT on the CD-ROM that accompanies this book. It organizes your sound files and makes it easy to play and trade them. Here are some of its features:

- It generates a sound request when you select a sound file from a list. You can add a message to the request or let WaVGeT randomly select a message from a list.

- It builds a list of who played what sounds that you don't have. You double-click an item on this list to generate a *!nick file* request.

- WaVGeT can generate *!nick file* requests automatically for files that you don't have.

- It can send automatic thank you messages to people who send you files.

- It can automatically play a sound after you receive it.

- It lets you organize your sound files into catalogs. You might, for example, create Rock, Jazz, Toons, Movie Clips, and Sound FX catalogs.

- It queues and manages other people's requests for you to send them files.

- It can interrupt a WAV.

- It can play sounds at random to one or more channels. You specify the time interval, the channels, and the list of sounds to choose from.

- It lets you play MP3, RealAudio, and other types of files that you couldn't ordinarily play in mIRC.
- It stores and accesses sound files in multiple directories.
- It lets you search for sound files in multiple directories.
- It can check new downloads for validity.
- It also organizes and "plays" text macros.

I can't devote an entire chapter to WaVGeT, so I'll just explain a few of its functions. Once you're comfortable with these functions, you should be able to learn more by exploring its Help library.

WaVGeT is shareware, and you may try it as long as you like. If you decide to keep it, the shareware fee is $10. (It nags you often to pay the fee.) WaVGeT for 32-bit Windows is on the CD-ROM for this book. Yes, you also can download a 16-bit version for Windows 3.1 from the WaVGeT Web site:

```
http://www.wavget.com
```

Playing sounds

After you install WaVGeT, you start it in the usual Windows ways:

- Open Windows Explorer or My Computer, open the folder containing WaVGeT, and then double-click the WaVGeT program icon.
- If you added it to your Start menu, open your Start menu and select it.

Or you can start mIRC first and then enter this command in any mIRC window:

```
/wavget
```

Figure 6-8 shows the main WaVGeT window, which acts as a sounds control panel. On the right is the list of sound files in your current catalog. Double-click a sound to preview it. To play it in the current channel, select it and then choose the speaker button, shown here.

Figure 6-8 *The main WaVGeT window acts as your sounds control panel.*

Notice the All Files item on the menu bar. That's the name of the current catalog. Clicking it opens a list of all your catalogs so you can select a different one. All Files is the default catalog that comes with WaVGeT and includes all the files in all your catalogs. How to create a catalog:

1. Choose Play ⇨ Catalog Manager to open the Catalog page in the WaVGeT Setup Dialog Box.

2. Choose Add to open a dialog box where you can assign a name to your new catalog.

3. Choose OK to close the dialog box.

4. Open the All Files catalog.

5. Select the files that you want to copy to your new catalog.

6. Right-click the file list to pop up your list of catalogs.

7. Choose your new catalog to copy all the selected files to it.

Configuring play messages

When WaVGeT generates a sound request, you don't see the usual /sound command in your chat window. Instead, you see a message like the following:

```
* yourname [trek.wav 334KB 31.0Sec 8bit Mono 11.0KHz]
```

You can configure the contents of the message, along with other options, in the WaVGeT Setup window, shown in Figure 6-9. Choose File ⇨ Setup to open the window. The buttons near the top determine which page of options appear in the window. In Figure 6-9, I have clicked the Play button to display the options affecting sound requests.

Figure 6-9 *You configure options in the WaVGeT Setup window.*

WaVGeT can generate a random message to go along with the sound request. It comes with two default messages, which you can see in the window. The sender's nickname, the filename, and WaVGeT's version number are filled into the message so that it appears like this:

```
* Grammy ! plays whoohoo.wav with WavGet V1.6
```

(The |*8* and *4* in the message are font commands for yellow text on a red background.)

The other message ends up looking like this:

```
* Grammy ! waves with WavGet V1.6
(http://www.en.com/users/pbeuger/wavget.html)
```

You don't have to send out an advertisement for WaVGeT with every sound request if you don't want. The three buttons beneath the list box let you add new play messages, delete the selected message, and edit the selected message. If you want to select just one message rather than letting WaVGeT select them randomly, disable

"Select random Play message" and select the message you want to send. You can disable play messages altogether by enabling "Do NOT send a Play message."

You can also attach a play message directly to a file in the main WaVGeT window. Select the file and type the message in the bottom box before sending it. WaVGeT remembers the message and shows it every time you play that WAV.

Sending file details

You can include file details like the following in your sound requests. These details help others decide if they want to ask you to send the file.

```
[explode.wav 293KB 54.5Sec 4bit Mono 11.0kHz]
```

To include the file details in your sound requests, choose File ⇨ Options, choose the Options button, and enable these two options: "Send file size" and "Send WaV info."

Getting sound files

The left-hand box in the WaVGet window builds up a list of the sounds that have been played that you don't have, along with the person who played them. Double-click a sound to generate a *!nick file* request to that person. Choosing File ⇨ Setup and choosing the Get button opens the dialog box shown in Figure 6-10, where you can configure the Get options.

Figure 6-10 *You configure your Get messages in this dialog box.*

As you can see, WaVGeT sends a message along with your !*nick file* request if you wish. You can use the messages provided by WaVGeT or create your own. To send the same message every time, select it from the list. To let WaVGeT randomly select messages, enable "Select random GET message." If you don't want to send a message, enable "Do not send a GET message." You can edit the list of messages by choosing the Add, Delete, and Edit buttons.

If you enable Auto GET, WaVGeT automatically generates a !*nick file* request for every sound you don't have. This can be a useful option in a channel where someone plays a sound every once in a while. But in a channel where people are playing sounds fast and furiously, you'll drive yourself and everyone else crazy with this option. Use the slider below the option to limit the number of GET sessions that you can have going at once. I have it set to 7 in the figure, but 3 or 4 would be more reasonable.

Tip

If you use Auto GET, create a catalog named Trash! – the name is important, be sure to include the ! – where you store sounds you *don't* want. When you store a file in the Trash! Catalog, WaVGeT deletes it from your hard drive but remembers the name so it will never request it again.

Sounds on Microsoft Network

The Microsoft Network (MSN) employs Web browser technology in its interface. Basically, it uses Microsoft Internet Explorer 4 (MSIE), although it replaces the usual MSIE window with the MSN Program Viewer (unless you request otherwise). This means that any type of Internet sound is possible as you travel around the service. When you access an area, you might hear a sampled sound file, synthesized music, and/or a streaming file or live broadcast. You'll also find it easy to preview and play sounds in an MSN chat room. Perhaps most exciting of all, you can add sounds right into your e-mail and newsgroup messages, but that subject is covered in Chapters 9 and 10.

The MSN sound events

MSN registers two sound events with Windows. Quick View Notification occurs when MSN pops up notices from the Quickview icon in your system tray (the inset at the right end of your taskbar). The default sound file is MSNNotif.wav, a soft chime — it sounds like a grandfather clock — which is stored in the C:\Program Files\OnMSN folder. Friends Online New Message occurs when one of your Friends Online sends you a message. Its default sound file is Folmsg.wav, a two-note chime, which is stored in the same folder. You can change the sound assigned to either of these events in the usual Windows ways. Some few sounds, such as the menu sounds, are built into the MSN Program Viewer and can't be replaced, although you can turn them on and off.

Sounds in chat rooms

You can play WAV files in an MSN chat room such as the one shown in Figure 6-11, either in text view or in comic view as shown in the figure. The Play Sound tool pops up the Play Sound dialog box where you select the sound you want to play. Choosing Test plays the sound on your computer so you can preview it. Choose OK to play the sound in the room. Other people hear the sound only if they have WAV files of the same name. They hear their own WAV files, which might be different from yours.

Figure 6-11 *The Play Sound tool opens the Play Sound dialog box so you can select a sound to play.*

Your sound files must be located in the sounds folder specified in your MSN options. This is your Windows\Media folder by default, but you can change to another folder if you prefer.
How to change the MSN sounds folder:

1. Choose View ➪ Options to open the Microsoft Chat Options window, shown in Figure 6-12.

2. Choose the Settings tab to open the Settings page, as shown in the figure.

3. Type the desired pathname in the Sound search path box at the bottom of the page.

You can also turn your chat sounds off by disabling the "Play sounds" option.

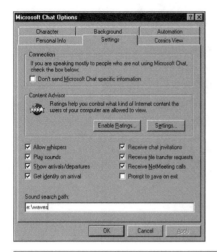

Figure 6-12 *You can change your chat room sounds folder in the Chat Options window.*

What's on the CD?

Ted's Sounds is a large collection of WAVs that are appropriate for AOL sound events, chat rooms, and many other uses.

What's Next?

Now that we've finished exploring sound files, it's time to look at a method of efficiently playing them over networks — streaming. Chapter 7 explains streaming media and shows you how to use them.

Chapter 7

RealAudio and Other Streaming Audio Applications

If you've ever waited for a huge WAV or SND file to download, you probably thought to yourself, "There's got to be a better way." Well, you were right — there is a better way to handle sampled files on the Internet. It's called *streaming audio,* and it lets you listen to files or even live broadcasts without long download times. This chapter features the primary streaming application, RealAudio, and introduces some of its up-and-coming competitors.

What you'll learn:

- What streaming is and how it works
- What RealAudio is and how to use it
- Who the major competitors are: Xing StreamWorks, Macromedia Shockwave, and Microsoft NetShow

What Is Streaming?

Streaming plays multimedia information — audio and/or video — while it is still being downloaded. You don't have to wait for an entire file to download before it starts to play, as you do with traditional audio files. Suppose you want to listen to a 400K file.

Without streaming, you could sit around twiddling your thumbs for what seems like forever while the file downloads. With streaming, you need wait only around a few seconds, barely time for a twiddle.

Note

In case you're not familiar with the server-client model, a *server* is a program that runs on a remote computer and makes various services available to a network. The Internet consists of Web servers, FTP servers, mail servers, gopher servers, newsgroup servers, and so on. A *client* is a program the runs on your PC and requests information from the server. In order to access a Web server, you must have a Web client. To access a newsgroup server, you must have a newsgroup client, and so on.

Why wait even a few seconds? Data does not flow smoothly across the Internet. It travels in *packets* — small chunks, each with an address and a sequence number. Your packets are mixed in with other people's packets, which often get into traffic jams. Each packet is routed dynamically, so one may travel by way of Chicago and New York, another by way of Timbuktu. Your Internet software then reassembles the packets into a file.

Imagine that you place a huge order with a company across the country. Your order is packed in hundreds of cartons, which are shipped via the Post Office and several other ground carriers. If you can imagine the various routes the packages take, the other packages that come and go, and the frequency and order in which yours arrive, you'll have a pretty good idea of how packets travel on the Internet. Of course, Internet packets travel much faster, even if it's still frustratingly slow.

How streaming works

If . . . you heard the sound data . . . as it . . . . arrived . . . it would sound . . . . . . like . . . this . . . . . . where the . . . dots . . . represent . . . . static. To smooth out the data flow and eliminate the static, streaming builds up several seconds' worth of sound in a buffer before beginning to play. (A *buffer* is simply a storage area in memory.) It then continues to drop arriving data into one end of the buffer while it pulls a smooth stream from the other end.

It's important to get the sound data through the Internet as efficiently as possible so your buffer doesn't run dry. Therefore, streamed data is compressed as much as possible, using a lossy compression scheme. Your streaming player's biggest task is to decompress it. Compression and decompression cause their own set of problems, as you'll see in the next section, but there's no better way to get a lot of data through the Internet as quickly as possible.

The pros and cons

Streaming offers two tremendous advantages. First, because you don't have to download an entire file before it starts to play, there's really no limit on file size. The 180K limit I suggested in earlier chapters does not apply to streamed files. A streamed file may contain a complete symphony, a ten-minute interview with your favorite star, a major news event, or an entire Shakespearean play.

Second, streaming enables live Internet broadcasting, much like radio and television except for the slight buffering delay. Hundreds of Internet "radio" stations are now transmitting, plus live audio and video broadcasts of events such as concerts, weddings, sports, and Mars landings. In Netspeak, a *live stream* is streamed data being broadcast as it happens. An *on-demand file* is a streamed recorded file, such as the symphony or Shakespearean play mentioned earlier.

As always, advantages are accompanied by disadvantages. When traffic is heavy on the Internet or the server is overloaded, you most likely will experience some *brownouts*—short periods where the buffer runs dry and you hear nothing but static. This can ruin the mood of a piece, to put it mildly. Brownouts can also happen when your processor can't decompress data quickly enough. Decompression requires intense computation, which eats up processing time. If you're doing any other computing while listening, you'll notice the difference. I currently have a Pentium 266, not as fast as they come these days, but pretty darn fast. I love to listen to Internet radio while I work. But when I do something that requires a lot of computation, such as scrolling or printing a large document, my radio broadcast turns to fuzz.

Another disadvantage is poor sound quality. Sometimes packets get lost entirely or arrive too late, making the audio sound choppy. Information lost during compression also contributes to poor sound quality. Speech comes through pretty well, but music sometimes sounds as if it's being played underwater.

These are early days for streaming technology, somewhat like radio in the 1920s. You'd better believe the major streaming companies are all scrambling to overcome the problems. I believe they'll succeed within the next few years, and someday we'll be able to say to our grandkids, "I remember when . . . ."

RealAudio

The biggest player in the streaming technology ballpark is RealNetworks, Inc., creator of RealAudio. They pioneered the technology and seized the lion's share of the market before anyone else really got into the game. Since they give away both their basic player and their encoder, they are likely to remain the king of the hill for quite some time. They make their money selling their enhanced player, their server, and a few other related products.

Early versions of RealAudio handled audio only, but video was added with version 4.0, and the player's name changed from RealAudio to RealPlayer. RealFlash, an animation viewer, was added with RealPlayer 5.0. Now RealPlayer G2 includes RealPix, a picture viewer, and RealText, a text viewer. Technically speaking, the name RealAudio is out-of-date, but it's still commonly used for the entire collection of streaming products and technologies from RealNetworks.

Another factor that keeps RealAudio on top is its flexibility. RealPlayer comes as a standalone player, a plug-in, and an ActiveX control, and it works not only with Windows and Macintosh, but also with several other platforms as well. Web designers who want to reach the widest audience for their streaming multimedia products usually choose RealAudio. This book's CD-ROM includes RealPlayer 5.0 for Windows 95, 98, and NT. If you have already installed RealPlayer 5.0 or earlier for Windows, you should definitely install the newer G2 version. It not only offers a lot more features, it also incorporates greatly improved technology.

Note

I'm sorry not to include a G2 RealAudio player on the CD-ROM, but RealNetworks has not yet finalized the G2 player. The CD-ROM includes the earlier RealPlayer 5.0. Check RealNetworks' Web site at the following address to see if the retail version of the G2 player is ready:

```
http://www.real.com/products/player/index.html
```

The fine print

The basic version of RealPlayer is free. (There's also a version with more features that you must pay for to use.) Its system requirements depend on your modem speed and the RealPlayer components you want to use. In general, you'll be fine in Windows if you have a Pentium 166, 16MB of RAM, a 28.8 Kbps modem, and 4MB of hard drive space. If your system falls short of these requirements, you might still be able to use parts of RealPlayer. You can check detailed requirements at this site:

```
http://www.real.com/products/player/50player/
sysreq.html
```

You might even be able to use RealPlayer behind your company's firewall. The following Web site offers some suggestions for dealing with firewalls:

```
http://www.real.com/help/firewall
```

RealAudio compression

Are you wondering why different modem speeds have different system requirements? Because RealAudio uses different *codecs* (defined in Chapter 1) for different modems speeds. The slower the speed, the more compression is needed to keep the data flowing fast enough. At 14.4 Kbps, data must be so highly compressed that the quality suffers — it's about equivalent to telephone quality. At 56 Kbps, much less compression is needed, and you'll find that the quality approaches that of a CD. With speeds of 64 Kbps or higher, stereo streams are possible.

The RealAudio file formats

A RealAudio sound clip was originally stored in an RA file. When video was added, the file extension was changed to RM for RealMedia. Basically, RA and RM files are sampled audio and video files that have been encoded for RealAudio streaming. An RM file may, however, contain several streams of audio, video, animation, and other data.

Two more RealAudio formats are RAM and RMM, for RealAudio Metafile and RealMedia Metafile. A *metafile* contains nothing but a link to an RA or RM file. The link could refer to a file on your hard drive or one on the Internet. When you open a metafile, RealPlayer knows to follow the link. This prevents you from saving a copy of the referenced file itself. If you save a copy, all you get is the link. Web designers use metafiles to protect their copyrights.

Here's another reason Web designers use metafiles. A Web site does not have to use the RealAudio server to make RealAudio files available. It can use HTML to link to RA or RM files just like WAV, MIDI, or any other type of file. But RA or RM files provided this way aren't streamed. RealPlayer downloads them entirely before starting them. When RealPlayer follows a link from a RAM file, however, it does stream the referenced RA or RM file. So Webmasters who don't want to pay the price for the RealAudio server can still provide streaming files by placing RAM files on the page and letting them link to RA or RM files. RealPlayer G2 recognizes another type of multimedia file. SMI files, which stand for the Synchronized Multimedia Integration Language, are files where two or more streams are synchronized to provide a complete multimedia presentation.

Streams, clips, and presentations

When talking about RealAudio, you'll often encounter these three terms:

- Presentation — A complete multimedia package, which may be made up of one or more clips; each RM or RA file contains a presentation.

- Clip — An integrated multimedia sequence, such as a song, a film preview, or a cartoon; a clip contains one or more streams.

- Stream — A single streaming component, such as an audio stream, video stream, or animation stream.

The RealPlayer window

You can download the free beta (test) version of RealPlayer G2 from http://www.real.com/products/player/index.html. Figure 7-1 shows what RealPlayer G2 looks like when playing a live audio stream. The window is divided into several sections. At the top are the title bar and menu bar. Below them appear the playback controls and position slider, which use the common icons for play, pause, stop, rewind, and fast forward. Rewind, fast forward, and the position slider work only with on-demand files, which is why they are dimmed in the figure. There's no way to change positions in a live stream.

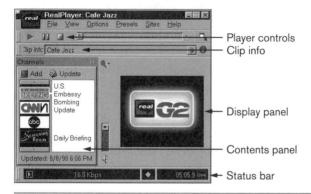

Figure 7-1 *RealPlayer G2's normal window looks like this.*

Clip Info bar

The bar below the playback controls is called the Clip Info bar. It typically shows the title of the clip. There may be more info lines that you can't see. You scroll through all the lines by choosing the Scroll Clip Info button, shown in the margin. The button on the far right, called About This Clip, pops up a separate window containing whatever information the clip's creators choose to share with you.

Contents Panel

In the free version of RealPlayer G2, the Contents Panel shows your channels. A *channel* is an Internet information service that is updated frequently. News channels could be updated several times a day, whereas other channels might be updated daily. The channels you can access with RealPlayer G2 tend to provide full multimedia content — video synchronized with audio, perhaps with animation, still pictures, and text as well. When you click a channel in the Contents Panel, its current show plays in the Display Panel.

Display Panel

The Display Panel shows the visual elements of a clip—video streams, animation streams, text, and still pictures. It displays the Real G2 logo in Figure 7-1 because the clip contains only an audio stream.

Status bar

The status bar displays status information as the clip plays. You may see these symbols at various times:

🕐

The timer appears while you're waiting for a connection or while-buffering.

`Connecting...`

The word "Connecting" appears while RealPlayer attempts to connect to a requested site.

▶ ◻ ⏸

When connected, the play, stop, or pause icon indicates the status of the clip.

▐▐▐▐▐▐▐▐▐▐▐

During buffering, this gauge shows the buffer filling up.

`45.5 Kbps`

This bandwidth indicator shows the bandwidth of the broadcast, in kilobytes per second. Typical bandwidths are 16.0 Kbps for mono and 20.0 Kbps for stereo. Some stations are now broadcasting at 80 or higher Kbps, for listeners with dual-channel ISDN, cable, and other high-speed connections.

`Stereo`

This tells you that you're listening to a stereo clip.

`Live`

This tells you that you're listening to a live stream.

`00:10.7/05:00.7`

The first number shows how much time has elapsed; the second number shows the total time of the clip and is omitted for live streams. Times are shown in minutes, seconds, and tenths of a

second until you pass one hour. Then they are shown in hours, minutes, and seconds.

The G2 logo appears when a clip uses features that are available
only with version G2.

The green "traffic" light indicates a good connection, yellow a fair
connection, and red a bad connection. A flashing light indicates that
RealPlayer is currently optimizing the stream, which could interrupt playback briefly but results in improved sound.

Configuring the window

You have quite a bit of control over what appears in the RealPlayer
G2 window. You can hide or show various elements and move them
around in the window. The Clip Info bar, Contents Panel, and
Status Bar are all optional. You hide and display them via the View
menu. For example, to hide the Clip Info bar, choose View ⇨ Clip
Info. Choose the same option again to redisplay the bar. The Clip
Info bar, Player Controls bar, and Status Bar can all be moved to
other positions by dragging them. A pair of vertical lines appears at
the left end of each bar. Grab the bar by those lines and drag it up or
down in the window to relocate it.

If you like to listen to RealAudio as you work at your computer, you can keep the window on top of your other applications.
Just choose View ⇨ On Top While Playing. Choose the same
option again to toggle this feature off. You might also want to
reduce the window to its smallest size. Clicking the Compact Mode
button, shown in the margin, reduces the window to the top view in
Figure 7-2. All you see are the most essential controls and information, and the window fits nicely in a corner of your screen However,
if you move your mouse pointer over the compact window, it
automatically jumps to the slightly larger view at the bottom in
Figure 7-2. This view gives you a title bar to drag around and a few
essential menus. As soon as you move your mouse away, the window

jumps back to the smaller view again. All this switching between two compact views happens automatically, but if you don't like it you can turn it off. Choose Options ⇨ Preferences and click the Display tab. Then disable the option that says "Auto-hide in compact mode."

When in compact mode, the Compact Mode button becomes a Normal Mode button, which you click to return to the full window.

Figure 7-2 *RealPlayer G2's compact window has two views, depending on the position of your mouse pointer.*

Playing audio clips

When you're browsing the Web and encounter a RealAudio clip, you can start RealPlayer simply by opening the clip. The player starts in its own window and plays the selected clip. You don't even have to stay on the original site. You can continue to surf while you listen. The window stays open so you can replay the same clip or play other clips that you find.

But you don't have to run your browser to access online clips. RealPlayer has some browser capabilities. As long as you are online somehow—an ISP or online service, for example—it can access RealAudio clips from sites. It can't display the Web pages, but it can play the clips. (Don't forget that the word *clip* can refer to an on-demand file or a live stream.) First, start up the standalone version of RealPlayer by choosing Start ⇨ RealAudio ⇨ RealPlayer G2.

Now you're ready to open a clip. RealAudio gives you several ways to do that:

- If you know the address of the clip, such as http://www.netradio.com/country.ram, choose File ⇨ Open Location, enter the address, and choose OK.

- If you played the clip recently, you might be able to recall it. RealPlayer G2 lists your recent clips at the bottom of the File menu. Simply choose one to reopen it. With RealPlayer 5.0, choose File ⇨ Open Recent, then choose the clip you want to reopen.

- Both versions of RealPlayer let you keep a list of your favorite clips. The next section explains how you save and access them.

If you're not online when you try to open a clip from an Internet site, RealPlayer will attempt to sign you on using your default service. You might have to enter your user name and password, of course.

If you want to play a clip from your own drive instead of the Internet, you don't have to be online. Just choose File ⇨ Open File and select the clip.

Can you save an online clip to your hard drive? Maybe or maybe not. You can't do it from the RealPlayer window, but you might be able to do it from the Web page where the clip is located. You can save the file just like you save any file from a Web page. (Chapter 9 shows you how to download and save files from a Web site.) If it's an RA or RM file, you save the actual clip. But if it's an RAM or RMM file, all you save is a link to the clip.

RealPlayer G2 presets

You use RealPlayer's Presets menu to store and access your favorite clips, including live broadcasts. Figure 7-3 shows an example of the Presets menu. To start a favorite clip, pull down the menu, point to one of the folders from the bottom of the list, then choose the desired clip.

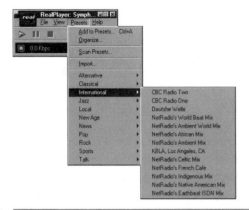

Figure 7-3 *You can add your favorite clips and Internet radio stations to RealPlayer G2's Presets menu.*

It's easy to add a new clip to the menu. While you're listening to it, choose Presets ➪ Add to Presets to open the dialog box shown in Figure 7-4. Change the default title, if you wish, and select one of the folders from the drop-down list.

Figure 7-4 *You use this dialog box to add another clip to the Presets menu.*

RealPlayer G2 starts you off with a good-sized collection of folders and clips. You don't have to keep the ones you don't want. Choose Presets ➪ Organize to open the Organize Presets dialog box. This dialog box is quite simple to use:

- To add a new folder, choose the New Folder button and enter a name for a folder.

- To delete a folder or a clip, select it and choose Delete.
- To change the name of a folder, select it and choose Edit.
- To change the name, the address, or the folder for a clip, select it and choose Edit.

Note

The RealPlayer G2 Sites menu contains links to Web sites, not clips. The sites are preprogrammed and you can't change them. Selecting a site points your browser to that address. (RealPlayer starts up your browser and signs you on, if necessary.)

Dealing with problems

If you're having trouble getting good sound from RealPlayer, there are several things you can try. Start by experimenting with your Connection preferences. Choose Options ➪ Preferences and click the Connection tab to open the dialog box shown in Figure 7-5. In the Bandwidth box, make sure you have set the correct speeds for your modem. For example, if you're using a 56K modem and never connect at any other speed, you would choose 56K modem for both the Normal and Maximum bandwidths. (Don't choose the other 56K option, 56K ISDN, unless you have an ISDN terminal that also acts as a 56K modem when necessary.)

If you're experiencing a lot of brownouts, try increasing your buffer size in the middle portion of the dialog box. If all else fails, try choosing "Buffer entire clip up to available memory." This could impede the performance of your other applications, however.

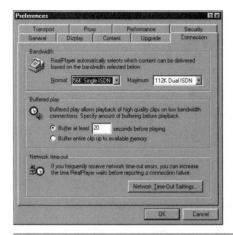

Figure 7-5 *You can often solve poor sound quality by adjusting your connection preferences.*

Also check out the options on the Performance tab, shown in Figure 7-6. As I said earlier, decompressing audio streams consumes huge amounts of processor time. If you find that the rest of your system is having problems because you're listening to RealAudio, you might want to give less processor time to the RealAudio stream. Adjust the slider in the Playback Performance box toward the left to give your other applications more time. But be aware when you do this that your playback quality will suffer. Keep adjusting the slider until you find the best trade-off between RealAudio quality and system performance.

As you can see in the Sound Card Compatibility box in the Performance preferences, sometimes poor quality can result from an incompatible sound card. If you can't find any other reason for poor performance, try pressing the Settings button to open the dialog box shown in Figure 7-7. You might need to limit clips to 8 bits if you have an older sound card. As it says in the dialog box, if audio sounds distorted or scratchy, try checking the box labeled "Disable 16-bit sound (use 8-bit only*).*" Check the box labeled "Disable custom sampling rates" if your audio often seems to play at the wrong speed or is distorted.

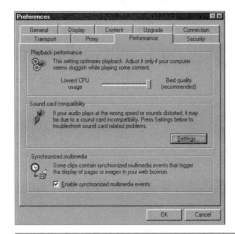

Figure 7-6 *The performance preferences can also help solve poor sound quality.*

Figure 7-7 *The Sound Card Compatibility settings might also improve sound quality.*

Sometimes you just can't get good performance because the Internet is too busy. You can check your network statistics by choosing View ⇨ Statistics to open the dialog box shown in Figure 7-8. You can get a lot of information about your connection from the Connection tab, which is shown in the figure. You can see how many packets have actually been lost or received late, how many had to be recovered, and so on. The statistics in the example are excellent. I was having no trouble listening to RealAudio that day. But sometimes, you just have to give it up and come back later.

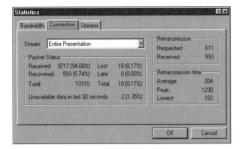

Figure 7-8 *RealPlayer's statistics can tell you that sound quality is poor because of Internet problems.*

Streaming other file types

You can set up RealPlayer G2 to stream non-RealAudio files. To do this, you have to download and install a plug-in for each file type you want to stream. A *plug-in* is a program component that extends RealPlayer's capabilities. As I write this, plug-ins are available for WAV, MIDI, AVI, and Vivo files. (Vivo Software is a company that creates video-related software.) RealNetworks continues to develop plug-ins, so by the time you read this, some more might be available. The easiest way to install a plug-in is to open a file that needs it. Suppose, for example, that you want to stream MIDI files. Use File ⇨ Open File to open any MIDI file on your hard drive. You'll see the dialog box shown in Figure 7-9, which offers to download the plug-in for you. Choose Yes to download and install it.

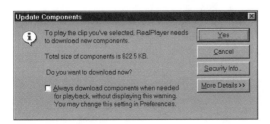

Figure 7-9 *RealPlayer displays this dialog box when you try to open a file type that requires a plug-in that you have not yet installed.*

Once the plug-in has been installed, it appears in the RealPlayer window whenever you play that type of file. Figure 7-10 shows an example of the MIDI plug-in — Crescendo Forte by LiveUpdate. You learn more about the regular Crescendo MIDI plug-in in Chapter 8.

Figure 7-10 *This shows the Crescendo Forte MIDI plug-in in the RealPlayer G2 window.*

To find out what plug-ins are already installed, choose Options ⇨ Preferences to open the Preferences window. Then choose the Upgrade tab to open the page shown in Figure 7-11. All your components are listed at the bottom of the page. The list includes the basic components for playing RealAudio, RealVideo, and so on, plus any plug-ins you have installed.

Figure 7-11 *You can see your list of components in RealPlayer's Content Preferences page.*

Playlists

Some files provide a playlist of several clips. For example, some sites let you "try before you buy" entire CDs online. There are sites where you can listen to complete audio books online, with a chapter per clip. The Playlist bar, shown in Figure 7-12, comes in handy when you're listening to a playlist. You display it by choosing View ⇨ Playlist. The title and number of the current clip appear in the bar. (The clips are often cleverly titled clip 1, clip 2, and so on.) You can change clips by clicking the previous and next icons or select a clip from the drop-down list.

Figure 7-12 *RealPlayer G2's Playlist bar gives you control over playlists.*

Tip

Clip 1 is often an advertisement. Just click the next clip icon to skip it.

Other ways to play RealAudio

You don't have to use RealPlayer to listen to RealAudio. Several third-party players can handle RealAudio files. Among the players described in this book, Media Player 5.2 and Jet-Audio can play RealAudio. However, neither of them can handle the new G2 features.

Other Streaming Applications

RealAudio isn't the only kid on the streaming block. Several other major players have come along in recent years, along with a host of minor players. Of these, the most important are StreamWorks, Shockwave, and NetShow. None of them approach the prominence of RealAudio on the Internet, although they all would like to. The following sections briefly describe these three streaming products and where you might run into them.

Xing StreamWorks

As specialists in data compression, it was only natural for Xing Technology Corporation to turn their attention to multimedia streaming, where compression is the name of the game. Their collection of streaming products and formats, called StreamWorks, uses MPEG compression with excellent results. They have extended the MPEG standard to handle exceptionally low bit-rates, down to 8 Kbps. Many music sites provide samples in StreamWorks XSM format, so I suggest that you install the StreamWorks player if you like to browse music sites. StreamWorks for Windows and Macintosh is included on this book's CD-ROM.

Macromedia Shockwave

Another extremely popular set of multimedia streaming products is Macromedia Shockwave. Like RealAudio, it handles audio, video, and animation. Some Web sites provide interactive experiences such as games via Shockwave. Shockwave players are built into Internet Explorer and Netscape Navigator, so I have not included any on this book's CD-ROM.

Microsoft NetShow

The new kid on the block comes from the Seattle area. Microsoft NetShow provides streaming multimedia presentations, or shows, in ASF and ASX format. You have already met NetShow's player, Media Player 5.2, which was designed specifically to play NetShow shows along with other popular file formats. Sites that are closely aligned with Microsoft tend to use NetShow rather than one of the other products for multimedia presentations. Figure 7-13 shows an example of a NetShow audio presentation playing in Media Player.

Figure 7-13 *Media Player 5.2 plays Microsoft NetShow presentations such as this audio presentation.*

As with RealPlayer, once you have started a presentation, NetShow continues to download and play the stream from that site, even if you browse to other sites or close your browser. You must stay online, however.

What's on the CD-ROM

Digiband Radio 3.3.0 for Windows provides a push-button interface to your favorite RealAudio Internet radio stations. Figure 7-14 shows an example of the Digiband window, which you can program with all your favorite stations.

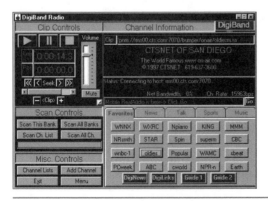

Figure 7-14 *Digiband Radio's window gives you push button access to RealAudio radio stations.*

iQ from QSound enhances all sampled sounds on your Windows system, including RealAudio. Try it; it's wild. (It runs in the background, so there's no window to show you.)

What's Next?

This chapter briefly introduced the concept of browser plug-ins. Chapter 8 explains a great deal more about how your browser plays audio.

Chapter 8

Audio and Your Web Browser

Your browser must use support programs to play audio files. You have a lot more options than you might think in what players your browser uses. This chapter explains how Netscape Navigator and Internet Explorer play audio, and how you can control the players.

What you'll learn:

- How Web browsers handle audio
- How to set up helper applications for Netscape and Internet Explorer
- How to use the most popular plug-ins: Media Player 5.2, Crescendo, and QuickTime
- Where to find and change information about your plug-ins and helper applications in Netscape Navigator

How Web Browsers Open and Play Audio Files

Web browsers do not provide their own audio playback capabilities. Instead, they call on external players to open and play audio files. Your browser might have a repertory of three or four players to handle different types of audio. A typical collection would include

Crescendo for MIDIs, Media Player for WAVs and other sampled sounds, and RealPlayer for RealAudio.

Plug-ins and helper applications

Browsers use two types of players: helper applications and plug-ins. A *helper application* is not connected with the browser in any way. It's a standalone application, such as Jet-Audio or SoundApp, that runs in its own window with its own menus, toolbar, and all its other features. Whenever you play a file that needs a helper application, you must wait while the browser starts the application and passes the file to it.

On the other hand, a *plug-in* is an extension of the browser's basic capabilities. Each plug-in you install becomes a part of the browser. The browser loads all its plug-ins when it starts — the more plug-ins you have, the longer your browser takes to start and the more memory it needs. On the plus side, the plug-in is ready to go when you call on it.

A plug-in often does not have a window to call its own. Its controls appear in the browser's window. Figure 8-1 shows an example of the Crescendo controls as they appear on a Web page displayed by Netscape. As with most audio plug-ins, the controls give you the ability to play, pause, and stop the sound. The size of the control graphic depends on how much room the Web page allocates to the plug-in. Some pages give no room for controls, and the sound plays without your being able to stop or control it. Others allocate less space than your controls need, and you see just a portion of your controls (or a distorted version). Others leave plenty of space and you may see your entire controls with some white space around them. Some Webmasters seem to think that everyone has the same controls they do. They put in just the right amount of space for their controls, which may not be the right amount for yours. (If you have your own Web page, you can avoid this problem by reading Appendix D on the CD-ROM.)

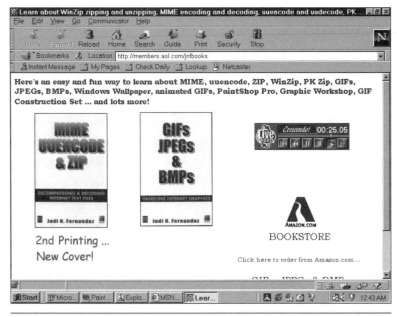

Figure 8-1 *Like all plug-ins, Crescendo appears in the browser's window.*

Since a helper application stands alone, any program can be designated as a helper application. But a plug-in must be specially written to fit with your browser, and it can't be used outside the browser because it can't stand alone. Some applications include both types of components, however. When you install QuickTime 3, for example, you get both a standalone program called Movie Player and the QuickTime plug-in.

A browser shows a strong preference for plug-ins over helper applications. When you ask it to open a file, it looks for a plug-in first. If it finds a plug-in, it automatically opens and plays the file without any fuss. On the other hand, it treats a helper application like a stranger coming to the back door asking for work. It looks for a helper application only if it can't find a plug-in. When it finds a helper application, it does not load and start it automatically. Instead, it displays a message suggesting that you save the file to disk rather than open it. Figure 8-2 shows Microsoft Internet

Explorer's version of this message. Notice that the default choice is to save the file.

Figure 8-2 *Internet Explorer displays this message when you try to open a file that uses a helper application.*

Of course, there's good reason for all this suspicion. Some files on the Internet carry viruses or their cousins (worms, Trojan horses, and the like). If there's any chance of infection, you should save a file to disk and scan it with at least two up-to-date virus scanners before attempting to open it. Fortunately, a sound file cannot be infected. It contains only audio information and no program instructions. So feel free to open a sound file immediately if you wish. You can avoid being asked about sound files in the future by disabling "Always ask before opening this type of file."

Caution

No virus scanner can catch 100 percent of today's epidemic of viruses. That's why I say you should use *at least* two scanners. Since you're most likely to catch the newest viruses, be sure to update all your scanners every two weeks or so. And by the way, files such as Microsoft Office documents, spreadsheets, and databases can carry viruses. Please don't assume they are safe because they're not programs. Many high-end office applications include macro programming features, and macros can be programmed to do a lot of damage to your files.

Most Web sites leave it up to you to use whatever player you prefer. But sometimes a site designates a particular plug-in for a file. Even though Crescendo is your chosen MIDI player, for example, a particular page may call on QuickTime to play its MIDIs. Usually, the site also provides a URL for downloading the player. If the download site is provided, your browser offers to download and install the plug-in for you. If a site does not specify a download site, your browser merely tells you that you need the plug-in and leaves it up to you to locate and install it.

Helper applications for Microsoft Internet Explorer and Netscape Navigator

When your browser can't find either a plug-in or a helper application for a file, it asks you what to do. Internet Explorer first displays the dialog box you see in Figure 8-2. (For safety's sake, the "Always ask" option cannot be disabled for unknown file types.) If you decide to open the file, Internet Explorer triggers the standard Windows dialog box for opening files of unknown types, shown in Figure 8-3, where you can select the application to open the file. If you leave "Always use this program to open this file" enabled, Internet Explorer registers the file type for the selected application. From then on, the registered program will be used as a helper application for that file type.

Netscape Navigator does not make so bold as to register a new file type for you. But it does give you a chance to set up a new helper application. Figure 8-4 shows the dialog box that Netscape Navigator displays for unknown file types. If you want to save the file without opening it, choose Save File to open a common Save As dialog box. To set up a helper application, choose Pick App to open a browse box where you can select the application. If you want to download and install a new plug-in for the file type, choose More Info to browse to Netscape's Plug-In Finder Web page, which is described under "Navigator's Helpful Plug-In Features" later in this chapter.

Figure 8-3 *You use this dialog box to tell Windows how to open an unregistered file type.*

Figure 8-4 *Netscape displays this dialog when you try to open a file type that it does not recognize.*

ActiveX

Some Web sites might play music on your system via Microsoft's ActiveX controls. *ActiveX* is a collection of technologies for turning a static Web site into a dynamic, interactive program. (*Technologies* is Microsoft's word for ActiveX. I wish I could come up with a less vague term, but it's such an all-encompassing collection that no other word really fits.) ActiveX is built into Internet Explorer 3.0 and higher but not Netscape Navigator, of course. So if you use Netscape Navigator exclusively, you won't get the advantage of sites programmed with ActiveX. Most ActiveX sites also are programmed via a language such as Java or Javascript to interact with

Navigator too, but often not as efficiently or as powerfully as with Internet Explorer.

Tip

The CaptiveX plug-in from NCompass Labs makes ActiveX controls work with Netscape Navigator. See Appendix E on the CD-ROM for the address where you can download it.

ActiveX *controls* are one of the ActiveX technologies. A control is a program module that can be inserted on a Web page, such as a stock ticker, an interactive map, or a live multimedia broadcast (or — to get back to the topic of this book — a sound player's control panel). Most of the popular players discussed in this chapter can be either plug-ins or ActiveX controls.

ActiveX gives the programmer a lot of power — perhaps too much power. Java and the scripting languages cannot write on your hard disk, for example, while ActiveX can. The possibility of destructive ActiveX controls is scary, although none have been reported. Each person or group who develops a control must sign it digitally. Internet Explorer displays a warning including the developer's signature whenever a site tries to use a control. Figure 8-5 shows a typical warning message. Notice that it includes links for more information about the control and its developer. You can also choose the More Info button to get help with the message. You choose Yes to accept the control or No to reject it. You can also enable "Always trust content from *so-and-so*," and Internet Explorer will no longer ask you about controls from that developer.

What does all this mean to you as you're browsing Web sites? At first, you may be aware of ActiveX controls because Internet Explorer must ask you about each one. You may also need to download a number of controls from the sites that use them. But as you build up a collection of controls and establish trust for certain developers, you'll become less aware of the difference between ActiveX controls and plug-ins.

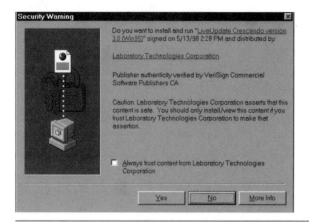

Figure 8-5 *Internet Explorer warns you when a site uses an ActiveX control.*

Some Popular Audio Plug-ins

Some people collect plug-ins like others do Beanie Babies. They have to have all the latest ones. Even if you aren't quite that avid a collector, you probably want to check out new releases every once in a while to see if you want some of the new features. Should you have more than one plug-in? You might need several to cover all the file types. Some handle several types, such as QuickTime and Media Player. Some handle specific types, like Crescendo for MIDIs. Some handle only their own proprietary types, like StreamWorks.

Windows Media Player

Chapter 2 introduced the standalone Media Player that comes with Windows 95 and 98 and plays WAVs plus a few other file formats. The new Windows Media Player is a much more comprehensive program, acting as both a standalone player and as a browser plug-in. Microsoft designed it to be the only player you need, and it handles a lot more formats than the old Media Player. But as you can see from the following list, it doesn't handle some of the popular emerging formats:

- Sampled formats: WAV, MP2, MP3, AIFF, AIFC, AU, and SND

- MIDI formats: MID and RMI using the Roland GS Sound Canvas (but not KAR or any of the MOD formats)

- Streaming formats: RealAudio and NetShow (but none of the other proprietary formats)

- Video formats: AVI, MPEG, and MOV

Figure 8-6 shows what the Windows Media Player plug-in control panel looks like when you open a Web page that calls for a multimedia file. (Don't forget that the control panel you see on a Web page depends not on the Web page but on what plug-in you have installed with your browser.) As you can see, Windows Media Player's plug-in control panel uses the standard icons for play, forward, backward, and so on. The speaker is a mute button. The slider at the right is a volume control, with low on the left and high on the right. If the Web page doesn't leave enough room for the entire control panel, Media Player shows the most important parts, the buttons for playing and stopping, and the slider.

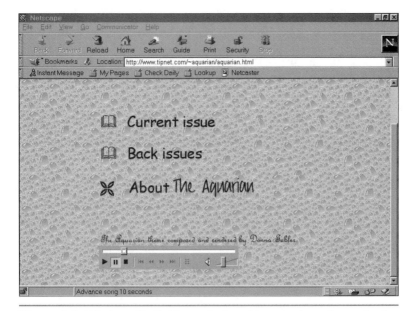

Figure 8-6 *Windows Media Player displays this control panel as a plug-in.*

Right-clicking the control panel pops up a context menu containing these options:

- Play/Pause — Same as the Play and Pause buttons
- Stop — Same as the Stop button
- Navigate — In media shows with marked sections, lets you select a section
- Language — Lets you select a language
- Volume — Same as the volume slider and mute button
- Full Screen — Expands a video to fill the screen (no function for audio)
- Zoom — Zooms a video (no function for audio)
- Properties — Displays the file's properties such as filename and length

- Statistics — For streaming audio, displays statistics such as frames skipped and frame rate
- More Information — Displays information about a NetShow show
- Options — Provides additional options such as left-right balance and Repeat Forever
- Error Details — Displays details about an error message
- Help — Opens the help library
- About — About Media Player

The new Media Player 5.2 came out too late to make it onto this book's CD-ROM, but you can download it from Microsoft's Web site:

`http://www.microsoft.com/windows/mediaplayer/default.asp`

(If the address has changed, please check my Web site at `http://members.aol.com/jnfbooks` for the updated address.)

QuickTime 3

QuickTime is Apple's multimedia player. This book's CD-ROM includes QuickTime 3 for both Windows and Macintosh. QuickTime acts as both a standalone player and a plug-in. It offers two major components: PictureViewer displays still pictures, while MoviePlayer plays movies and sounds. You saw in Chapter 3 that MoviePlayer plays karaoke files. It plays a few other formats as well:

- Sampled formats: AIFF, AIFC, WAV, AU, and MP2
- Synthesizer formats: MIDI (using the Roland GS Sound Canvas)

The fine print

The basic version of QuickTime is free. The Windows version works with Windows 95, 98, and NT 4.0. It requires a 486-DX2/66 or higher, 16MB RAM, a Sound Blaster compatible card. Also, the following are recommended for better performance: DirectX 3.0, DirectDraw, and DirectSound. (These can all be downloaded from Microsoft's Web site.) The Macintosh version works with 7.1 or higher. It requires 16MB RAM for PowerPC or 8MB RAM for 68K machines; 68K-based computers must also support Color QuickDraw.

Figure 8-7 shows the QuickTime plug-in control panel on a Web page. The Volume button pops up a small volume slider. The Play button turns into a Stop button when the sound is playing. Rewind and Fast Forward move a few seconds back and forward in the file. You can also change positions by dragging the slider.

The menu button pops up a small menu with these items:

- Open this Link — If the plug-in is linked to a site
- Plug-in Settings — To configure the plug-in
- About QuickTime Plug-in — About the plug-in

Figure 8-8 shows the Plug-in Settings dialog box, which opens when you choose the Plug-in Settings option. If you don't want sounds to start automatically — perhaps you're browsing at the office — disable the "Play movies automatically" option. You can keep movie and sound files out of your browser's cache by disabling "Save movies in disk cache." But since QuickTime doesn't give you a Save As option, you may want to cache movies and sounds. As Chapter 9 explains in more detail, you can save movie and sound files by copying them from your cache to some other folder.

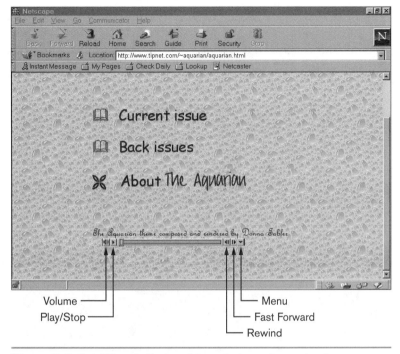

Figure 8-7 *QuickTime 3 displays this control panel as a plug-in.*

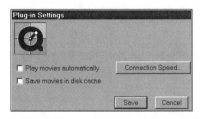

Figure 8-8 *You use the Plug-in Settings dialog box to configure QuickTime's plug-in options.*

Crescendo

LiveUpdate's Crescendo is a MIDI player with some special features. I particularly like the way you can detach the plug-in from a

Web page and float it on your desktop. That way, it continues to play a MIDI even when you leave the original site and continue browsing other sites. This book's CD-ROM includes both the Windows and the Macintosh version of Crescendo.

Crescendo's streaming feature starts playing a MIDI file before it finishes downloading. This typically cuts your waiting time in half. Crescendo offers two streaming levels. The free version, which is included on this book's disk, can respond to sites that use the SiteStream feature—in other words, the streaming is done from the site. The Crescendo Plus version, which costs $29.95, can stream MIDIs from any site—the streaming is done at your end. (Only the free version is included on the book's CD-ROM. See Appendix E on the CD-ROM for the address where you can order Crescendo Plus.)

The fine print

The Crescendo 3.0 plug-in for Windows works with Windows 95, 98, or NT and Netscape Navigator 2.0 and higher; it also works with Microsoft Internet Explorer. The Crescendo 3.0 ActiveX control for Windows works with Internet Explorer 3.0 and higher. The Crescendo 2.0 plug-in for Macintosh works with System 7.1 and higher and requires QuickTime 2.1 or higher. (QuickTime 3.0 is included on this book's CD-ROM.)

Figure 8-9 shows the Crescendo plug-in as part of a Web page displayed by Netscape Navigator. The ActiveX control looks exactly the same. As you can see from the labels in the figure, the buttons use the common icons. The button labeled Rewind returns to the beginning of the song. The Back and Forward buttons each move 10 seconds backward or forward. Unlike many other players, there is no position slider—the counter shows you where you are in the song. Crescendo's slider controls the volume of your MIDI device.

Figure 8-9 shows the full Crescendo control panel. Depending
on how much space a Web site allocates, you may see a smaller control panel or just a piece of the control panel. You can right-click any
of these to pop up Crescendo's context menu.

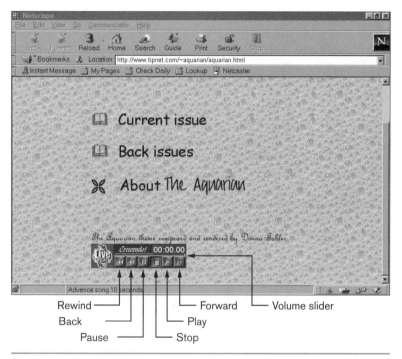

Figure 8-9 *Crescendo's control panel includes typical playback buttons.*

You float the Crescendo plug-in or control by right-clicking the
plug-in and choosing Detach (float). Figure 8-10 shows an example
of the floating plug-in, which has its own window, menu bar, and so
on. In the figure, it is sitting on top of the Netscape Navigator window, but you can move it, minimize it, and otherwise treat it like the
independent window that it is.

Tip

Crescendo's Auto-Detach option automatically floats the plug-in or control every time. To enable Auto-Detach, right-click the control panel and choose Options ⇨ Allow Auto-Detach. Or in the detached window, choose Options ⇨ Allow Auto-Detach.

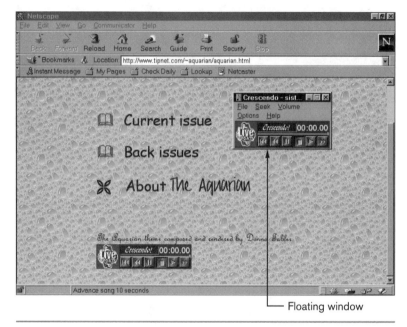

— Floating window

Figure 8-10 *When you float the Crescendo plug-in, it appears in its own window.*

Some Crescendo stream sites play not just a single song but a playlist, also known as a *jukebox*. You can skip ahead to the next song or back to the previous one. Right-clicking the Crescendo control panel brings up a context menu with options to control a single song or a playlist:

■ Previous Song — Returns to the previous song in a playlist

■ Rewind Song — Same as the Rewind button

- Back 10 sec — Same as the Back button
- Pause — Same as the Pause button
- Stop — Same as the Stop button
- Play — Same as the Play button
- Forward 10 sec — Same as the Forward button
- Next Song — Skip to the next song in a playlist
- Detach (float) — Floats the control panel
- Stop All — Stops the playlist
- MIDI Reset — Resets your MIDI device
- Save As — Lets you save the current MIDI
- Volume — Adjusts the volume
- Options — Lets you select options such as Allow Looping and Allow Auto-Detach
- Help — Links to LiveUpdate's online help site
- Buy Crescendo Plus! — Links to LiveUpdate's page where you can buy Crescendo Plus!
- About — About Crescendo
- Go to LiveUpdate — Links to LiveUpdate's home page

Tip

When you float Crescendo, you can access these commands via the menu bar in the floating window.

Netscape Navigator's Helpful Plug-In Features

If you choose not to install any third-party plug-ins, Netscape Navigator can still play audio files using its own LiveConnect plug-ins: LiveAudio, Netscape Media Player, and RealPlayer LiveConnect-enabled plug-in. LiveAudio handles WAV, AU,

AIFF, MIDI, and Netscape's own sampled format, called *Netscape Packetized Audio* (LA or LMA). Netscape Media Player handles Netscape's own streaming format, *Streaming Audio Metafiles* (LAM). The RealPlayer LiveConnect-enabled plug-in handles files in RPM format.

Figure 8-11 shows the LiveAudio plug-in on a page displayed by Netscape Navigator. As you can see, it provides the basic controls and little else. Right-clicking the plug-in pops up a context menu where you can choose Play, Pause, Stop, Save As, and About. Save As comes in handy for saving background music files from Web sites, as detailed in Chapter 9.

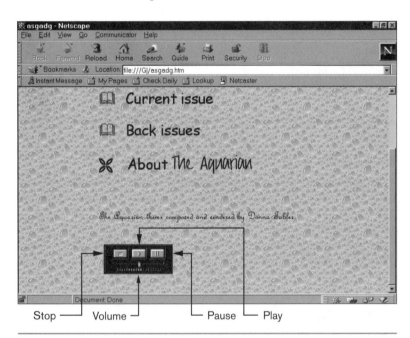

Figure 8-11 *This is Netscape's LiveAudio plug-in.*

With so many possible plug-ins, how do you manage the ones you have installed? Fortunately, Netscape Navigator lets you see what you have installed, and their order of priority. Figure 8-12 shows the page that opens in Navigator when you choose Help ⟿

About Plug-Ins in the either the Windows version or the Macintosh version of Navigator 4.0*x*. It lists all your installed plug-ins in their order of priority, with a detailed list of the file formats they support. The example in Figure 8-12 lists QuickTime as the first plug-in, so QuickTime will be used for any files it supports. When you open a file that QuickTime doesn't support, Navigator continues down the list until it finds the first plug-in that handles that format.

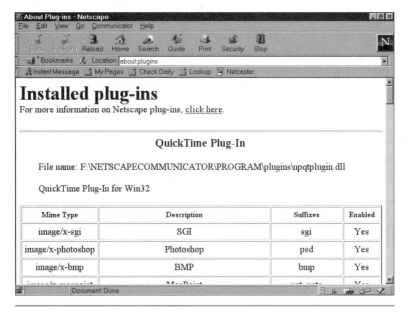

Figure 8-12 *In Windows, Netscape Navigator's About Plug-ins feature lists your plug-ins in order of priority.*

Tip

You do not have to be online to open About Plug-Ins. It's on your computer.

Notice that About Plug-Ins shows the full pathname for the plug-in. In Figure 8-12, the QuickTime plug-in is in the file named F:\NETSCAPECOMMUNICATOR\PROGRAM\plugins\npqtplugin.dll. You could remove a plug-in by deleting its DLL file if it doesn't have an uninstall feature as QuickTime does. Suppose you want to temporarily disable a plug-in, perhaps to try out another one that's lower down on the list. You could exit Navigator, change the file's name, and then restart Navigator. To restore the plug-in, exit Navigator, restore the file's original name, and restart Navigator.

Tip

Netscape maintains a Web site of Navigator-compatible plug-ins. You can read up on all the latest plug-ins and download the ones you'd like to try. To open the page from the About Plug-Ins page, click "For more information on Netscape plug-ins, click here."

To find out what helper applications you have set up with Netscape Navigator, choose Edit ⇨ Preferences to open the dialog box shown in Figure 8-13. In the Category panel on the left, open the Navigator group and select Applications, as shown in the figure. The boxes on the right show all your helper applications — your plug-ins, too. When you select a type of file in the list, the File Type Details box shows the Windows filename extension for that file type, along with the helper application or plug-in for it. Not only can you view your helper applications and plug-ins in the Preferences dialog box, you can also edit them.

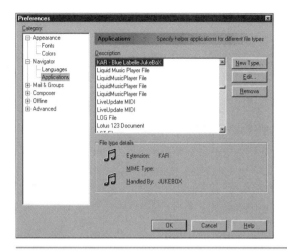

Figure 8-13 *You can view and change your Netscape Navigator helper applications and plug-ins in the Preferences dialog box (Windows version).*

Figure 8-14 shows the Macintosh version of the Preferences dialog box. It contains the same information, although it's laid out a little differently. (I find its table layout easier to work with.)

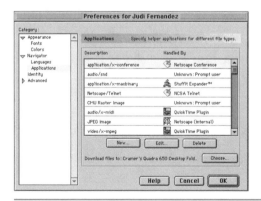

Figure 8-14 *You can view and change your Netscape Navigator helper applications and plug-ins in the Preferences dialog box (Macintosh version).*

How to edit an application or plug-in assignment in Netscape Navigator:

1. Choose Edit ⇨ Preferences to open the Preferences dialog box.

2. In the Category list, open Navigator and select Applications. All the current applications are listed in the Applications box.

3. Locate and select the application you want to edit.

4. Choose Edit to open the Edit Type dialog box. Figure 8-15 shows the Windows version of this dialog box. The Macintosh version is similar.

5. If you don't want to assign an application to the file type, select Save to Disk.

6. To assign an application to the file type:

   a. Select Application.

   b. Choose the Browse button to open a browse box where you can select the application.

   c. Choose Open to close the browse box and return to the Edit type dialog box.

7. If desired, enable "Ask me before opening downloaded files of this type." (For Macintosh, select "Unknown: Prompt user.")

8. Choose OK to close the Edit Type dialog box.

9. Repeat steps 3 through 8 for each file type you want to change.

Figure 8-15 *You edit a Netscape Navigator helper application or plug-in assignment in this dialog box (Windows version).*

Beatnik

Beatnik from HeadSpace, shown in Figure 8-16, is a multiformat player for both Macintosh and Windows. It handles many of the standard audio formats such as MIDI, WAV, AU, AIFF, and several of the MOD formats. It also plays its own Rich Music File (RMF) format. This is a MOD type of format, which incorporates a software synthesizer and built-in wavetable, along with copyright information and other documentation. Beatnik also lets Web designers add sound for events such as clicking a button or moving the mouse over an icon.

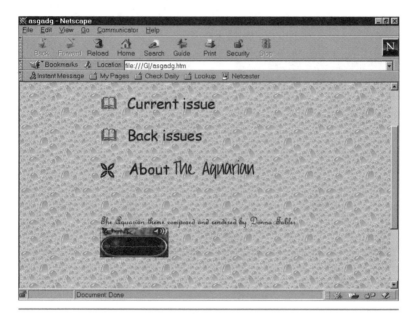

Figure 8-16 *Beatnik's player offers three views, including this waveform view.*

The fine print

Beatnik is free, but it expires in 180 days to encourage you to download the latest version. Both the Windows and the Macintosh version work with Netscape Navigator but not Microsoft Internet Explorer. (Headspace says their ActiveX control for Internet Explorer will be released soon.) The Windows version runs on Windows 95, 98, and NT and requires a Pentium 90 or faster and Netscape Navigator 3.01 or higher. The Macintosh version runs on a PowerPC running Sound Manager 3.1 or higher and Netscape Navigator 3.01 or higher. Please note that Beatnik runs into serious problems with Netscape Navigator 3.0!

MacZilla

Knowledge Engineering's MacZilla, shown in Figure 8-17, is a Macintosh product only. It acts as both a plug-in and a standalone player, handling a variety of multimedia files, including AVI, MPEG, and MIDI. MacZilla's claim to fame is that it downloads multimedia files in the background while you continue to browse. The player pops to the front in a free-floating window when the file has finished downloading. MacZilla can also extract multimedia files from Netscape Communicator e-mail and ZIP archives.

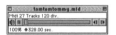

Figure 8-17 *MacZilla is shown here as a Netscape plug-in.*

The fine print

MacZilla works on 68K and PowerPC CPUs. It requires QuickTime 2.1 or higher. It works with Netscape Navigator 2.0 and Microsoft Internet Explorer. The shareware fee is $10.

What's Next?

Now that you've got great music playing in your browser, how can you download and save it on your hard drive? Chapter 10 explains how to download audio files from Web sites, FTP sites, newsgroups, and e-mail.

Chapter 9

Downloading Sound Files

Internet Web sites, FTP sites, and newsgroups contain hundreds of thousands of sound files. You can download the ones you like and build your own local collection. This chapter shows you how. And since you may want to share some of your favorites with others, it also covers how to post them to a newsgroup.

What you'll learn:

- How to download sound files from Web sites using Netscape Navigator and Microsoft Internet Explorer
- How to download sound files from an FTP site
- How to download sound files from a newsgroup using Outlook Express, Netscape Messenger, and CompuServe
- How to post sounds on a newsgroup using the same newsreaders

Downloading from Web Sites

The way that you download a file from a Web site depends on two factors: first, whether it is a background sound or a linked file, and second, which browser you're using. Linked files are easier in both browsers, so let's tackle them first.

Downloading linked files

Figure 9-1 shows an example of a Web page that offers sound files to play or download. The links such as "Lincoln's Gettysburg Address" and "FDR's Pearl Harbor Speech" refer to files instead of other pages. How can you tell? When you pause your mouse pointer over a link, both Netscape Navigator and Microsoft Internet Explorer display the linked URL in the status bar. In Figure 9-1, I paused the mouse pointer over "Lincoln's Gettysburg Address," and you can see "http://www.ptu.edu/media/~knudsen/speeches/gettysburg.ra" in the status bar. The filename `gettysburg.ra` tells you that this refers to a RealAudio sound file. As explained in Chapter 8, RA files are downloadable, but RAM files are not.

Note

Please don't try to access this Web site, as it's not real. I made it up for this example.

Downloading the linked file is simple as long as you don't want to preview it first. In Windows, right-click the link to pop up a context menu. Figure 9-2 shows Netscape Navigator's version of the context menu, where you would choose Save Link As. Internet Explorer's context menu is similar, but the option is called Save Target As. A common Save As dialog box appears so that you can select a name and location for the file. With Macintosh, hold down the Option key and click the link to open the Save As dialog box.

Link address

Figure 9-1 *"Lincoln's Gettysburg Address" links to an RA file, not an Internet site.*

Figure 9-2 *This context menu pops up in Netscape Navigator when you right-click a link to a filename.*

If you want to listen to the file before deciding to download it, simply click the link instead of right-clicking it or holding down the Option key. When you click a link to a filename, instead of a link to another site, your browser reacts in one of three ways:

- If it can find a plug-in for the file's type, it downloads and opens (plays) the file.

- If it finds a helper application instead of a plug-in, it displays a dialog box asking if you want to save the file on your hard drive or open it right away.

- If it can't find either a plug-in or a helper application, it asks you what to do with the file.

File types that are handled by plug-ins

When you play a sound file that is handled by a plug-in, both Netscape Navigator and Microsoft Internet Explorer launch a new window for the plug-in. The new window may not give you a chance to save the file. Navigator's does — the File menu includes a Save As option. Internet Explorer's doesn't, but the plug-in itself might. For example, right-clicking the Crescendo control panel pops up a menu that includes a Save As option. QuickTime and Media Player, however, do not provide such an option. Try right-clicking your plug-in's control panel to see what options it gives you.

What if you have Internet Explorer and your plug-in doesn't give you a way to save the file? Fortunately, Internet Explorer maintains a cache on your hard drive where it temporarily stores all the files that it opens. Figure 9-3 shows an example of Internet Explorer's cache. It removes files from the cache after a few days or if it needs room for new files. When you open a file handled by a plug-in, Internet Explorer downloads the file to its cache before the plug-in can play it. It shows a Downloading message while it's download-ing, but for a short file the message flashes by too fast to read. Most of the work of downloading the file is done, but you still haven't managed to save it permanently on your hard drive — remember, it's going to disappear from the cache in just a few days. But you can copy the file from the cache into a more permanent folder on your hard drive.

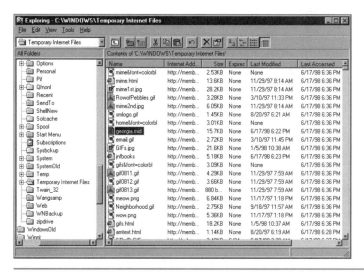

Figure 9-3 *Notice the MIDI file in my Internet Explorer cache.*

How to locate Internet Explorer's cache in Windows 95, 98, and NT:

1. Start Internet Explorer and choose View ➪ Internet Options to open the Internet Options dialog box. (You can do this offline.)

2. The General page includes a group called Temporary Internet Files. Choose the Settings button in that group to open the Settings dialog box shown in Figure 9-4.

3. Choose View Files to open the cache.

Figure 9-4 *Internet Explorer's Settings dialog box gives you access to your cache.*

Tip

Your browser cache fills up quickly, and sometimes it's hard to spot the file you want. Try choosing View ⇨ Details to show the file details, as in Figure 9-3. Then sort the files in reverse chronological order by clicking the Last Accessed header twice. The files you opened last will be at the top of the list.

How to locate Macintosh Internet Explorer's cache:

1. Start Internet Explorer and choose Edit ⇨ Preferences to open the Internet Explorer Preferences dialog box. (You can do this offline.)

2. In the panel on the left, choose Advanced in the Web Browser group to display the Advanced Preferences.

3. The Cache preferences describe the location of your cache.

4. Now that you know where your cache is, use Finder to open it.

By the way, Netscape Navigator also maintains a cache from which you can copy files. If you decide to save a file after the plug-in window closes, you don't have to go back to the Web to find it. You have a few days to copy it from your cache. Unfortunately,

Navigator assigns generic names to the files in its cache, which makes it a bit harder to find what you're looking for. Figure 9-5 shows an example of Navigator's cache, where I have highlighted a MIDI file. As you can see, the file's name is meaningless to anyone but Navigator, but at least you can find it by its file type. If there are several files of the same type in the cache, and if you can't tell by the Modified date and time (in Details view) which one you want, you can try out each one by double-clicking it.

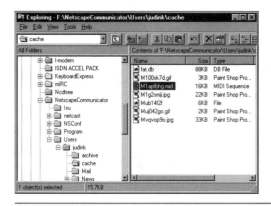

Figure 9-5 *Netscape Navigator's habit of assigning generic names to the files in its cache makes it harder to find the file you want.*

Navigator usually keeps its cache in the folder Netscape Communicator\Users*yourname*\cache, where *yourname* stands for your user name. If you can't find it there, the following procedure helps you find it.

How to locate Netscape Navigator's cache:

1. Start Netscape Navigator and choose Edit ➪ Preferences to open the Preferences dialog box, shown in Figure 9-6. (You can do this offline.)

2. Click the icon next to Advanced to expand that item, as shown in the figure.

3. Select Cache to display your cache preferences in the dialog box. The location of your cache folder is shown in Disk Cache Folder.

4. If you can't see the entire location, in Windows click the text box to place a typing cursor in it, then press the End key on your keyboard to scroll to the end of the pathname. In Macintosh, click the Choose button, then use the pop-up menu to figure out where the cache is.

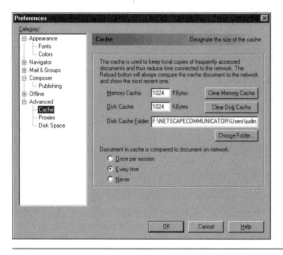

Figure 9-6 *Netscape Navigator's Preferences dialog shows you where the cache is located.*

File types that are handled by helper applications

Most types of audio files are handled by plug-ins in your browser, but you may run into some rare type that needs a helper application such as Jet-Audio. When your browser uses a helper application instead of a plug-in, it does not automatically start up the helper application. Instead, it asks you whether you want to open the file or save it on your hard drive. Figure 9-7 shows the dialog box that Netscape Navigator uses for this function. Microsoft Internet

Explorer's dialog box is similar, although the wording is different. If you choose "Save it to disk," your browser next displays a common browse dialog box so you can specify a name and location for the file. Then it downloads and saves the file. On the other hand, choosing "Open it" downloads the file to your cache and starts up the helper application to open and play it. If you decide that you want to save the file, you can most likely do so by using the helper application's File menu. Or you can copy the file from your cache as explained before.

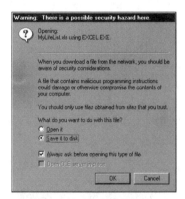

Figure 9-7 *Netscape displays this Warning dialog box when it finds a helper application for a file.*

Your browser puts you through this extra step for security reasons. As Navigator advises you in the Warning dialog box, opening files that you get from the Internet is risky business. They could contain viruses or other nasty surprises. It is much safer to save them and scan them with a virus scanner or two before opening them. That's why the default choice is "Save it to disk." I recommend using two virus-scanning programs that have been updated no more than two weeks ago. The types of files we are dealing with in this book — WAVs, MIDIs, RealAudio files, and their cousins — pose no threat. There is no way they can contain any program commands, so they cannot contain viruses. At most, they could crank up your speaker volume higher than you'd like. So you can feel safe in choosing "Open it" if you want to listen to a file before you download it.

In the dialog box in Figure 9-7, the option called "Always ask before opening this type of file" is enabled, the default setting. When this option is enabled, your browser always displays this Warning dialog box whenever you click a link to this type of file. If you decide that this file type is safe, and you want to always open it without being asked, you can bypass this dialog box in the future by disabling "Always ask before opening this type of file." Since audio files cannot contain viruses, you can safely disable this check box for them.

Note

"Always ask before opening this type of file" cannot be disabled for certain high-risk file types, such as program files with extension .exe or .com. You cannot bypass the File Download dialog box for such files.

If I'm connected at 33.6 Kbps, how come I'm downloading at 3.2 Kbps?

This disparity perplexes and irritates a lot of folks. It sounds like you're using only one tenth of your bandwidth, but that's not really true. You're not connected at 33.6 kilo*bytes* per second but 33.6 kilo*bits* per second. Modem speeds are stated in kilobits per second – what the heck, it sounds faster. But your browser shows your download speed in kilobytes per second so you can estimate how long a download will take. Downloading at 33.6 kilobits per second works out to approximately 3.4 kilobytes per second. (It takes about ten bits to send a byte over a modem.) So 3.2 kilobytes per second comes close to your maximum speed. Doesn't that make you feel better?

You may be able to achieve maximum speed downloading from a nearby site at 3 a.m. But the traffic being handled by your ISP, the server you're accessing, and the Internet nodes your data must travel through all serve to slow things down. At each step, your data must wait its turn. Hence, your speed is often short of the maximum.

More factors intervene when you're connected at today's high speeds of 56 Kbps or faster. The server you're requesting data from may have slower modems than you do, so you may be stuck with a 33.6 Kbps rate even though your modem can go much faster. Even if the server also has 56 Kbps modems, FCC regulations currently prohibit servers using *plain old telephone service* (POTS – it's a technical term, honest) to transmit data faster than 53 Kbps, so that becomes the ultimate limit unless the server has digital phone service. (The same FCC regulations prohibit you from uploading any faster than 33.6 Kbps via POTS.) Other factors may also slow you down, in particular your own serial port's capabilities, as well as the number of connection points between you and your phone company. If you're managing to download at a rate between 6 and 7K per second, you're close to the maximum speed for a 56 Kbps modem via POTS.

Downloading background sounds from a Web site

When a sound plays in the background of a Web page, how can you download and save it? The site may not display a control panel for the background sound. If it does give you a control panel, you can try right-clicking the control panel to look for a Save As option. If not, the easiest way to save the sound is to copy it from the browser's cache as described earlier. Since you don't know the name of the file — which wouldn't help you in Netscape Navigator anyway — use the date and time to locate the right one. You can play any sound file in the cache by double-clicking it.

Downloading Files from FTP

Have you ever clicked a link on a Web site and ended up on a page like the one in Figure 9-8? This is an FTP (File Transfer Protocol) site, not a Web site. The Web has become so popular that newcomers tend to think it's synonymous with the Internet, but it's not. FTP is another service that gives people a way to share files over the Internet. It's a no-frills service — no graphics, no background sounds, no fancy fonts, no hyperlinks to other sites. Just a directory full of files for you to open or download. And because it doesn't have any frills, it's a lot faster.

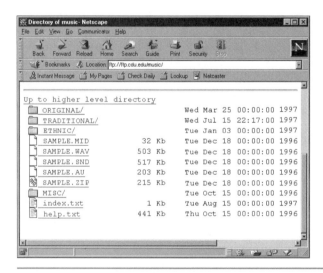

Figure 9-8 *Sometimes you end up on an FTP site when looking for files to download.*

An FTP site looks and behaves much like a directory tree. It might contain several subdirectories and/or files that you can open by clicking. If the directory you're currently viewing is a subdirectory, the entry at the top takes you up to the parent directory. There is often a text file called index.txt or readme.txt that describes what's in the directory, since the directory itself contains only filenames with no explanations.

When you access an FTP site via your Web browser, all the files listed are linked files and you can preview, download, and save them the same way you do linked files on a Web page.

Downloading Files from Newsgroups

A *newsgroup* is an Internet service where people post messages that anyone else can read and respond to, kind of like a bulletin board at the grocery store. In fact, newsgroups are often called bulletin boards. Figure 9-9 shows an example of a newsgroup devoted to bluegrass music. The example shows just the subject headings of the messages that are currently posted. You use the buttons at the bottom of the window to read or otherwise handle messages, as well as posting your own messages.

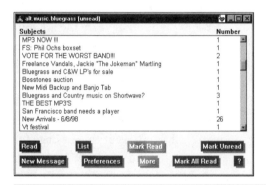

Figure 9-9 *This newsgroup is for fans of bluegrass music.*

To access a newsgroup, you need a *newsreader*—a program that formats and displays the contents of newsgroups, like the one shown in Figure 9-9. America Online and CompuServe both include built-in newsreaders—that's AOL's in Figure 9-9. The Microsoft Network doesn't provide a newsreader. You use your own newsreader, probably the one built into Outlook Express if you have installed that feature. If you don't have any of these services, but you do have an Internet service, you can access newsgroups by using an independent newsreader.

Newsgroups on the Internet can handle text data only, causing tons of complications and hassle for people who want to post pictures or songs. Graphics and sound files are binary files, not text files. Theoretically, you can't post them in a newsgroup. But you can get around the limitation by encoding the file. Encoding turns a binary file into a text file. You can't read the text file — it looks like nonsense data — but when you decode it, it turns back into the original binary file. I don't want to get too deeply into encoding here. If you want to learn more about it, please see my book *MIME, UUENCODE & ZIP: Decompressing & Decoding Internet Files* (MIS:Press, 1997). Fortunately, most newsreaders now encode and decode binary files automatically, so you need only to be aware of the process.

Another problem with newsgroups is that they limit the amount of data you can send in a single message. Encoded binary files often exceed the limit, and you have to divide them into several messages to upload them. When you download them, you have to combine them again before decoding them. Fortunately again, most newsreaders now split messages automatically. Combining them is not so automatic, since you have to identify all the parts of the message for the newsreader. Take a look at the example in Figure 9-10, which shows a newsgroup where people post a lot of graphics and music files. When messages are split into parts, each part is marked [1/3], [2/3], and so on. I'll show you how to reassemble the parts when I talk about specific newsreaders in the following sections.

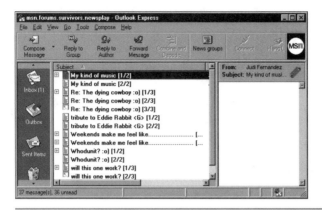

Figure 9-10 *These are all multipart messages as indicated by the [n/n] markers.*

Microsoft Outlook Express

Microsoft Outlook Express includes both an e-mail handler and a newsreader that are Internet capable—they can interpret HTML and Java scripts. You end up with colorful e-mail and newsgroups, because you can include photos, animated GIFs, and Java applets right in a message. This chapter shows you how to use the Outlook Express newsreader; the e-mail handler is covered in Chapter 10.

Only people who are also using Outlook Express or another newsreader with HTML capabilities can receive the graphics and sound files in their messages. Depending on their newsreader, other people may receive the files as attachments, which is fine, or they may receive unintelligible code, which they probably won't appreciate. Most of the people on the Microsoft Network (MSN) are using Outlook Express, so you can feel safe in posting messages containing HTML and Java scripts to MSN newsgroups, or to any newsgroup about MSN, Microsoft Outlook, or Microsoft Outlook Express.

MSN has many newsgroups related to sound. Here are a few of my favorite sound-oriented newsgroups to get you started. These are all on the `msnnews.msn.com` server, for MSN members only:

Some serious MIDI composers post their new works here:

`msn.computingcentral.electronicmusic.featured.performances`

People discuss MODs and post new works here:

`msn.computingcentral.electronicmusic.mod.music`

No files here, but lots of questions and answers about sound hardware, software, and files:

`msn.computingcentral.multimedia.sound`

When a file is attached to a newsgroup message instead of embedded in it, the message looks something like the one in Figure 9-11. You can see the attached file in the bottom pane of the window. Double-click the file to play it. To save it on your hard drive, right-click it to pop up a context menu where you can choose Save As.

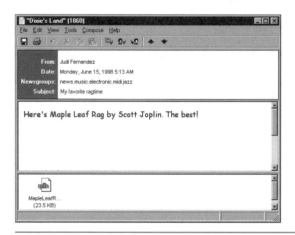

Figure 9-11 *The file attached to this message shows up in the bottom pane.*

If a message contains an embedded sound, you'll hear it when you read the message. But it's a little harder to save it on your hard drive. You can extract it from the background by forwarding the message to yourself as a plain text e-mail. Because plain text messages cannot contain embedded files, Outlook Express changes all embedded files into attached files when converting a message to plain text. The following procedure shows the exact steps to follow. How to extract a background sound from an Outlook Express message:

1. Choose Tools ➪ Options to open the Options dialog box.

2. Choose the Send tab to open the Send options.

3. In the "Mail sending format" box, select Plain Text.

4. Choose OK to close the Options dialog box.

5. Open the message with the embedded sound.

6. Choose the Forward Message icon. Outlook Express opens the message in a mail window. The bottom pane shows the sound file, which is now attached instead of embedded.

7. Right-click the file's icon in the bottom pane and then choose Save As.

8. You don't need to actually send the file to yourself. You can close the window after you save the file.

When you want to read a split message, you must first select all the parts of the message. The following procedure shows you how. How to combine and decode a multipart message in Outlook Express:

1. Click the first part of the message.

2. Hold down Ctrl while you click the remaining parts of the message.

3. Choose Combine and Decode. Outlook Express opens a dialog box listing the messages you have chosen.

4. Drag the parts up and down as necessary to put them in the correct numerical order.

5. Choose OK to combine and decode the message. Outlook Express does the rest of the work and displays the finished message.

When you want to post a sound file to a newsgroup, you can either embed it in the message or attach it to the message. If you embed it, it plays automatically when someone reads the message, much like the background sound on a Web page. An attached sound must be downloaded and saved by readers who want to hear it. It's easier for your recipients to listen to an embedded sound but easier to save an attached one.

Tip

Figure out the "rules" of a newsgroup before posting a message with embedded sound. If all the other messages are plain text, and any sound files or graphics are attached, the people in that newsgroup probably don't want to be bothered with the extra time it takes to download messages with HTML content. But if you see that other people are embedding sounds, feel free to express your creativity and entertain your readers.

It's easy to embed a sound with Outlook Express 5.0 — choose Format ↪ Background ↪ Sound and select the file. For earlier versions of Outlook Express, you have to use a rather intimidating Javascript if you want to embed a sound. You can find the instructions and the script at this Web site:

```
http://www.okinfoWeb.com/moe/format/format_008.htm
```

How to attach a sound file to a newsgroup posting using Outlook Express:

1. Choose Compose Message to start a new message or Reply to Group to respond to the current message. A new message window opens. Figure 9-12 shows what this dialog box looks like when the message is ready to send.

2. Write the message.

3. Choose the Insert File tool, shown in Figure 9-12. This opens an Insert Attachment dialog box.

4. Locate and select the file that you want to attach. When you choose Attach, the dialog box closes and the file appears in the bottom pane of the window, as in Figure 9-12.

5. Choose Post to post the message. Outlook Express takes care of encoding and splitting the attached file as needed.

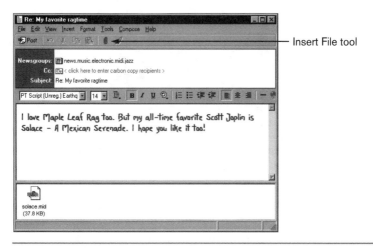

Figure 9-12 *The Outlook Express Insert File tool lets you attach files to the messages you post.*

Netscape Messenger

Messenger is the Netscape equivalent of Outlook Express for Communicator 4.0 and later versions. Like Outlook Express, it interprets HTML and Java. Figure 9-13 shows what a message looks like with an attached MIDI file. Notice the attachment icon next to the Subject. The details of the attachment are spelled out below the message, along with a link to the file. Clicking the link plays the file using your Netscape plug-in. Right-click the link and choose Save Link As to save the file on your hard drive.

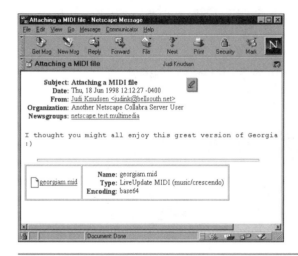

Figure 9-13 *You download an attached file by right-clicking the link at the bottom of the message.*

Suppose you want to post a file by attaching it. After you open the Composition window by choosing New Message or Reply, click the Attach tool and select the file you want to attach. It's as easy as that. There is a way to embed sounds in a newsgroup message, but it's hard to do. If you're interested in trying, Chapter 10 contains a step-by-step procedure for embedding sounds in Netscape Messenger e-mail. The process is nearly identical for newsgroup messages.

CompuServe's CIM newsreader

CompuServe's newsreaders are much more primitive than Outlook Express. Figure 9-14 shows an example of a newsgroup displayed in CompuServe's CIM newsreader. I have set it up to retrieve and decode a MIDI file attached to a message. (There's no way to preview a sound before downloading it.) You click the box next to the message to place an *X* in it. You also select the "Decoded" option so the newsreader will decode the file. Then you click Retrieve to download the file. When CompuServe displays the Save As dialog box, be sure to add the right extension to the filename if it doesn't already have one. After retrieving the file, use Windows Explorer or My Computer to locate and play it.

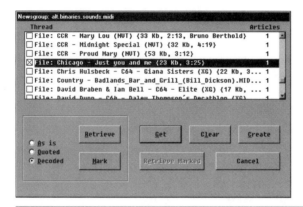

Figure 9-14 *CompuServe's CIM newsreader can retrieve and decode sound files posted in messages.*

Posting a sound file, or any binary file, to a newsgroup by using the CIM newsreader is not so easy, because you must encode and split the file yourself. I don't have room here to explain how to do that, as it's a huge topic, and you'll need some special software. For more information on how to post a sound file or a binary file to a newsgroup by using the CIM newsreader, see my book *MIME, UUENCODE & ZIP: Decompressing & Decoding Internet Files,* mentioned earlier in this chapter.

What's Next?

In Chapter 10, you'll learn how to send sound files to your friends via e-mail, as well as how to download the ones they send you.

Chapter 10

Exchanging Sound Files via E-mail

Suppose you want to send your best online buddy a birthday greeting or a new MIDI you just sequenced. You can attach the sound file to an e-mail message and send it on its merry way. With some mailing programs, you can even embed a sound right into the message just like the background sound on a Web page — it plays when your buddy opens the message. This chapter shows you how to send sound files either as attachments or as background sounds. It also shows you what to do when you receive a sound file. We'll cover the most popular mailing programs: America Online, CompuServe, Outlook Express, and Netscape Messenger.

What you'll learn:

- Why sound files must be encoded
- How to attach sound files to an e-mail message using America Online, CompuServe, Outlook Express, and Netscape Messenger
- How to receive, listen to, and save attached sound files with all four mailing programs
- How to insert background sound files with Outlook Express and Netscape Messenger
- How to extract and save a background sound file with Outlook Express and Netscape Messenger

You may be wondering why this chapter doesn't cover voice e-mail. A lot of people are talking about it, but so far it's not a practical alternative to regular e-mail. Basically, *voice e-mail* is a voice-quality recording attached to an e-mail message. And, as Shakespeare said, " . . . there's the rub." As long as we're stuck with WAV and SND files for recorded messages, you wouldn't want to send anyone a message longer than, "Hi, it's me. Bye." When we reach the point where everyone can play back MP3 files — and I think that will happen in the next couple of years — voice e-mail may then come into its own.

How the Internet Handles E-mail

Were you surprised to learn in Chapter 9 that newsgroups can handle text data only? The same is true for Internet e-mail. If you try to e-mail any other kind of data, such as a sound file, it doesn't go through properly. So you must convert your sound files — along with any other kinds of nontext files, such as images, videos, and spreadsheets — to text data before sending them. You must encode a file before sending it, and the people who receive it must decode it. *Encoding* converts any file to text data, and *decoding* restores it to its original form.

Your e-mail program probably handles encoding and decoding for you — most of the time. Every once in a while, it can't figure out how to decode a file and gives you the encoded data. If you ever receive an e-mail message full of gobbledygook, it's probably an encoded file that your mail handler couldn't decode. The easiest solution? Ask the sender to send it again. If that doesn't work, you may be able to decode the file yourself. I can't show you how to decode and encode files here — it's too big a topic. I devote several chapters to it in *MIME, UUENCODE & ZIP: Decompressing & Decoding Internet Files* (MIS:Press, 1997). But the MIME and uuencode information in the following sidebar briefly describes the two most popular encoding schemes.

MIME and uuencode

The two most popular schemes for encoding binary files for the Internet are called *uuencode* and *Multipurpose Internet Mailing Extensions* (MIME). The uuencode method came first, back in the days when the Internet was young and mostly UNIX computers used it. (The *uu* in uuencode stands for "UNIX-to-UNIX" because files were being transferred from one UNIX machine to another.) It encodes using a fairly simply scheme called Base64 encoding. Most programs that do uuencoding produce a file with a .uue extension.

MIME is a more modern and sophisticated encoding system, which most of today's high-end newsreader and mailing programs use. It offers the choice of several encoding schemes, including Base64. Another handy encoding scheme, called *Quoted Printable*, encodes just the binary characters in an otherwise text document. It's meant for documents that are mostly text but contain an occasional ñ or © Quoted Printable encoding should not be used for binary files such as sound files because it would triple the size of the file.

One important feature of MIME is that it permits multipart encoded files. If you send a message with three files attached, for example, your mailer encodes the message and files into one four-part MIME file. It might use Quoted Printable encoding for the message and Base64 encoding for the attached files. The receiving mailer separates and decodes the four parts again, if it's capable of handling multipart MIME files. One extremely popular mailer that cannot decode a multipart mailer is AOL's built-in mail handler. It can handle a message and one attachment, but if there are more attachments it makes no attempt to decode any part of the message. Instead, it attaches the entire multipart MIME file to a generic message and leaves it up to the recipient to handle the decoding. This has always surprised me, as AOL was designed mostly for people who are not Internet sophisticated and wouldn't know what to do with a MIME file if it bit them on the nose.

Continued

MIME is much more than an encoding scheme. It also identifies each file's type, such as audio/midi or image/gif, and includes that information in the encoded file. Mailers and newsreaders that decode MIME often go on to load a plug-in or helper application to play the file based on its MIME type. MIME types have become so useful that they have grown beyond their original use with encoded files. For example, Web browsers use a file's MIME type, rather than its file extension, to decide how to open it. Windows also keeps track of the MIME types of registered file extensions, although it still uses the extension to determine how to open a file.

Sending and receiving sound files

When you want to send a sound file to a friend via e-mail, you must attach it to an e-mail message. Your friend then downloads the attached file to his or her hard drive. In this section, I show you how to send and receive files using some popular mailers: America Online, CompuServe, Outlook Express, and Netscape Messenger. These mailers automatically encode and decode using MIME encoding.

Keep in mind that your recipient may have a slow connection. Most people don't want to spend 20 minutes or more downloading a file just to hear you sing "Happy Birthday" to them. Here's a good rule of thumb: Assume that your recipients can download at about 3 kilobytes per second. That's nearly full speed when they're connected at 33,600 bits per second. At that rate, an attachment under 180K downloads in less than a minute.

Should you zip or stuff the sound files that you send? You could save 50 percent to 80 percent of a MIDI file's size by compressing it. A WAV compresses by about 25 percent to 50 percent. MP3s don't compress much at all as they are already highly compressed. But the advantages of an uncompressed file might outweigh the advantages of a compressed file. If a sound file is not compressed, most mailers can recognize its MIME type and make it easy for the recipient to listen to it. AOL, for example, automatically displays a playback control when you download a sound file from an e-mail. But if the file is zipped or stuffed, most mailers simply save it without decompressing or playing it. It's up to you to decide how well your recipients can handle compressed as opposed to uncompressed sound files.

Here's another reason not to bother zipping or stuffing sound files. Modems often compress files automatically. When two modems that use the same protocol are connected, the sending modem compresses the data and the receiving modem decompresses it again. The users aren't even aware of the process, but it can save a lot of transmission time. So when your recipients download files you send, they may get the advantage of compression without any of the disadvantages.

When someone sends you a sound file, you don't need to worry about viruses. An audio file contains data only and cannot contain a virus. But if someone sends you an EXE file as a self-extracting ZIP file containing audio files, take extreme care. Never download and start up an EXE file without checking it first — not even if your best friend sends it to you. Open it in an unzipping program such as WinZip, where you can examine its contents to make sure it really is a self-extracting ZIP file.

Using America Online

The America Online 4.0 for Windows (WAOL 4.0) built-in mailer lets you attach one or more files, which it automatically encodes before sending. If you attach more than one file, it zips them into a single file. When you receive a single attached sound file, it automatically decodes it. It cannot decode multiple attachments. If it recognizes the sound file's type, it also displays a playback control so you can click the Play button to listen to it. The following sections explain in detail how to send and receive sound files on America Online 4.0 for Windows.

Sending sound files

WAOL 4.0 gives you an Attachments button to attach one or more files. Figure 10-1 shows the Write Mail form that you use to compose a new letter. In the example, I have attached several files. Two of them are shown next to the Attachments button. When you send an e-mail with multiple attachments, AOL automatically zips them into a single ZIP file, assigning the first attachment's name to the file. In the example in Figure 10-1, AOL will create a file named `medb.zip`, because the first attachment is named `medb.mid`. If you suspect that your recipients might not know how to deal with a zipped file, don't attach multiple files in AOL. Instead, send a separate e-mail for each attachment.

Tip

There's another advantage to sending unzipped files to AOL members. In addition to saving a downloaded sound file, AOL automatically opens and plays it. But if the file is zipped, AOL doesn't recognize it as a sound file and simply saves it without playing it.

Figure 10-1 *With America Online's mailer, you choose the Attachments button to attach a file to an e-mail message.*

How to send sound files with WAOL 4.0:

1. In the main AOL window, choose the Write Mail tool to open a blank Write Mail form.

2. Address and write the message.

3. Choose the Attachments button to open the Attachments dialog box. Figure 10-2 shows an example of the Attachments dialog box after some files have been attached.

4. Choose Attach to open a common Windows browse box.

5. Select a file and choose Open. The browse box closes and the Attachments dialog box shows the attached file in its list box.

6. Repeat steps 4 and 5 until you have attached all the desired files.

7. Choose OK to close the Attachments dialog box and return to the Compose Mail window.

8. Send the letter.

If you change your mind about an attached file before you send the letter, you can detach it by choosing Attachments, selecting the file, and choosing Detach.

Figure 10-2 *WAOL 4.0's Attachments dialog box lists your attachments and lets you attach and detach files.*

Receiving and saving sound files

Now suppose you receive e-mail with an attached file. WAOL 4.0 gives you several clues that a file is attached. First, you'll see an attached file icon next to the message in your mailbox. When you open the letter, it looks something like Figure 10-3, where you can see the name of the attached file as well as buttons to download the file now or later.

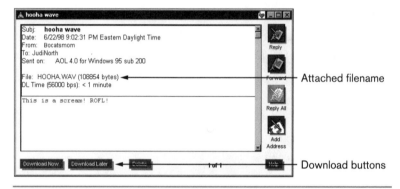

Figure 10-3 *AOL gives you several clues that a file is attached.*

Clicking the Download Now button opens a common Windows browse box where you can select a name and folder for the file. As long as the file isn't zipped, AOL downloads it, decodes it, saves it in the selected folder, and then starts up your default player to play it. The Download Later button adds the file to your Download Manager list. Unfortunately, Download Manager is another topic that I don't have room to cover in this book. (I'm sorry, but I haven't written a book about it — yet.) Here are a few survival tips for Download Manager:

- When you try to sign off, Download Manager interrupts to ask if you want to download files now. If you say yes, all the files on your Download Manager list are downloaded.

- The files being downloaded receive their default names and go into the default download folder, which is probably the download folder in your AOL folder, unless someone has changed it.

- Download Manager does not play files. You must locate them on your hard drive and play them yourself.

- Choose My Files ⇨ Download Manager for information about the files that have been downloaded or are waiting to be downloaded.

When you download a zipped attachment, AOL can unzip it for you when you sign off. To enable or disable this feature, go to keyword: PREFERENCES and open Download Preferences. Two options control AOL automatic unzipping:

- "Automatically decompress files at sign-off" — Enable this option if you want AOL to unzip your files automatically when you sign off.

- "Delete ZIP files after decompression" — Enable this option if you want AOL to delete a file after unzipping it. Otherwise the ZIP file remains in your download folder.

When you enable these features, you'll see an extra sign-off message listing the files that were unzipped. AOL creates a new folder in your default download folder for each ZIP file it unzips. If it unzips `medb.zip`, for example, the new folder is called simply `medb` and contains all the files that were extracted from `medb.zip`.

Using CompuServe

CompuServe 3.0.4 for Windows lets you send and receive multiple sound files attached to a single e-mail message. It encodes and decodes automatically, which simplifies playing and saving the files you receive. If you receive a zipped file, CompuServe automatically starts a program to unzip it. The following sections explain in detail how to send and receive sounds on CompuServe.

Sending sound files

CompuServe's Create Mail form includes an Attach File button that serves two functions. First, it opens a dialog box where you can attach and detach files. Second, it shows how many files are attached. Figure 10-4 shows an example of the Create Mail form with three attached files.

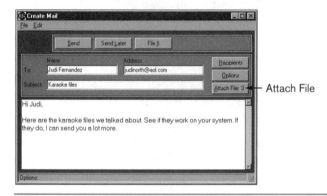

Figure 10-4 *CompuServe's Attach File button shows how many files are currently attached.*

How to send sound files with CompuServe 3.0.4:

1. On the Home Desktop, choose Mail Center to open the Mail Center.
2. Choose Create to open the Create page.
3. Choose New to open a blank Create Mail form.
4. Address and write the message.
5. Choose Attach File to open the Attach Files dialog box, shown in Figure 10-5.
6. Choose Add to List to open a common browse box.
7. Select a file and then choose Open. The browse box closes and the Attach Files dialog box shows the attached file in its list box.

8. Repeat steps 6 and 7 until you have attached all the desired files.

9. Choose OK to close the Attach Files dialog box and return to the Compose Mail window.

10. Send the letter.

If you change your mind about an attached file before you send the letter, you can detach it by choosing Attach File, selecting the file, and choosing Remove.

Figure 10-5 *CompuServe's Attach Files dialog box lists your attachments and lets you attach and detach files.*

Receiving and saving sound files

Now suppose you receive an e-mail with attached files. When you open the letter, you'll see in the header box that you're reading Part 1 of so many parts. Figure 10-6 shows an example where three files are attached, for a total of four parts. The figure shows Part 2, which is an attached file named `bluetailfly.kar`. The arrow icons take you to the previous and next parts. Choose Open to listen to the file using your default player. Choose Save to save the file on one of your drives.

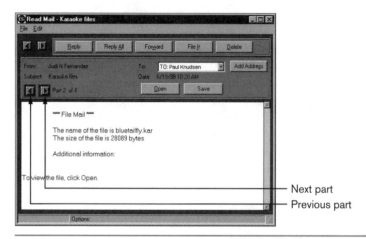

Next part

Previous part

Figure 10-6 *This message displays information about the first of three attached files.*

If you open a ZIP file, CompuServe unzips it and displays the contents. If you have a default unzipping program set up on your system, CompuServe calls on your program. Otherwise it uses its own unzipping facility.

Using Outlook Express

In Chapter 9, you saw how Microsoft's Outlook Express 5.0 acts as a newsreader. It also handles e-mail, permitting you to send and receive messages containing HTML code and scripts. As long as you're corresponding with other people whose mail handler also interprets HTML and scripts, your e-mail can be quite colorful. Keep in mind, though, that some people would rather receive plain old text that downloads quickly. To send a message including HTML code, enable Format ⇨ Rich Text (HTML) in the message window.

Sending sound files

When you want to send a sound file to some friends, you can choose between embedding it as a background sound or attaching it. A background sound plays as soon as someone opens the message, just like the background sound on a Web page. An attached sound file simply appears as an attachment to the message. It's easier for your recipients to listen to a background sound but easier to save an attached one.

If your purpose is to entertain or dazzle the recipient, and you know that they also use Outlook Express, try using a background sound. Outlook Express can receive and play background sounds, as can Netscape Communicator. But people on America Online or CompuServe would receive something strange, such as your HTML source file or a multipart MIME message.

With Outlook Express 5.0, inserting a background sound in a message at last becomes easy. You simply choose Format ➪ Background ➪ Sound to select a background sound file. You can insert sounds with earlier versions of Outlook Express, too, but not as easily. You must trick the mail handler into treating the sound file as an image file via a rather complex procedure. If you want more information about how to embed sounds in Outlook Express 4 and earlier versions, you'll find the instructions and the necessary script at this Web site:

http://www.okinfoWeb.com/moe/format/format_008.htm

If your purpose is to transmit a sound file rather than entertain, it's better to attach the file. Your recipient can easily download an attached file, whereas extracting a background sound takes extra steps as well as extra knowledge. (Hint: Send all your friends copies of this book.) To attach a sound file, choose the Attach File tool, shown here, to open a browse box where you can select the file.

Saving sound files

Now suppose you receive a sound file that you want to save on your hard drive. If it's attached, and if you're using Outlook Express 5.0, you'll see it listed next to Attach in the headers for the message, as shown in Figure 10-7. Double-click a file to preview it. To download it, right-click it and then choose Save As.

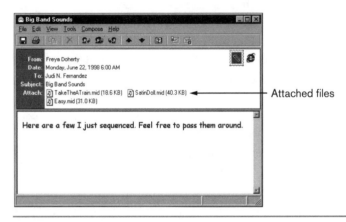

Attached files

Figure 10-7 *Outlook Express 5.0 lists attached files in the message headers.*

If you want to save a background sound, you can extract it by converting the message to plain text. Changing the message to plain text converts the background sound to an attached file. The following procedure explains exactly what to do.

How to extract a background sound from an Outlook Express message:

1. Choose Forward Message to open a forward window.

2. Choose Format ➪ Plain Text.

3. When Outlook Express asks if you're sure you want to do this, choose Yes. The message changes to plain text in the window and the embedded file becomes an attached file.

4. Right-click the attached file to save it.

Using Netscape Messenger

Netscape Messenger 4.0x acts as both a newsreader, as you saw in Chapter 9, and an e-mail handler. It offers many of the same functions as the Netscape Navigator browser. It can interpret HTML code and scripts, and it can display graphics and play sound files by using the same plug-ins and helper applications as Navigator. In this section, you'll learn how to both send and receive sound files with Netscape Messenger 4.0x.

Sending sound files

The easiest way to send sound files to someone is to attach them to a message. The headers area of the Composition window includes three icons that change the contents of the area. From top to bottom, they are:

Address Message — Displays the addressing fields (the default display)

Attach Files and Documents — Displays attached files and documents

Message Sending Options — Displays options such as format and priority

When you start a new message, the Address Message icon is automatically selected so you can address the message. Complete the address first. Then choose the Attach Files and Documents icon to attach files to the message. The addresses disappear when you choose Attach Files and Documents. (They're still valid, you just can't see them.) Instead, the header area lists the attached files, as in Figure 10-8. The list is blank, of course, until you attach at least one file.

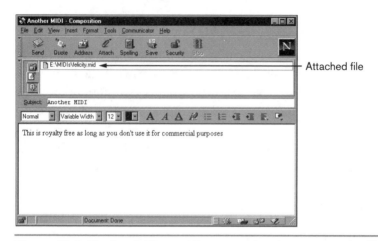

Attached file

Figure 10-8 *The Attach Files and Documents icon lets you see what files are attached and add more attachments.*

To attach a file, click anywhere in the file list to pop up a browse box where you can select the file. You can attach as many files as you wish, but keep in mind that your recipient's mail handler may not be able to receive multiple files.

If the recipient's mail handler also interprets HTML and is capable of playing background sounds, it is possible to insert a sound into the background with Netscape Messenger. Messenger by nature ignores background sounds that you insert into the HTML document. It does not encode or transmit them. But there's a way to trick it into encoding the file as an image file and then editing the encoded file to change it into an embedded sound file before you send it. It's a complex process, and it's easy to make a mistake and end up with garbage. But if you're willing to try it, here are the instructions.

How to embed a background sound file in a Messenger message:

1. Choose File ⇨ Compress Folders to remove all the old messages from your Unsent Messages folder. (You'll use this folder to store your new message while you edit it, and you don't want any old messages in there.)

2. In the Compose Mail window, choose Insert ⇨ Image to open the Image properties dialog box.

3. Choose the Choose File button to open a common browse box.

4. Locate and select the sound file. (Hint: You must set the "Files of Type" option to "All files (*.*)" in order to see sound files in the browse box.)

5. In the Dimensions group, disable Constrain and set the Height to 100 pixels and the Width to 300 pixels.

6. Choose OK to close the Image Properties dialog box.

7. Choose Format ⇨ Page Colors and Properties and either choose a background color for the page or insert a background picture. (This doesn't sound like an important step, but it forces Netscape to generate the HTML you need to make the background sound work.)

8. Choose the Message Sending Options icon to display the options.

9. In the Format drop-down list, choose HTML text only.

10. Choose File ⇨ Send Later. Happily, Messenger encodes the sound file before placing it in your Unsent Messages folder.

11. In a plain text editor such as Windows Notepad, open the Netscape Communicator Folder, then the Users folder, then the folder for your user name, then the Mail folder, and finally the document called Unsent Messages. What you'll see is the encoded version of your message and the attached file. Don't worry — you don't really have to read it. You just have to change one line. (If there is more than one unsent message in the document, the one you just added will be the last one in the document.)

12. Find the line that looks something like this, where xxxxxx indicates information supplied by Netscape :

```
<IMG SRC="cid:xxxxxx.xxxxxx.xxxxxx.@xxxxxx.xxxxxx"
HEIGHT=100 WIDTH=300>
```

13. Change "IMG" to "EMBED" and add LOOP=1 before the ending bracket. Don't change anything else! The result should look like this:

```
<EMBED SRC="cid:
xxxxxx.xxxxxx.xxxxxx.@xxxxxx.xxxxxx" HEIGHT=100
WIDTH=300 LOOP=1>
```

14. Save the changed file as a text file. Important! It's crucial that you save this file as an ordinary text file. Since you opened the document as a text file, you should be able to use the Save function to save it in the same format. But if you decide to use Save As for some reason, be sure to follow these two rules:

- Select "text" from the "Files of Type" drop-down list.

- Do not let the editor change the file's name or add .txt to the end.

15. Return to Messenger and send the file. If all went well, you'll hear the background sound and see your plug-in's control panel when you open the message to send it.

Note

HTML's <EMBED> tag is explained in Appendix D on the CD-ROM.

If something goes wrong and Messenger chokes on the edited Unsent Messages folder, the easiest solution is to delete these two files from the Netscape Communicator\Users\yourname\Mail folder: Unsent Messages and Unsent Messages.snm. Messenger generates a new, empty Unsent Messages folder for you after you delete those two files. (You lose any unsent messages that were in the old folder.)

Saving sound files

Figure 10-9 shows what a message looks like when you receive an attached sound file. An attachment icon appears next to the Subject, and the file appears below the message. Click the file to listen to it. To save it, right-click it and choose Save Link As.

Figure 10-9 *Netscape Messenger gives you a link to an attached file below the message.*

If a sound file is embedded in a message as a background sound, the message window does not show a link. You'll hear the sound as soon as you open the message. To save it, choose File ⇨ Open Attachments, which displays a list of the attachments to the letter, including the background sound. Select the background sound to open it in a separate window where you can choose File ⇨ Save As. The file will have a generic name, assigned by Netscape Messenger, so you'll probably want to rename it when you save it.

What's Next?

How about recording your own sound files to share with your friends in newsgroups and e-mail? Chapter 11 shows you how to record sound files from CDs, from a microphone, or from the Line In port of your sound board.

Chapter 11

Recording Your Own Sampled Sounds

Now that you know how to send sounds to your friends, how about sharing some sounds that you record yourself? This chapter shows you how to record sounds in both Windows and Mac OS. You can record from a microphone, a CD, a MIDI or other file, or any device connected to your sound board's input jack. You can even record from two or more devices at once, so you can sing along with your favorite song, if you'd like. This chapter covers sampled sounds only, not MIDIs, MODs, or proprietary formats such as Shockwave or NetShow, all of which require special software.

What you'll learn:

- A bit about copyright law—what the law permits you to record and what it doesn't

- How to choose the audio properties for a recording (file format, sampling rate, and so on)

- How to use Windows Sound Recorder to record a new sound

- How to use Cool Edit 96 for Windows to record a new sound

- How to use SndSampler for Mac OS to record a new sound

What You Should Know about Copyrights

Many of my Net friends would never think of breaking a law. In fact, some of them are in law enforcement and are rather uptight about it. Yet they quite casually record and pass around sound bites from movies, cartoons, popular songs, and other copyrighted material. They even publish copyrighted sounds on their Web sites. I don't think they would do this if they knew they were breaking the law.

Some Net users really don't care about copyrights. They freely copy whatever pleases them with the full knowledge that it is protected material. But I believe that most copyright infringement on the Net is casual and unintentional — people just don't realize they are breaking copyright laws. To keep you out of that category, this section briefly explains copyrights. From now on, if you infringe on someone else's copyright, at least it will be your conscious decision.

U.S. copyright law is quite complex, and international copyrights are even more so. There's no way I can explain it all here. All I can do is give you a few guidelines. You'll find links to some excellent Web sites on copyrights in Appendix D on the CD-ROM.

Any new work automatically has several rights associated with it, which are generally referred to as the copyright: the right to make reproductions, the right to perform it, the right to distribute it, the right to adapt or edit it, and so on. These rights are originally owned by the creators — the authors, composers, arrangers, performers — but are often sold to publishers or producers. Basically, you cannot record or distribute something that was written, composed, arranged, and/or performed by someone else unless you get proper permission from the copyright owners.

Copyright laws are softened a bit by the concept of "fair use," which says that you may quote part of a copyrighted work for educational purposes. In addition, the Audio Home Recording Act of 1992 extends fair use to enable us to copy songs to audiotape for our own personal use. Can we stretch "audiotape" to include electronic formats that weren't considered in 1992, such as sampled and streaming audio files? The experts are wrestling with that alligator now.

Copyrights don't last forever. When a work's rights expire, it passes into the *public domain*, meaning that it is owned by all of us and we are free to use it. In the United States, a work created before 1978 was automatically copyrighted for 28 years, and the copyright owner could extend it for another 28 years. Since the U.S. copyright laws changed in 1978, a work is protected for 50 years after the death of the creators. But there was a gray area in the '60s and '70s when expiring copyrights were extended so they would be covered by the new law when it went into effect. So it's not always easy to determine whether a particular work written earlier in this century is in the public domain. Works composed in earlier centuries — the music of Tchaikovsky, Mozart, Beethoven, and Verdi, for example — are clearly in the public domain. A recent recording of a public domain work, however, is copyrighted for the performers and arrangers.

What this boils down to is that you have the right to record, publish, perform, distribute, and so on, anything that you compose and arrange yourself. You can record, publish, and so on, public domain works as long as you're not using someone else's arrangement or performance.

Note

Any works created by the U.S. government are automatically in the public domain.

How likely are you to get caught infringing a copyright? If you record a ten-second sound bite of Daffy Duck and pass it around to your chat buddies, your chances of getting caught are near zero. But if you create a large Web site offering thousands of downloadable sound bites from Warner Brothers cartoons, the next sound you hear might be a clutch of Warner Brothers lawyers knocking at your door. Copyright owners no longer ignore what is happening on the Internet, not even on "amateur" sites.

Deciding on Audio Properties

Before you begin a new recording, you need to decide what audio properties you want to use — the file format, the encoding, and properties such as sampling rate and sample size. Always keep in mind that you have to trade quality for size. For your own use, if you have enough disk space and RAM, you might prefer the highest quality you can achieve no matter how big the file gets. For exchanging on the Internet, small file size is more important than quality.

 Tip

You may make a high-quality recording for yourself and then convert it to a smaller size for sharing with others.

Should you make WAVs? Or perhaps SNDs or MP3s would be best? It depends on how you want to use the sounds you're about to record. If you're going to post them to a site that features a particular format — an MP3 newsgroup, perhaps — the answer is obvious. But what if you want to use a sound for the background of your own Web site? Or e-mail it to a group of friends?

If you're making a short recording to share with Mac users, use the Macintosh SND or AIFF format. Choose WAV format for Windows users. If your audience will have both Windows and Mac users, I suggest that you use WAV, as that is the most common format on the Internet and many Mac users know how to deal with it.

Suppose you're recording a sound to play in chat rooms. Choose the right format for your own system. If you'll be sharing the sound with people on both systems, make a WAV version and a SND version.

But what about a long file — perhaps an entire song or a long voice message? Certainly you don't want to make your friends download a multimegabyte WAV or SND file. Consider using MP3 for a much smaller file. The drawback to the MP3 format, of course, is that some people can't play it yet. But that is changing rapidly. Windows 98's Media Player can handle MP3, for example. So can many third party players such as Jet-Audio. I suggest that you record the long version in MP3 format. Also, record a short version as a WAV and accompany it with a note about the MP3 version and where people can download MP3 players.

Windows Sound Recorder

Windows comes with Sound Recorder, which provides basic recording features. For more advanced recording and editing, you'll need a third-party recorder. I have included one called Cool Edit on the book's CD-ROM. In the following sections, I'll show you how to use Sound Recorder first, then Cool Edit 96.

Windows Sound Recorder, shown in Figure 11-1, is a fairly simple application for recording WAVs up to 60 seconds long. You can start it by choosing Start ⇨ Programs ⇨ Accessories ⇨ Multimedia ⇨ Sound Recorder (Windows 95 or Windows NT) or Start ⇨ Programs ⇨ Accessories ⇨ Entertainment ⇨ Sound Recorder (Windows 98). If Sound Recorder isn't on your Start menu, I suggest you read through this section, including the description of Cool Edit 96, before you decide to install it. If you do want to install it, you'll need your Windows 95 or 98 installation disk(s) and the following instructions.

Figure 11-1 *Sound Recorder is included with Windows 95, 98, and NT.*

How to install Sound Recorder:

1. Choose Start ⇨ Settings ⇨ Control Panel to open the Control Panel.

2. Open Add/Remove Programs.

3. Choose the Windows Setup tab.

4. Open Multimedia by double-clicking it.

5. Select Sound Recorder.

 Caution

Be careful not to select or deselect any other item. If you add a check mark to another item, Windows installs that item. Worse, if you accidentally remove an existing check mark, Windows uninstalls that item.

6. Choose OK to close the Multimedia dialog box. Then choose OK to close the Add/Remove Programs Properties window.

7. At this point, Windows installs the items you selected. Follow the directions on the screen that tell you when to insert the Windows disk(s).

Configuring your recording device

Before you can record, you need to tell Sound Recorder from which device to record. Double-click the Volume Control icon in your system tray to open your Volume Control window. Choose Options ⇨ Properties to open the Properties dialog box and then select Recording and choose OK. Now Volume Control displays your various recording sources in the Recording Control window, as shown in Figure 11-2. Select the devices you want to use in this recording by enabling the Select box below each device. You can select multiple devices, such as the CD audio and microphone. Then close the window.

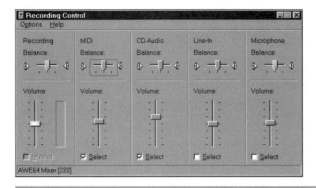

Figure 11-2 *You select the devices you want to record from in the Recording Control window.*

 Note

If your system tray doesn't show a Volume Control icon, you can start Volume Control in Windows 95 and Windows NT by choosing Start ⇨ Programs ⇨ Accessories ⇨ Multimedia ⇨ Volume Control. For Windows 98, choose Entertainment instead of Multimedia.

Setting the recording properties

The next step is to set the recording properties for your upcoming recording. In the Sound Recorder window, choosing File ⇨ Properties opens the Properties for Sound dialog box, shown in Figure 11-3. Select Recording Formats from the Format Conversion drop-down list. Then choose Convert Now to open the Sound Selection dialog box, also shown in Figure 11-3.

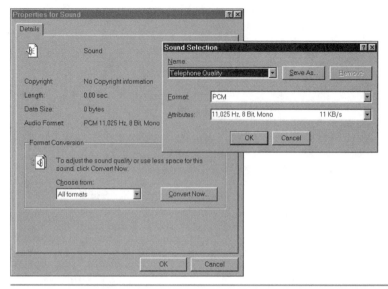

Figure 11-3 *Sound Recorder uses these dialog boxes to set the properties for the upcoming recording.*

In the Sound Selection dialog box, the Name drop-down list provides these named setups:

- CD Quality — 44 kHz sampling rate, 16-bit samples, stereo, PCM encoding

- Radio Quality — 22 kHz sampling rate, 8-bit samples, mono, PCM encoding

- Telephone Quality — 11 kHz sampling rate, 8-bit samples, mono, PCM encoding

If you don't want to use one of these, you can select your own settings in the Format and Attributes drop-down lists. Notice in particular that all three named setups use PCM encoding, which offers no compression. The Format drop-down lists all the codecs available on your system. You may want to select a codec that will compress your recording to keep the file size small. But stick to the popular codecs — described in Chapter 1 — which other people are likely to have. You can assign a name to your own setup by choosing the Save As button. Then your setup will appear in the Name drop-down list for future recordings.

Tip

The Remove button becomes available only when you select one of your own named setups. You cannot remove CD Quality, Radio Quality, or Telephone Quality.

Making the recording

Now you're ready to make your recording using the controls in the Sound Recorder window. The following two procedures show you step-by-step how to record from the microphone and from the CD-ROM drive.

How to record from your microphone using Sound Recorder:

1. Make sure your microphone is plugged into the microphone jack at the back of your computer.

2. Select Microphone and set its volume in the Recording Control window (refer back to Figure 11-2).

3. Set the recording properties (refer back to Figure 11-3).

4. Choose the Record button to start recording.

5. Make your recording.

6. Choose the Stop button to stop recording.

7. Choose the Play button to listen to your recording.

Tip

If you can hear your breath hitting the microphone, try getting farther away from the mic next time. If that doesn't work, place the mic to one side of your mouth. Or tape something over the mic, such as a tissue, a piece of paper, or a piece of cloth.

How to record from a CD using Sound Recorder:

1. Get Sound Recorder ready by following these steps:

   a. Select CD Audio and set its volume in the Recording Control window (refer back to Figure 11-2). Make sure Microphone is not selected unless you want to sing along.

   b. Set the recording properties.

2. Get the CD ready by following these steps:

   a. Place it in your CD-ROM drive.

   b. Start up your CD player program. (It probably starts automatically when you put the CD in the drive.)

   c. Locate the point on the CD where you want to start recording.

   d. Pause the CD at that point.

3. Choose Sound Recorder's Record button, then quickly start the CD.

4. When you have recorded the sound you want, choose Sound Recorder's Stop button to stop recording.

5. Choose the CD player's stop button to stop playing the CD.

6. Choose Sound Recorder's Play button to listen to your recording.

Any device attached to your sound board's Line In jack, such as a radio, TV, or tape player, can be used as a sound source by choosing Line-In in the Recording Control window. You can also record MIDIs played on your sound board's synthesizer. In Figure 11-4, I am using Media Player to play a MIDI while I record it with Sound Recorder. Keep in mind that a MIDI file is much, much smaller than a sampled recording, so there's little reason to make a sampled recording of a MIDI unless you want to change it somehow. You might, for example, want to sing along with it.

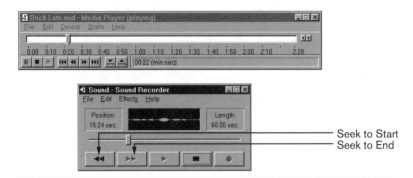

Figure 11-4 *You can record MIDIs played by your sound board.*

If you're not satisfied with your recording, you can record over it by choosing the Seek to Start button, shown in Figure 11-4. Then choose the Record button and record it again. If you want to add to the end of the current recording, choose the Seek to End button, also shown in the margin, and then choose Record to continue recording. You can also change just a portion of the recording. You'll see how to do that in Chapter 12, which shows you how to edit sound files.

When you're satisfied with your recording, choose File ⇨ Save to save it. A common Save As box lets you choose a file format, give it a name, and select a folder for it.

Overcoming Sound Recorder's time limit

Unfortunately, Sound Recorder places a time limit on your recordings. The maximum time depends on your recording properties. A Telephone Quality recording, for example, is limited to 60 seconds. Higher quality recordings have shorter time limits. As soon as you click the record button, you'll see the Length value jump from 0.00 seconds to the time limit, expressed in seconds. The best way around the time limit is to use a different recorder, such as Cool

Edit. But if you don't want to do that for some reason, you can work around Sound Recorder's time limit.

Assume that you are using Telephone Quality recording with a 60-second time limit. For voice recordings, start the recording as normal. At 60 seconds, the recorder turns itself off automatically. Simply stop talking while you click the record button again, then keep on going. Sound Recorder extends the time limit by another 60 seconds. You can keep on extending the time limit in 60-second increments until you finish your recording.

But what if you're making a recording where you don't want to pause every 60 seconds? Perhaps you're trying to record a 3 minute and 12 second song (192 seconds), and you don't want three little gaps in it. Go ahead and record the song as described above, with the gaps. Keep recording at the end until Sound Recorder's Position shows 192.00 seconds and then click the stop button. (You probably won't stop it right on 192.00, but you'll be close.) Now you've got a file of exactly the right length in memory. Simply click the Seek to Start button to return to the beginning of the file, then record over it. This time, you'll be able to record the entire file without pausing.

Another way to make a longer recording is to open one that's at least that long, then record over it. You can use any file that's long enough. Be sure to choose Save As instead of Save so you don't overwrite the original recording. When you use this method, you may need to trim the end of the recording, where your new sound ended and the original sound continues to the end of the file. You'll see how to trim recordings in Chapter 12.

Note

Long recordings eat up memory. Be sure to close all other applications to free up as much memory as possible before starting to record. If you get an out-of-memory message, you may have to add more memory before you can make the recording.

Cool Edit 96 for Windows

The easiest way around Sound Recorder's limitations is to use a third-party program such as Cool Edit 96 from Syntrillium. I chose Cool Edit 96 because it offers so many features. Let's take a quick look at the full range of Cool Edit 96's features and how you can use them:

- It can play, edit, mix, and convert many sound formats: WAV, AIFF, Macintosh SND (only PCM encoding), AU, Raw PCM, RealAudio 3.0, MP1, and MP2, among others.

- You can edit all or any portion of a sound. For a stereo recording, you can edit the channels separately.

- You can work on several files at once.

- Special effects include Reverb, Delay, Echo, 3D Echo Chamber, Flanging, and Distortion.

- Other transformations include Reverse, Inverse, adding silence, modifying the amplitude, and adjusting the time and the pitch.

- You can generate specific tones by frequency and amplitude, DTMF tones (telephone touch tones), brainwave sounds (sounds that induce relaxation, sleep, and meditation), or just plain noise. You can also select a clipping, such as a dog bark, and use it as a sound sample to generate music. Now *your* dog can sing "Jingle Bells."

- You can filter out specific frequencies or filter out noise.

- You have the choice of several different views: waveform, spectral analysis, frequency analysis, and statistics.

This chapter, however, merely shows you how to make a sampled recording with Cool Edit 96. Chapter 12 shows you some basic editing tools. Then you'll be on your own to explore Cool Edit 96's advanced features.

The fine print

Cool Edit 96's shareware fee is $25 for the Lite version or $50 for the full version. It works with Windows 95, 98, and NT. Until you register Cool Edit 96, you can use only a few functions at a time, an extremely effective way to get you to register.

Getting ready to record

Before recording in Cool Edit 96, select your source device in the Recording Control window (refer back to Figure 11-2). When you start the unregistered version of Cool Edit 96, you must select which functions you want to use. Be sure to select the group that includes Save so you can save your new recording. When you get to the Cool Edit 96 window, choose File ➪ New to open the dialog box shown in Figure 11-5. Select your recording properties and choose OK. When you return to the main Cool Edit 96 window, you'll see the properties in the status area.

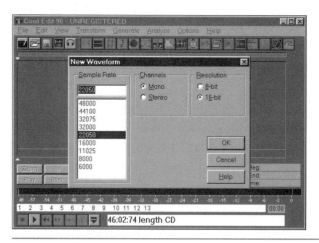

Figure 11-5 *You select the recording properties for a new sound recording in Cool Edit 96's New Waveform window.*

Using the VU meters

To check your volume level, start the source and double-click Cool Edit 96's VU meter window, shown in Figure 11-6, to start the VU meters. The example in the figure is for a stereo recording, with the left track on top and the right on the bottom. For a mono recording, only one meter appears in the VU meter window.

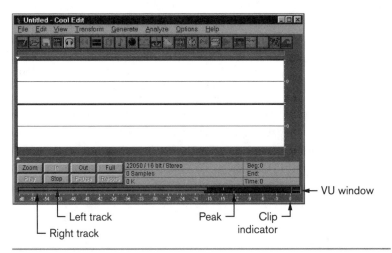

Figure 11-6 *The VU meters monitor the volume of the sound source.*

The decibel markings in the VU window are negative numbers because they express the relationship to the maximum volume, indicated by 0dB. Anything above the maximum volume is clipped—it is not recorded. A track's clip indicator lights up when the track gets clipped; it stays lit until you turn it off again by clicking it.

The peak indicators show where each track recently peaked in volume. Each peak indicator moves up with the volume, but as the volume drops back, the peak indicator sticks for about 1.5 seconds to give you a chance to see exactly where the peak occurred.

Adjust the source device's volume until you're satisfied with the result on the VU meters. After your sound check, double-click the meters again to stop them. (The Record and Play buttons won't become available again until you stop the meters.)

Making the recording

At last you're ready to start recording. Choose the Record button and start the sound source. As you record, you'll see the current time, number of samples, and file size in the status area. The waveform display doesn't react unless you choose Options ➪ Settings and enable Live Update During Record. Choose the Stop button to stop recording. Then choose the Play button to hear the results.

 Tip

If you decide to rerecord the sound, choose File ➪ New to get rid of the current recording and start over. (You don't need to repeat the volume test.)

When you are satisfied with your recording, choose File ➪ Save As to open a Save As box. When you select the file type, if the Options button becomes available, choose it to configure options for the format. Figure 11-7 shows an example of the options for the AU format, where you can choose which form of encoding you want to use.

Figure 11-7 *Cool Edit 96 displays these options for the AU file format.*

And that's it as far as making a new recording goes. Obviously, there's a lot more to Cool Edit 96, but most of its features help you edit sound files. You learn more about them in Chapter 12.

Recording Mac Sounds with SndSampler

In Chapter 5, you saw how to record a new system alert sound using the recorder in the Alert Sounds panel. But since that limits you to recording a ten-second snd resource in the System file, you'll probably want some other way to record sounds that aren't alerts. This book's CD-ROM includes a shareware sound editor called SndSampler 3.5.2 by Alan Glenn and M. Q. Edison. Briefly, here's what it can do:

- Record sounds from the selected sound source in AIFF or System 7 SND format

- Edit sounds in AIFF or System 7 format

- Add special effects: Reverse, Echo, Reverb, Chorus, and a few others

- Import (convert) WAVs, AUs, Sun, NeXT, and raw audios to AIFF format

- If you have QuickTime 1.6 or later, import QuickTime movie sound tracks and CD audio tracks into AIFF format

- Export sounds to WAV, Sun, NeXT, and raw audio format

You learn about its importing, exporting, and editing capabilities in Chapter 12. This chapter shows you how to use SndSampler to record sounds.

My one big complaint about SndSampler is that it does not give you much help. It has no balloon help or Guide. It does provide an electronic user's manual, but it's not thorough. So you're often on your own to figure out how to use it. I hope this book fills in some of the gaps.

The fine print

SndSampler's shareware registration fee is $20 (U.S.). You can try it out free of charge for 30 days. It works on any Mac running System 7.0 or later. If your Mac doesn't have 16-bit audio hardware, you must have Sound Manager 3.0 or later installed in order to play 16-bit sounds.

Recording sounds

To record a new sound, start SndSampler and Choose File ⇨ New to open the window in Figure 11-8, where you select the input device, the sound properties, and a few other recording options. Notice in particular the option called "Record directly to disk." Normally, sound data is stored in memory as you record it. Its size is limited by the amount of available memory. You can work around size problems by bypassing memory and recording directly to disk. But you might not care for the results, because you can't open, play, or edit sounds that don't fit in memory.

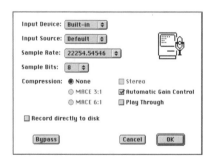

Figure 11-8 *SndSampler displays this window to collect information for a new recording.*

Caution

If the dialog box does not seem to recognize your selected input device – if it offers the wrong options, for example – it's better to choose Bypass than OK. Bypass retains the default recording parameters, while OK changes them to the ones indicated in the dialog box.

When you choose OK, the recording window opens, as you can see in Figure 11-9. The title bar shows your recording properties. You can also see how long your sound can be based on your selected properties and the amount of available memory. In the example, I can record a 1 minute and 6 second sound with a 22 kHz sampling rate, 8-bit sample size, and one channel.

Figure 11-9 *SndSampler's recording windows gives you the controls to make a recording (but not play it back).*

The two rows of blocks near the middle of the dialog box are your volume meters. The top row is labeled "L/m" for left/mono because it displays the volume of the left track for a stereo recording or the only track for a monaural recording. The bottom row is labeled "R" for right. The volume indicators work even when you're not recording, so you can test and adjust the volume before you start. Just start the sound source and watch the volume levels. The blocks light up from left to right to show the volume level. Most of the blocks are green, for normal volume, but the last two are red to warn you that the volume is too high. Adjust the volume of the sound source as needed until the blocks stay in the green zone.

When you're ready to record, choose the Record button and start the sound source. Record Time Remaining and Data Bytes Recorded update constantly as the recording progresses. The Pause button pauses the recording without stopping it; click it again to continue recording. Choose Stop when you're done. Then your only choice is OK to close the Recording window.

When the window closes, SndSampler's two editing windows appear, as shown in Figure 11-10. The top window displays the sound sample as a waveform. It's interesting to look at, but it doesn't provide much useful information when you're recording. It becomes valuable when you edit the sound, because you can select portions of the wave to work on. You'll learn how to do that in Chapter 12, the editing chapter.

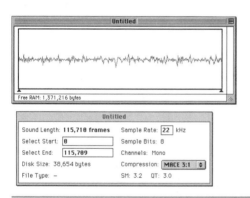

Figure 11-10 *SndSampler displays a waveform window on top and a statistics window below.*

The bottom window displays statistics for the sound:

- Sound Length shows the number of recorded frames. A *frame* consists of one sample from each track. The first frame of a stereo recording, for example, contains sample 1 for the left track followed by sample 1 for the right track. In the example in Figure 11-10, there are 115,710 frames. Since it is a mono recording, that means there are also 115,710 samples in the recording.

- Sample Rate shows the sampling rate, which is 22 kHz in the example.

- Sample Bits shows the sample size, which is 8 bits in the example.

- Channels shows mono or stereo.

- Compression shows the compression method, which is MACE 3:1 in the example. You can convert to a different method by selecting another one from the pop-up menu.

- SM and QT show your current versions of Sound Manager and QuickTime, which are Sound Manager 3.2 and QuickTime 3 in the example. SndSampler relies on Sound Manager and QuickTime for part of its function, so these version numbers can be important.

- Select Start and Select End come into use when you select part of the waveform to edit. They're explained in Chapter 12.

- Disk Size shows the file size, in bytes. It is 38,654 in the example, or about 38K. (That is roughly the 115,710 samples divided by the compression ratio of 3:1, give or take a few bytes.)

- File Type shows the file's type, AIFF or System 7. The example shows no file type because this recording has not yet been saved.

To listen to your new recording, choose File ➪ Play. If you decide you don't like it and want to rerecord it, choose File ➪ New to start over. When you're satisfied with it, choose File ➪ Save As so you can select a file type (AIFF or System 7), give it a name, and choose a folder for it.

What's Next?

Recording your own sounds is fun, but what about adding special effects like echo and reverse? How about fading in and out? Or mixing two or more files together? Chapter 12 explains all these editing techniques and more.

Chapter 12

Editing Sound Files

Unless you are much better at recording than I am, you probably need to clean up your recordings after you make them. Perhaps you need to trim the beginning and the end. You may want to add a little echo or other sound effects. You may also want to mix two sounds together. This chapter shows you how to do these and other basic editing tasks using the editors introduced in Chapter 11: Sound Recorder and Cool Edit 96 for Windows and SndSampler for Macintosh.

What you'll learn:

- How to edit sounds using Windows Sound Recorder
- How to edit sounds using Cool Edit 96 for Windows
- How to edit sounds using SndSampler for Macintosh

Don't forget that you are free to edit your own original work as much as possible, but other people's works are copyrighted and you are not supposed to copy or edit them. (End of lecture for this chapter. Refer to Chapter 11 for a brief discussion of copyright laws.)

 Tip

Whenever you edit a sound, make a copy first and then edit the copy. That way, you can always get back to the original sound if need be.

Using Windows Sound Recorder

Windows Sound Recorder provides a few simple editing facilities for WAV files. It can

- Change the properties of the WAV
- Copy all or part of a WAV
- Delete all or part of a WAV
- Add to the WAV
- Insert or mix in another file
- Increase and decrease the volume and speed
- Add echo to all or part of the WAV
- Reverse all or part of the WAV

You can edit only uncompressed (PCM) sound files. If you don't see a green waveform when you open the file, it is compressed and can't be modified as is. You can uncompress it by changing its format to PCM, as explained in the next section.

Converting audio properties

You change the audio properties of a WAV in the Sound Selection dialog box, shown in Figure 12-1. Open the desired WAV in Sound Recorder and then choose File ➪ Properties to see its current properties. Then choose the Convert Now button to open the Sound Selection dialog box. You can select new properties in the Format and Attributes drop-down list or select one of the named setups from the Name list. (The Name list is explained under the "Setting the recording properties" section in Chapter 11.)

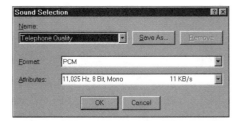

Figure 12-1 *Sound Recorder's Sound Selection dialog box lets you change a sound's properties.*

You may not like what you hear after changing a sound's properties. If you try to increase its quality — from mono to stereo, from 8-bit to 16-bit, or from 11 kHz to 22 kHz, for example — Sound Recorder must generate new sound samples based on the current ones. This is definitely not the same as recording the needed samples to start with. The result can sound pretty bad. Reducing the sound quality works better, as Sound Recorder merely needs to remove existing sound samples.

Selecting and replacing all or part of a sound

You can apply some editing functions to the entire sound or just part of it. For example, you can replace the beginning or mix in another file starting at a specific point. Sound Recorder gives you limited ability to select part of a sound for editing. All you can do is place the position slider where you want to start editing. In Figure 12-2, I placed the slider at .13 second.

Figure 12-2 *To edit part of a sound, you position Sound Recorder's slider where you want to edit your sound.*

Tip

Positioning the slider at just the right point is often a matter of trial and error. Drag the slider and listen to the result. Then drag the slider again. Use the Position time and the waveform display as guides.

To record over any part of a sound, simply position the slider where you want the replacement to begin and start recording. If the replacement is longer than the original file, Sound Recorder extends the file up to a point. As I explain in Chapter 11, Sound Recorder limits the length of a new recording, and you have to press the Record button again each time you reach the limit.

Inserting and mixing files

You can add other sounds to your current sound by inserting or mixing. Figure 12-3 shows the difference between these two techniques. In the figure, Sound A represents the currently open file — the sound being edited. The gray dotted line marks the current position in this file, right after the first of four loud bangs. Sound B is another sound — perhaps another file or something on the Windows clipboard.

Inserting a sound is much like inserting text in a document. As you can see in Figure 12-3, Sound B is inserted after the first bang, and the rest of Sound A is moved over to make room for it. The result is a longer file. If you played the file, you would hear Sound A up through the first bang, then Sound B, and then the three remaining bangs and the rest of Sound A.

Mixing two sounds adds them together, starting at the current position. If you examine the mixed sound carefully in Figure 12-3, you can see how the softer sounds from Sound B were blended right in with the four bangs. The file might or might not be longer, depending on the length of Sound B. In the example, Sound B is considerably shorter than Sound A, so it did not extend the file's length.

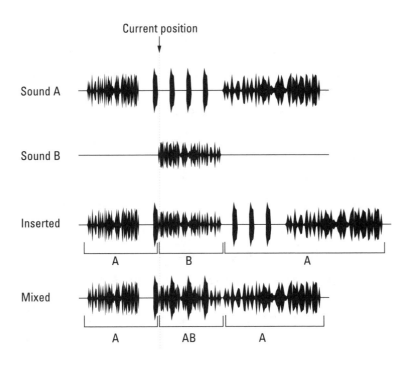

Figure 12-3 *You can insert or mix a second sound into the current sound.*

How to insert or mix another file into the current file:

1. Open the sound to be edited.
2. Position the slider.
3. Choose Edit ⇨ Insert File or Edit ⇨ Mix with File to open a common browse box.
4. Select the file to be inserted or mixed and choose Open.

Deleting the beginning or end of a sound

Sometimes when you make a new recording, you accidentally record a second or two of silence at the beginning, perhaps followed by the sound of you picking up the microphone and clearing your throat. You don't have to rerecord the sound to get rid of the rubble at the beginning. You just delete the part you don't want. Sound Recorder gives you the option of deleting the beginning or the end of a sound. Unfortunately, you can't delete a middle part.

How to delete the beginning of a recording:

1. Position the slider where you want the edited sound to start.

2. Choose Edit ⇨ Delete Before Current Position. A message box asks you to confirm the deletion.

3. Choose OK in the message box to confirm the deletion.

How to delete the end of a recording:

1. Position the slider where you want the edited sound to end.

2. Choose Edit ⇨ Delete After Current Position. A message box asks you to confirm the deletion.

3. Choose OK in the message box to confirm the deletion.

Adding sound effects

Sound Recorder's Effects menu offers a limited number of effects:

- Increase and decrease volume
- Increase and decrease speed
- Echo
- Reverse

They all affect the complete sound. You can't add an effect to just a portion of the file in Sound Recorder. To use one of these effects, just select it from the Effects menu and then listen to the result. If you find you don't like it, the next section shows you how to get rid of it.

Discarding and saving changes

Sound Recorder does not have an Undo feature. If you decide to discard the changes you have made, choose File ➪ Revert to get rid of them. This command returns to the last saved version of the file so you can continue editing.

When you're satisfied with your changes, choose File ➪ Save to replace the former version with the new one. Or choose File ➪ Save As to create a new file out of the edited version.

Using Cool Edit 96 for Windows

As you can see in the last section, Sound Recorder is pretty limited. Cool Edit 96, on the other hand, has more features than I can hope to cover here. It's great for casually playing around with sounds, as it offers lots of special effects. But it's also an excellent tool for heavy-duty editing, such as filtering out the background noise from an on-the-street interview and equalizing the volume to eliminate sudden lows and highs. This chapter concentrates on the more casual and fun editing functions such as the special effects.

Until you register Cool Edit 96, the dialog box shown in Figure 12-4 appears each time you start it. You may select only two groups of functions to work with. Always select the first group because it includes the Save function. Otherwise, you won't be able to save your editing. The other group is up to you. In the example in Figure 12-4, I chose a group of effects that I was planning to use in that session.

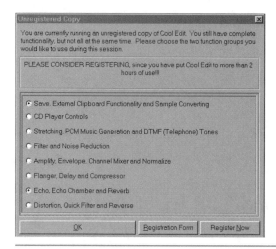

Figure 12-4 *Cool Edit 96 encourages you to register by permitting only two function groups at a time in the unregistered version.*

Converting sound files

Cool Edit 96 makes converting a sound file to another format simple. Just open the file and choose File ⇨ Save As to open the Save Waveform As box shown in Figure 12-5. You can select a different file type and give the file a new name and location in this box. For example, you might open a WAV file, choose File ⇨ Save As, and then select Apple AIFF from the "Save as type" drop-down list. Now you have both the WAV and the AIFF versions.

Suppose you want to change an uncompressed WAV into a compressed WAV using μ-law compression. Open the WAV, choose File ⇨ Save As to open the Save As box, and choose A/mu-law Wave. The Options button in the Save As box becomes available when you select this file type. Choose it to pop up a dialog box where you can select between a-law and mu-law.

Figure 12-5 *Cool Edit 96's Save As box lets you convert files from one type to another.*

Suppose instead that you want to change the sound's properties. Choose Edit ➪ Convert Sample Type to open the dialog box shown in Figure 12-6. As you can see, you can change the sampling rate, sample size, and number of channels.

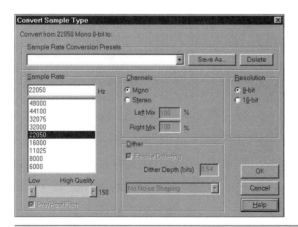

Figure 12-6 *You use Cool Edit 96's Convert Sample Type dialog box to change a sound's properties.*

If you change the number of channels, you indicate the volume mix in the Left Mix and Right Mix boxes. When you go from mono to stereo, use the Left Mix and Right Mix boxes to indicate the relative volume of the channels. You can also assign -100% to one channel for an "inverse mono" effect, where each channel is the inverse of the other. When going from stereo to mono, the Left Mix and Right Mix boxes determine how the two channels are mixed into one.

The Quality setting determines the overall quality of the converted sound. The higher the setting, the longer the conversion takes. When you are *upsampling*—that is, increasing the sampling rate or sample size—there's not much difference between the low and high settings, so try a setting around 100. When you are *downsampling*—decreasing the sampling rate or sample size—higher quality settings produce a better result. Try a setting around 400 to start with. If the result sounds muffled, undo the conversion and try it again with a higher quality setting.

Working with a selection

You can select any portion of a sound for editing. Just drag your mouse pointer across the desired area in the waveform display. In Figure 12-7, I have selected the samples from 80,000 to 130,000. The selected portion is shaded by default in light blue. Yellow markers above and below the waveform display also indicate the selected area.

When an area is selected, many of Cool Edit 96's commands apply only to the selection. If you choose the Play button, for example, only the selection is played. Transformations such as stretching and echo apply only to the selection by default.

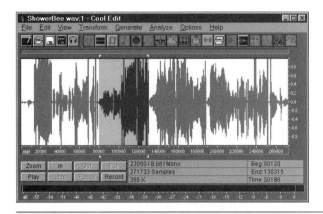

Figure 12-7 *Shading indicates the selected portion of the sound wave.*

The Zoom button lets you examine the current selection close up by expanding it to fill the waveform window. Choose the In button to get even closer — you can click it several times to keep expanding the wave. The Out button reverses the effect of the In button. Or you can use Zoom to return the entire selection to the window. The Full button restores the original view of the complete waveform.

Tip

An easy way to select the portion of the wave that appears in the window is to double-click it.

If instead you just want to position the pointer at a specific spot, click that spot on the waveform. A dotted line appears in the waveform to mark the spot, and the yellow markers appear above and below it. Any editing applies from that point to the end of the sound. The zooming commands try to keep the selected spot centered in the window.

When working with a stereo sound, you can edit one or both channels. To select both channels, drag or double-click somewhere near the middle of the waveform window. To select a single channel, drag or double-click somewhere near its outside edge. To select part of the left channel, for example, you would drag near the top of the waveform window. To select the entire visible portion of the bottom channel, you would double-click near the bottom of the waveform window. The letter *L* or *R* attaches to your mouse pointer when you're in the proper position to select just the left or right channel.

Pasting and mixing a selection

When you cut or copy a selection, you can paste it somewhere else in the same file or another file. All the commands you need are on the Edit menu: Cut, Copy, Paste, and Mix Paste. The effect of the Paste command depends on whether something is selected. With no selection, the sound is inserted at the current position. With a selection, the sound replaces the selection.

When you choose Mix Paste, the dialog box shown in Figure 12-8 opens so you can choose how you want the sound to be inserted or mixed. If you choose Insert, the effect is much the same as the Paste command. The Overlap function mixes the two sounds. Modulating is similar to Overlap—the samples are multiplied by each other instead of added. You might try both methods to see which produces the result you want.

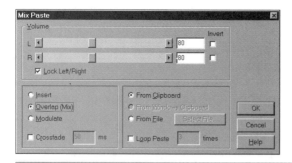

Figure 12-8 *The Mix Paste dialog box gives you control over how a clipboard sound is pasted into the current sound.*

When you Overlap or Modulate, the Volume sliders adjust the volume of the sound from the clipboard. Use Lock Left/Right to keep the two sliders together. If you want different volumes for the left and right tracks, disable Lock Left/Right.

Tip

Notice that the Mix Paste function also gives you the ability to select a file to mix into your current file. Just enable "From File" and then click the Select File button.

Undo, reverting, and saving

Cool Edit 96 keeps track of your edits and lets you undo them by choosing Edit ➪ Undo *edit*, where *edit* is the action to be undone, as in Undo Delete or Undo Record. You must undo edits in reverse order. Suppose you change the format, then delete a section, then record a section. To undo the changed format, you must first undo the recording, then undo the deletion, then undo the format change. The number of actions that Cool Edit 96 can undo is dictated by the amount of space available in your Windows temporary folder. By default, Cool Edit 96 will warn you if it cannot keep track of at least five actions. Usually, there is plenty of room for at least five edits.

If you want to undo all the changes you have made so far, the File ➪ Revert to Saved command is the easiest way. This restores the file to its last saved condition. You can't undo any editing that has been saved, of course.

You save your editing just as you do with most Windows programs, with File ➪ Save to replace the current file or File ➪ Save As to create a new file. You can also save the current selection as a separate file with File ➪ Save Selection. Don't forget that saving is one function that must be enabled when you start up the unregistered version of Cool Edit 96. If you don't enable it during startup, you won't be able to save your work.

Basic editing operations

Many of Cool Edit 96's basic editing operations are the same as in word processing. After selecting part of a sound, you cut, copy, delete, or replace it. But there are a couple of functions unique to sound files, such as trim and silence. The following list reviews the basic editing functions:

- To delete the selection, press the Delete key. If the selection involves only one track of a stereo recording, Cool Edit 96 replaces it with silence, rather than deleting it, to keep the two tracks in sync.

- To replace the selection with silence, choose Transform ⇨ Silence.

- You record over the selection simply by choosing the Record button and recording something else. Recording automatically stops when you reach the end of the selection.

- To copy the selection, choose Edit ⇨ Copy.

- To cut the selection, choose Edit ⇨ Cut. As with deleting, if the selection is limited to one track of a stereo recording, Cool Edit 96 replaces it with silence rather than deleting it.

- To trim the selection, choose Edit ⇨ Trim. Trimming deletes everything *but* the selection — the opposite of deleting.

Note

In the unregistered version of Cool Edit 96, unavailable functions appear dimmed on the menus and in the toolbar. You may need to restart Cool Edit 96 with a different set of functions to access the one you want.

Adding sound effects with Cool Edit 96's Transform menu

Cool Edit 96's Transform menu offers many ways to manipulate (or *transform*) a sound, from reversing it to stretching it. Some are fairly easy to learn and to use, while others are much too complex to cover here. This section shows you some basic transforms: inverting, reversing, and delays (which include echoes and reverb).

Inverting

Inverting a selection essentially turns the waveform upside down. The peaks become valleys and the valleys become peaks. Interestingly, if you invert a mono wave or both tracks of a stereo wave, you probably won't be able to hear a difference. The difference becomes noticeable when you invert just one channel of a stereo recording. Choose Transform ➪ Invert to invert the selection.

Reversing

Reversing a selection turns it backwards. If you want to check out a rumor that a certain song includes hidden messages, try reversing it by choosing Transform ➪ Reverse. You may also need to speed it up or slow it down using the Stretch transform (explained in the "Stretch" section below).

Stretch

Stretching a selection changes its tempo and/or pitch. It comes in especially handy when editing a song you want to sing along with. When you choose Transform ➪ Time/Pitch ➪ Stretch, you can set sliders to slow the selection down, speed it up, lower its pitch, or raise its pitch. You can even use the Gliding Stretch feature to have it gradually become slower or faster, lower or higher, rather than change the entire selection at once. (Try singing along with that!)

Delay

The Delay option lets you insert so many milliseconds of silence at the beginning of the selection. Transform ➪ Delay Effects ➪ Delay opens the dialog box shown in Figure 12-9, where you set up the delay. The Delay slider and text box indicate how much delay you want. The maximum slider value is 500 ms, but you can type a larger value in the text box.

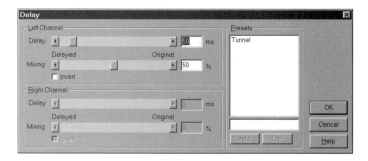

Figure 12-9 *The Delay dialog lets you specify the details of a delay effect.*

You can replace the selection with the delayed sound, or mix the delayed sound into the original sound for an echo effect. If you don't want to mix the delayed sound into the original sound, set the Mixing slider and text box to zero percent. A value above zero indicates how much of the original sound to include in the mix. A value of 50 percent mixes the two sounds equally. Seventy-five percent gives prominence to the original sound, with the delayed version sounding like a distant echo. When working on a stereo sound, you can delay and mix the two channels separately.

Presets are a handy feature of Cool Edit 96. When you create an effect you like, you can give it a name so you can recall it later without having to remember all the settings. Cool Edit 96 starts you off with a few presets in many of the Transform dialog boxes. For example, it provides the Delay preset called Tunnel, which sets the delay to 26 ms and the mix to 60 percent. To use a preset, double-click its name in the Presets list. To create your own preset, set up the desired values in the dialog box, choose Add, and give it a name. To remove a preset, select it and then click the Del button.

Echo

The Echo effect creates a more sophisticated echo than a simple delay. It provides continuous echoing, with each echo fading away at the rate you specify. Figure 12-10 shows the dialog box that opens when you choose Transform ⇨ Delay Effects ⇨ Echo with a stereo selection. (When only one track is selected, the Echo Characteristics section shows sliders and text boxes for only one track.)

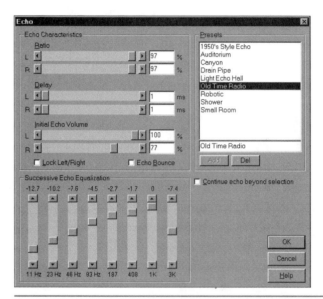

Figure 12-10 *You use Cool Edit 96's Echo dialog box to set up the properties of an echo.*

The three main settings are Ratio, Delay, and Initial Echo Volume. Ratio determines how the echoes fade out. If you set it to 50 percent, each echo will be 50 percent softer than the preceding one until they fade out entirely. At 100 percent the echoes never fade, whereas at 0 percent they never appear. Delay determines how quickly the echoes follow each other, in milliseconds. Initial Echo Volume specifies the first echo's volume as a percentage of the original sound's volume.

Echo Chamber

The Echo Chamber function also creates a complex echo. But instead of calculating factors such as Ratio, Delay, and Initial Echo Volume yourself, you specify the characteristics of a room and the location of the microphones, and it calculates the echo for you. Figure 12-11 shows the dialog box that open when you choose Transform ➪ Delay Effects ➪ Echo Chamber. Notice that Cool Edit 96 gives you a number of presets that you might find handy as an alternative to setting these options yourself.

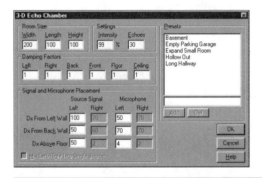

Figure 12-11 *The Echo Chamber dialog box lets you add an echo effect to the selection by specifying the characteristics of the "room."*

If you want to try your hand at your own settings, try to imagine a place that gives the effect you want to create. Suppose, for example, you want the effect of a cavern. The dimensions are set in feet, so you might decide that your cavern is 200 feet long, 100 feet wide, and 100 feet high.

Damping factors indicate the sound absorption of the various surfaces of the room, from 0 (total absorption — imagine heavy velvet drapes) to 1 (no absorption). Your cavern, with its slimy wet walls, ceiling, and floor, has no absorption, so you might set all the damping factors to 1.

Intensity determines the volume of the echoes as a percentage of the original sound. Because each echo adds to the overall volume of the sound, you can end up with too much volume, which results in clipping, if you set the intensity too high. I find that a number between 80 and 99 works best.

Echoes specifies the number of echoes that you want to produce. Cool Edit 96 suggests using at least 300 echoes for good reverb. A cavern would probably produce some distinct echoes rather than a general reverb, so you might try around 30 echoes to start with. You can use numbers as high as 25,000 or so if you have enough RAM for Cool Edit 96 to do the calculations.

You'll find the greatest differences in effect result from the source and microphone placement. The source placement determines where the sound is coming from. You specify it in feet from the left wall, the back wall, and the floor. To place the sound source in the exact middle of the cavern, you would put it 100 feet from the left wall, 50 feet from the back wall, and 50 feet above the floor. The microphone placement indicates where the microphone is located, in feet. The further it is from the sound source, the more echoing you'll get. In your cavern, you could try placing the microphone 50 feet from the left wall, 70 feet from the back wall, and 4 feet above the floor for a start. Then move it around until you get the effect you want.

When you have completed the settings, choose OK to close the dialog box. Cool Edit 96 calculates the new wave. The more echoes you specified, the longer the calculations take, but it's only a matter of seconds with a reasonably fast Pentium. Then choose Play to hear the transformed sound. If you decide to try again, choose Edit ⇨ Undo Echo Chamber to return to the previous version. Then choose Transform ⇨ Delay Effects ⇨ Echo Chamber to reopen the Echo Chamber dialog box. Cool Edit 96 remembers your previous settings, so it's easy to make a few adjustments and try again.

When you find the settings you like, you might want to turn them into a preset for future use. Simply type a name such as Cavern at the bottom of the preset box and choose Add.

Flanger

The Flanger effect is difficult to describe. It sounds like someone was fiddling with the dials on the recording equipment while the recording was being made. Basically, it plays around with the speed of the recording by creating a varying delayed signal and mixing it with the original. Flanger effects were popular in the psychedelic era, and can still be fun to experiment with. Figure 12-12 shows the dialog box that opens when you choose Transform ⇨ Delay Effects ⇨ Flanger. As always, the presets provided by Cool Edit 96 can save you the bother of trying to create your own flanger effects.

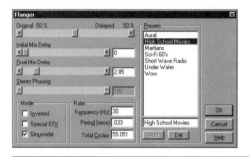

Figure 12-12 *The Flanger dialog box lets you add a psychedelic effect to the selection.*

The top slider determines the mix between the original signal and the delayed signal. Try setting it to the middle to start with, then adjust it left or right as desired.

The Initial Mix Delay slider indicates how many milliseconds to delay the flanged signal initially. The Final Mix Delay slider indicates how many milliseconds the flanged signal will be delayed by the end of the sound selection. The change from the initial delay to the final delay is what causes the flanger effect. The bigger the change, the more flanging you get. If you specify the same number of milliseconds for both settings, you'll end up with a simple echo instead of flanging.

The Stereo Phasing setting is available only when you're editing a stereo selection. It determines the delay settings for the two channels in relationship to each other. If you set it to 0, both channels use exactly the same delay settings. But if you set it to 180, one channel starts off with the initial delay setting and moves to the final delay setting, while the other channel does just the opposite. This is a fun setting to play around with for some interesting effects.

The Rate settings determine how fast the flanged signal moves from the initial delay setting to the final delay setting and back again—which is considered one complete cycle. You can set it in terms of cycles per second, or the number of seconds to complete a cycle, or the number of cycles to complete during the entire time of the selected sound. Whichever one you set, Cool Edit 96 automatically sets the other two.

The Invert option inverts the flanged signal, which causes the waves to cancel each other out periodically, resulting in brief periods of silence.

The Special EFX option mixes both normal and inverted flanging, with a few other transformations as well. All I can say is, try it and see if it works for you.

The Sinusoidal option affects the rate of change from the initial delay to the final delay. When this option is disabled, the rate of change is constant. In other words, the delay increases and decreases steadily. But when this option is enabled, the rate of change follows a sine curve, sometimes increasing or decreasing faster that at other times. Flanging is more noticeable and more psychedelic when you enable the Sinusoidal option.

As with other transformations, you probably have to experiment to find the effect you want. Be sure to use Edit ⇨ Undo Flanger in between trials. When you find an effect you like, you can save it as a named preset by typing a name at the bottom of the Presets box and choosing Add.

Reverb

Reverb differs from echo because it does not produce specific echo waves at regular intervals. Instead, it makes the audio sound bigger and more natural—more like you're in the same room with the original source. You can create the sound of a specific type of room or hall by using Echo Chamber first and then using Reverb to "smooth out" the echo. Figure 12-13 shows the dialog box that opens when you choose Transform ➪ Delay Effects ➪ Reverb. Cool Edit 96 supplies several preset Reverb effects, shown in the figure, to get you started.

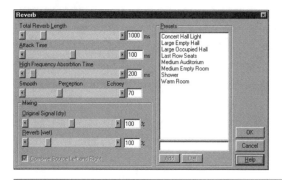

Figure 12-13 *The Reverb dialog box lets you select or set reverb effects for your sound selection.*

 Tip

Reverb helps to create a more natural stereo effect when you convert a mono recording to stereo. After converting the sound, add in some reverb to get a larger effect.

The Total Reverb Length specifies how long the reverb lasts, in milliseconds. The signal trails off after the specified amount of time. The reverb length creates the effect of being in a specific size of room. The shorter the length, the smaller the room. The following numbers are estimates to give you a starting point in creating the effect you want:

Less than 400	Small room
400 to 800	Medium room
800 to 1600	Large room
1600 to 3000	Huge room (concert hall)
Over 3000	Amphitheater

Attack Time specifies how long it takes for the Reverb effect to go from zero to full strength. The shorter the time, the sharper the attack. Try an attack time that is approximately 10 percent of the reverb length to start with. Make it longer for a softer effect or shorter for a more pronounced effect.

The High Frequency Absorption Time determines how soon the high frequencies disappear. In most rooms, high frequencies are the first to be absorbed by the objects in the room, and the low frequencies reverberate a little longer. The more furnishings and people are in the room, the faster the high frequencies are absorbed. By adjusting this setting, you can create the effect of a crowded concert hall (a low setting) or a sparsely furnished basement (a high setting). As with most of these settings, you have to experiment to create the effect you want.

The Perception slider adjusts the prominence of echoing. The more you move it to the left, the mellower the reverb. Move it to the right to create more noticeable waves of echoes, as in a larger concert hall.

The reverb signal, based on all your other settings, is mixed into the original signal. The Original Signal (dry) slider determines what percentage of your original signal should be used in the mix. You can go up to 200 percent, but watch out for clipping. The Reverb Signal (wet) determines the volume of the reverb signal in the mix. Generally, it should be lower than the Original Signal, but you might want to create the effect of great distance by giving it more prominence than the Original Signal. If you end up with a clipping problem, reduce both signals.

For stereo recordings, the Combine Source Left and Right option helps to save computation time by combining the left and right tracks before the reverb is calculated. If your left and right tracks are the same anyway, you might as well enable this option. But if your left and right tracks are different, and if you have a fast enough processor, disable the option to calculate the reverb for each track separately. The reverb is mixed into both tracks to produce an enhanced stereo effect.

A final word on Cool Edit 96

I have shown you the Cool Edit 96 features that most people want to use at first. But it has a lot more features that you'll probably want to try out eventually, such as the brainwave generator or the noise reduction options. Cool Edit 96's Help library can help get you started with a new feature, although it's often couched in unfamiliar audio jargon that is less than helpful to people who are not audio engineers. In my opinion, the best way to learn what a feature does is experiment, undo, experiment, undo, experiment, undo ... until you have found the effect you want. Have fun!

Using SndSampler for Macintosh

In Chapter 11, you learned how to record sounds using SndSampler 3.5.2. Now let's look at how you use SndSampler as an editor. I can only cover some of the basic SndSampler editing functions in this chapter, but here's a brief overview of what it can do:

- Convert a sound from stereo to mono and vice versa, change the sampling rate (resample), and convert it from 8-bit to 16-bit samples and vice versa
- Cut, copy, paste, and mix to create the sound you want
- Add the following effects: echo, reverb, chorus, flange, tremolo, and backwards (reverse)

- Adjust amplitude (including fade-ins and fade-outs) and the pitch
- Generate tones from scratch
- Edit movie soundtracks and convert a sound to movie soundtrack format (requires QuickTime 1.6 or later)
- Edit a file that is larger than your RAM by breaking it into segments
- Convert batches of files

Plus, SndSampler provides some miscellaneous functions such as editing snd resource headers extract snd resources from files.

Working with files in SndSampler

SndSampler works only on System 7 or AIFF sound files, but you can import files from these formats: WAV, Sun, NeXT AU, raw audio, QuickTime movies, and CD audio tracks. You can also extract a snd resource from another file to work on. After editing, you can export to these formats: WAV, Sun, NeXT, and raw audio. You can work on several files at once, and copy sounds from one to another.

Opening files

To open one or more files, drag and drop them on the SndSampler icon. Or start SndSampler first and use File ⇨ Open to select them from the file list. Use File ⇨ Import to import another type of sound file, such as a WAV or AU file. You can access snd resources with the File ⇨ Extract command. This opens a dialog box where you select the file from which to extract the snd resources — usually a program file. Then you see a list of snd resources for that file, and you choose the ones you want to open.

Working with the selection

With SndSampler, almost all editing takes place on the current selection, not the whole file. The selection is marked in SndSampler's sample window both by color and by two markers below the waveform. You can see them in Figure 12-14. The status window also shows the frame numbers for the start and end of the selection. In Figure 12-14, the selection starts at frame 9,205 and ends at frame 14,339.

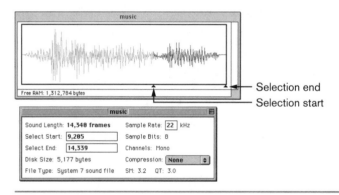

Figure 12-14 *The selection is clearly marked in the sample window and identified in the status window.*

There are several ways to make a selection:

- Drag the markers.
- Click the waveform where you want the selection to start; double-click where you want it to end.
- Type the start and end frame numbers in the Select Start and Select End boxes in the status window.

To make sure your selection is just right, choose Sound ➪ Play to listen to the selection. You might also try Sound ➪ Play Unselected to listen to everything else.

Tip

Play Unselected comes in particularly handy when you are planning to delete the selection. You can hear what the remainder will sound like after the deletion.

Many of the commands on the Edit menu work with the selection. Copy copies it to the clipboard. Cut also copies it to the clipboard, but then deletes it. Delete simply deletes it. Make Selection New creates a new file out of it. The new file becomes the current file, which is untitled until you save it.

Working with the clipboard

Once a selection is on the clipboard, you can paste it into the current sound using these commands from the Edit menu:

Paste	Replaces the current selection with whatever is on the clipboard
Paste New	Creates a new, untitled sound file from the clipboard
Insert Start	Inserts the sound from the clipboard at the start of the current sound
Insert End	Inserts the sound from the clipboard at the end of the current sound
Mix Start	Mixes the sound from the clipboard with the current sound, matching their start points
Mix End	Mixes the sound from the clipboard with the current sound, matching their end points

SndSampler uses its own clipboard, which can hold much more data than Finder's clipboard. If you forget what's on the clipboard, choose Edit ➪ Play Clipboard Sound to hear it. You can clear the clipboard by choosing Edit ➪ Clear Clipboard.

Changing the audio properties

Several commands on the FX menu really have nothing to do with effects. Instead, they let you change the audio properties, the number of channels, the sampling rate, and the sample size.

Changing the number of channels

The Stereo to Mono option combines two tracks into one. When you choose FX ⇨ Stereo to Mono, the dialog box shown in Figure 12-15 opens. You can choose to equally mix the left and right tracks to create the new single track, or to simply use the left or right track. If you enable "Make into new sound," the mono recording becomes a new file in memory that won't have a filename until you save it. (The previous file still exists on disk and will not be replaced by the new file.) If you disable this option, the mono recording replaces the previous stereo in memory, and when you choose Save, it replaces the previous file on disk.

Figure 12-15 *The Stereo to Mono dialog box lets you choose how to reduce two tracks to one.*

The Mono to Stereo option is doesn't offer as many choices. A slider appears so that you can set the volume mix between the left and right channels. Other than volume, the two channels will be the same. As usual, "Make into new sound" means that the original file will not be replaced when you save the new recording.

Changing the sampling rate

Two options let you change the sampling rate of the selection. Both work on the entire sound, not the selection. (You can't have different sampling rates in different parts of a sound file.)

Selecting Downsample cuts the sampling rate in half, which not only reduces the quality of the sound but also cuts the file size in half. It offers no options, and the downsampled sound replaces the original sound. The Resample option provides a more flexible way to change the sampling rate. It opens the dialog box shown in Figure 12-16 so you can set the new sampling rate. You can use the pop-up menu to select one of the standard sampling rates, or use the slider to set the rate as a percentage of the current rate.

Each time you resample a sound, whether you increase the sampling rate or decrease it, the quality of the sound deteriorates to a certain extent. Try to avoid resampling a sound more than once. Instead, choose Edit ➪ Undo Resample to restore the original resampling rate before using the Resample option a second time.

Figure 12-16 *The Resample option opens this dialog box so you can select a new sampling rate.*

Changing the sample size

The 16 ➪ 8-bit option reduces the sample size from 16 bits to 8 bits. Likewise, the 8 ➪ 16-bit increases the sample size from 8 bits to 16 bits.

Adjusting amplitude

Use the commands on the Sound ⇨ Amplitude submenu to adjust
the volume of the selection. Choose X 2 to double the amplitude or
÷ 2 to cut it in half. If you don't want to multiply or divide it by two,
use one of the other options on the menu.

The three other options on the menu are initially labeled User
Amplitude 1, User Amplitude 2, and User Amplitude 3. You can set
these three options to any values you'd like, and they become menu
items that you can use in the future. For example, you could create a
menu item that says X 3 or Very Soft.

How to set a user amplitude:

1. Choose Sound ⇨ Amplitude ⇨ User Amplitude 1, 2, or 3 to
   open the window shown in Figure 12-17.

2. Type your name for this amplitude in the Amplitude box.

3. Select Multiply or Divide.

4. Type an amount in the By box. SndSampler automatically
   fills in the Percent amount.

5. Choose OK to close the window and place your new option
   on the Amplitude submenu. (The selection is not changed
   until you select the new option from the submenu.)

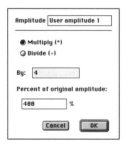

Figure 12-17 *You create your own User Amplitude setting in this dialog
box.*

Tip

Replace User Amplitude 1 with the user amplitude setting you'll use more often, because that option has a shortcut key combo assigned to it, ⌘+G.

When you're increasing amplitude, especially when you're multiplying it by a factor of 2 or greater, it's easy to get extremes that are so loud that clipping occurs. You can spot possible clipping problems in the waveform window when the graph touches the top and bottom of the window. One way to avoid clipping is to *normalize* the selection. Normalizing amplifies the sound just below the point where it would get clipped. Choose Sound ⇨ Normalize ⇨ Integer if you want SndSampler to multiply the amplitude by an integer only. This eliminates distortion but might not produce the loudest sound. Choose Sound ⇨ Normalize ⇨ Fraction to permit SndSampler to select a fractional multiplier for the loudest possible sound, with some possible distortion.

If you want to make your sound fade in, select the beginning portion of the file and choose Sound ⇨ Fade In. SndSampler adjusts the amplitude of the selection so it increases from zero to its original volume. You control the speed of the fade by the size of the portion you select. Similarly, to fade out at the end, select an ending portion and then choose Fade Out.

Adding sound effects

At last we come to the fun part — adding in sound effects. They are all located in the top section of the FX menu. Five of the effects — Echo, Reverb, Chorus, Flange, and Tremolo — open submenus with five User Effect options. The first option on each submenu has a shortcut key combo. The last effect, Backwards, simply reverses the selection and needs no options.

Caution

While SndSampler is performing a complex effect on a large sound selection, you can cancel it by pressing Escape. But if you cancel it, you could corrupt the original sound. Always choose Undo after canceling any effect in midstream, just to make sure the original sound was not corrupted.

Echo

The Echo command cascades a submenu with five commands: My Echo and User Effect 2 through 5. Any of the five submenu commands opens the Echo dialog box shown in Figure 12-18, where you can set the parameters for the echo. Enter a name in the Echo FX box to replace the name on the Echo submenu. The Decay Factor indicates how fast the echoes die away. The higher the number, the faster they die. The Delay value determines the time between echoes. Enable Auto Extend to increase the length of the file to enable the last echo to die away.

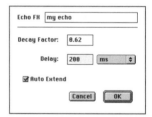

Figure 12-18 *You specify the parameters for an echo effect in the Echo dialog box.*

Reverb

Reverb provides a smoother, more random echo effect, much like being in a large hall. Figure 12-19 shows the dialog box that opens when you choose any one of the five User Effect options for the first time.

Figure 12-19 *You set the options for a reverb effect in this dialog box.*

The Gain Factor determines the mix of the original sound to the reverb sound. Raise the gain factor to hear more of the original sound and less of the reverb sound. Or lower it to give more emphasis to the reverb sound. When you use a low factor, it sounds as if you are far away from the sound source in a large hall or amphitheater.

The Delay indicates how much delay is built into the reverb effect, in milliseconds. The longer the delay, the more extreme the reverb effect will be. This is easier to understand if you consider a single echo effect. Suppose you holler "hello" down a well and the echo returns to you in about one second. You know it's not a deep well. But if the echo doesn't return to you for 20 seconds or longer, you get the feeling of a deep well. You can create similar feelings of size with your reverb by adjusting the length of the delay before the echoing starts.

Auto Extend is directly related to Delay. Each echo that makes up the reverb dies away at the end. If you want to hear the last ones die, enable Auto Extend so that SndSampler can extend the length of the selection to make room for the dying echoes. If you don't use Auto Extend, the echoes cut off when the selection ends, which might not sound natural. Even if you don't enable Auto Extend, SndSampler extends the length of the selection by the length of the delay.

The two filters, Allpass and Comb, affect the way in which the reverb is calculated. It's a matter of experimentation to decide which provides the effect you're looking for. By the way, you can use the reverb function many times on a selection to compound the echoing effects and combine the Allpass effect with the Comb effect.

Chorus

Chorus makes the selection sound like it comes from multiple voices. You can choose the number of voices (up to 20). To create the multiple voice effect, a slight delay is used between voices. You can set the size of the delay for the first voice, such as 10 milliseconds. But to make things realistic, that value will be varied somewhat for additional voices. You can also set the speed that the delay is varied, with 100 percent being the default speed.

Flange

Flange provides a somewhat psychedelic effect, with the sound speeding up, slowing down, and speeding up again. The flanged signal is mixed with the original signal to produce the final result. To me, it sounds like the file is slightly damaged, but sometimes you want that effect. As with Chorus, you specify both Delay and Speed. Delay specifies in milliseconds how far behind the original track the flanged track begins. Speed determines the rate at which the flanged track varies in speed. You also specify Gain Factor to control the mix between the original sound and the flanged sound. Auto Extend extends the selection to permit the delayed flanged track to join up smoothly with the next section (or the end of the recording).

Tremolo

Tremolo mixes a tremolo or vibrato effect into the selection by rapidly varying the amplitude of the original wave. You can choose the frequency of the variation; the higher the frequency, the more the tremolo effect. You can also set the minimum amplitude of the variations; the amplitude varies from 100 percent down to your minimum. The Smooth Junction option returns the amplitude to 100 percent at the end of the selection to phase smoothly into the next part of the sound.

Undoing, redoing, and reverting

Happily, SndSampler includes an Undo option to remove the previous editing action. Choose Edit ⇨ Undo *action*, where *action* is your most recent edit, such as Undo Delete or Undo Echo. You'll find Undo handy when you're experimenting with a sound effect to see what its various settings do. Finding the exact right combination of settings can often take a lot of trial and error.

If you change your mind again after undoing an edit, you can redo it by choosing Edit ⇨ Redo *action*. Undo and Redo keep track of the most recent action only. If you want to undo a whole series of edits, you may need to choose File ⇨ Revert to Saved to get back to the last saved version of the file. This removes all editing that you haven't saved.

Saving files

Eventually, you'll want to save your edited sound. Use File ⇨ Save to save the selection (only) in the current file. Use File ⇨ Save As to save the selection (only) as a new file, which becomes the current file. Use File ⇨ Save In to save the current selection in another file's resource fork, the opposite of the Extract command. Use File ⇨ Export to export the current selection to another format, such as WAV or AU.

By the way, unlike most programs, SndSampler lets you undo a save command. Saving a sound saves only the selected portion. If you want to recover the part that wasn't saved, undo the save. This restores the former sound in memory only. The version on disk still reflects the last save. But now you can change the selection and save it again.

Caution

Be especially careful with the File ⇨ Save command, as SndSampler saves or exports only the current selection. Since only the selection is saved, you might replace the whole sound with just part of it. Fortunately, you can undo saves to recover sounds you accidentally damage this way.

A final word on SndSampler

This chapter has explained the SndSampler features that you most likely want to use at the beginning. But eventually, you'll probably want to try out some other features, such as the tone generator or the Pitch Bend feature. SndSampler comes with a User's Guide that can help get you started with a new feature. Unfortunately, it often breaks into jargon that only an audio engineer could love or understand. But it never hurts to experiment. Just keep trying out options and undoing them until you have created the effect you want. It's a fun program, and I hope you'll have fun with it.

What's Next?

Nothing's next — you have finished the book. Congratulations! I hope you are already having more fun with your computer and the Internet sound. Please write to me at judinorth@aol.com with any comments, questions, or criticisms. I really do read and answer my e-mail!

Appendix A

What's on the CD-ROM

The CD-ROM that accompanies this book contains more than 20 applications and plug-ins for Windows and Macintosh computers. This appendix describes each program. To find a particular application on the CD-ROM, open the Windows Software or Macintosh Software folder and then open the folder with the desired program's name.

Windows Software

Beatnik 1.3.2

Beatnik is an audio plug-in that handles many of the standard audio formats such as MIDI, WAV, AU, AIFF, and several of the MOD formats. It also plays its own Rich Music File (RMF) format. The version included here works with Netscape Navigator but not Internet Explorer. Check the Headspace Web site to see if the Beatnik ActiveX control has been released.

System requirements: Windows 95/98/NT, Pentium 90, Netscape Navigator 3.01 or higher.

Shareware info: Beatnik is freeware, but it expires in 180 days.

Web site: `http://www.headspace.com`.

Installation: Double-click `Beatnik132.exe`.

CD/Spectrum Pro 3.4 – Psychedelic Screen Saver 4.0 – Kinemorphic Screen Saver 3.0

This virtual stereo rack system from Synthesoft includes players for CDs, WAVs, MP3s, and RealAudio, a sound mixer, a spectrum analyzer, and a visual display of the screen saver output (when the screen saver isn't running). You can program the CD player and create playlists of audio files. The CD player downloads track information from the online CD database (CDDB). The Kinemorphics 3D screen saver creates animated 3D patterns synchronized with the music played by CD/Spectrum Pro. The Psychedelic screen saver is an outstanding kaleidoscopic screen saver that synchronizes with the music played by CD/Spectrum Pro. Both screen savers give you a nearly overwhelming amount of control in creating your own patterns.

System requirements: Windows 95/98/NT 4.*x*; Kinemorphics requires Open GL 1.1 or higher, which is included in the installer. The software will run on a 486, but a Pentium 90 or higher is recommended for the visuals.

Shareware info: Registration fee $20 U.S. for each component or $30 U.S. for CD/Spectrum Pro plus one screen saver; the programs display reminder messages until you register them.

Web site: http://www.synthesoft.com.

Installation: To install with Kinemorphics screen saver, double-click Kinemorphic.OpenGL30.exe. To install with Psychedelic screen saver, double-click Psychedelic40.exe.

Cool Edit 96

Cool Edit 96 from Syntrillium is a sound editor that can record, play, edit, mix, and convert WAV, AIFF, Macintosh SND (only PCM encoding), AU, Raw PCM, RealAudio 3.0, MP1, and MP2, and other sound formats. Special effects include Reverb, Delay, Echo, 3D Echo Chamber, Flanging, and Distortion. Other transformations include Reverse, Inverse, adding silence, and adjusting the amplitude, time and pitch. You can generate specific tones by frequency and amplitude, DTMF tones (telephone touch tones), brain wave sounds (sounds that induce relaxation, sleep, and meditation), and noise. You can use a sound clip as a sound sample to generate music. Filters help you get rid of specific frequencies or noise.

System requirements: Windows 3.1/95/98/NT, 4MB RAM, 2MB free hard disk space; a sound card, speakers or headphones, and mouse are recommended.

Shareware info: The registration fee is $25 U.S. for the Lite version or $50 U.S. for the full version; until you register Cool Edit 96, you can use only a few functions per session.

Web site: `http://www.syntrillium.com/cooledit`.

Installation: Double-click `CoolEdit96.exe`.

Cool Edit is described in Chapters 11 and 12.

Crescendo 3.0

LiveUpdate's Crescendo is a browser plug-in MIDI player that is capable of playing MIDIs before they completely download, by using streaming technology. You can detach the plug-in from a Web page and float it on your desktop to continue listening to a MIDI while you browse other sites. It installs as a plug-in for Netscape Navigator 2.0 or higher and as an ActiveX control for Microsoft Internet Explorer 3.0 and higher.

System requirements: Windows 95, 98, or NT, Netscape Navigator or Microsoft Internet Explorer. The Crescendo 3.0 ActiveX control for Windows works with Internet Explorer 3.0 and higher.

Web site: `http://www.liveupdate.com`.

Shareware info: Crescendo us freeware.

Installation: Double-click `Crescendo30.exe`.

Crescendo is described in Chapter 8.

DigiBand Radio 3.3.0

DigiBand Radio for Windows from DigiBand is a RealAudio player with a push-button interface to your favorite RealAudio Internet radio stations. You can program up to 100 push buttons arranged in five banks. It provides an updateable list of hundreds of operating Internet radio channels. A scan feature lets you scan stations to find one that you want to listen to. Please note that this version of DigiBand Radio does not support the new RealAudio G2 standard. Check DigiBand's Web site to see if their new player has been released.

System requirements: Windows 95/98/NT, 486-DX2/66 or better, 4MB of RAM, 5MB of hard drive space, sound card, and 14.4 Kbps modem (28.8 Kbps recommended).

Shareware info: The registration fee $18.95 U.S. and includes a 15-day trial.

Web site: `http://www.digiband.com`.

Installation: Double-click `DigiBandradio330.exe`.

Digital Peace (Light version)

Digital Peace from the Plastic Factory plays soft environmental WAVs (rain forest, forest stream, ocean) continuously while you work. It's a nice change of pace.

System Requirements: Windows 96/98/NT and a sound card.

Shareware info: The registration fee is $10 U.S.

Web site: `http://www.rmaonline.net/hippies/theplasticfactory/`.

Installation: Double-click `DigitalPeaceLight10.exe`.

iQ 1.17

iQ from QSound Labs, Inc., enhances all sampled sounds on your Windows system, including RealAudio, for a 3D effect. (It cannot enhance ADPCM encoded files, though.) It enhances sound played by your standalone players, your Web browsers, and games.

System requirements: Windows 95/98, Pentium 90 or higher, 8MB of RAM, and stereo sound card.

Shareware info: The registration fee is $24.95 U.S.

Web site: http:\\www.qsound.ca.

Installation: Double-click iQ117.exe.

Jet-Audio 3.12

Designed to resemble a stereo rack system, Jet-Audio from COWON includes players for sampled files (including MP3s), MIDIs and other synthesizer files, RealAudio, audio CDs, and digital videos. You can organize your sound files into albums and create playlists. The CD player downloads track information from the online CD database (CDDB). Records in WAV and RealAudio formats. Other features include a volume mixer with attenuation switch, graphic equalizer, digital signal processor, spectrum analyzer, remote control, and sleep timer.

System requirements: Windows 95/98/NT; 486-DX2/66 or higher (Pentium 90 or higher recommended to play MP3 or RealAudio); 8MB RAM (16MB recommended); 4MB disk space.

Shareware info: The registration fee is $29 U.S. Software expires after 30-day trial.

Web site: http://www.cowon.com.

Installation: Double-click Jet-Audio312.exe.

Jet-Audio described in Chapters 2, 3, and Appendix C on the CD-ROM.

Media Blaze 98 1.5-SP1

Media Blaze from Dryad Systems helps you manage your sound files when they're starting to overwhelm you.

System Requirements: Windows 95/98/NT.

Shareware info: The registration fee is $14.95 U.S. and includes 30-day free trial.

Web site: http://www.dryad.com.

Installation: Double-click MediaBlaze98.exe.

mIRC 5.41

mIRC by Khaled Mardam-Bey gives you the ability to chat on Internet Relay Chat (IRC) with a Windows GUI interface. Its menus and dialog boxes make it easy to enter those Byzantine IRC commands, including the ones to play, hear, and trade chat sounds.

System requirements: mIRC needs Windows 95 or 98 and your own Internet access, such as an ISP account, that provides a 32-bit winsock.

Web site: `http://www.mirc.co.uk`.

Shareware info: The registration fee is $20 U.S. and includes a 30-day free trial.

Installation: Double-click `mIRC.exe`.

mIRC is described in Chapter 6.

QuickTime 3

QuickTime is Apple's multimedia player. It acts as both a stand-alone player and a browser plug-in. The PictureViewer component displays still pictures, and the MoviePlayer component plays movies and sounds. It plays audio files in AIFF, AIFC, WAV, AU, MP2, MIDI, and KAR format. It uses the Roland SoundCanvas wavetable for MIDI files.

System requirements: QuickTime requires Windows 95, 98, NT 4.0; a 486-DX2/66 or higher, 16MB RAM, and a Sound Blaster-compatible card. Also, the following are recommended for better performance: DirectX 3.0, DirectDraw, and DirectSound.

Shareware info: QuickTime is freeware.

Web site: `http://www.apple.com/quicktime/`.

Installation: Double-click `QuickTime3.exe`.

QuickTime is described in Chapters 3 and 8.

RealPlayer 5.0

This player from RealNetworks plays multimedia streaming presentations. RealNetworks' Web site provides links to sites that are broadcasting live or recorded presentations in RealPlayer format.

System requirements: Windows 95, 98, or NT. Hardware requirements depend on modem speed and the RealPlayer components you want to use. Maximum requirements are Pentium 166, 16MB of RAM, 28.8 Kbps modem, and 4MB of hard drive space. Check RealNetworks' Web site for specific requirements.

Web site: `http://www.real.com`.

Shareware info: RealPlayer is freeware.

Installation: Double-click `rp32_50.exe`.

RealPlayer is described in Chapter 7.

The RealPlayer is included under license from RealNetworks, Inc. Copyright 1995–1998, RealNetworks, Inc. All rights reserved.

StreamWorks Player 3.1

The StreamWorks Player from Xing Technology Corporation plays multimedia presentations in StreamWorks XSM format as well as audio files in MP3 format. It installs as a plug-in for Netscape Navigator and an ActiveX control for Internet Explorer 3.0 and higher.

System requirements: Windows 95/98/NT, 486-DX2/66 processor (Pentium 166 recommended) with 16MB RAM, sound card (16-bit sound card recommended). A Video Accelerated VGA card with current DirectDraw drivers is recommended for playing StreamWorks video.

Web site: `http://www.xingtech.com`.

Shareware info: StreamWorks is freeware.

Installation: Double-click `streamworksplayer31.exe`.

StreamWorks is described in Chapter 7.

Ted's Sounds

Ted's Sounds from Ted Tatman is a large collection of WAVs that are appropriate for AOL sound events, chat rooms, and many other uses.

System requirements: The ability to play WAVs.

Shareware info: Ted's Sounds is freeware.

Web site: http://members.aol.com/tedt13/.

Installation: No installation is needed. All the sound files contained in the Ted's Sounds folder in the Windows Software folder on the CD-ROM. Double-click a sound to listen to it. You can copy it to your hard drive using Windows Explorer or My Computer.

WaveEvents 2.0

WaveEvents by Gregory Jones makes it easier to edit your Windows 95 or 98 sound events. You can edit sound events for specific applications, screen savers, and shortcuts. You can also randomize sound event assignments.

System requirements: Windows 95 or 98.

Shareware info: WaveEvents includes a 30-day tryout. Some functions are disabled until you pay the $10 U.S. registration fee.

Web site: http://www.waveevents.com.

Installation: Double-click WaveEvents20.exe.

WaveEvents is described in Chapter 4.

WaVGeT 1.7

This add-on for mIRC and ViRC helps you organize, play, and trade massive amounts of sound files. It issues sound commands for you, keeps track of sounds that have been played that you don't have, automatically requests sound files from other chatters, and automatically sends sound files to other requesters. It even automatically thanks people who send you sound files. WaVGeT also gives you the ability to play and hear MP3 and RealAudio sound files in chat rooms. It also includes a text macro feature.

System requirements: Windows 95/98/NT; mIRC 3.92, 4.*xx*, 5.*xx*, or ViRC.

Web site: `http://www.wavget.com`.

Shareware info: Registration fee $10 U.S.; no limitation on the tryout period, but it nags you often to register.

Installation: Double-click `WaVGeT17.exe`.

WaVGeT is described in Chapter 6.

Macintosh Software

Agent Audio 1.2

Agent Audio from Clixsounds lets you manage System 7 snd resources. You can view and play sound resources from programs and other files, convert sound resources to standalone System 7 sound files, replace snd resources in a program's resource fork, and archive snd resources.

System requirements: Mac OS 7.1 or higher; 2MB of RAM; 2MB space on hard drive.

Shareware info: Registration fee $12 U.S., one week trial period.

Web site: `http://www.clixsounds.com`.

Installation: Double-click `AgentAudio12`.

Agent Audio is described in Chapter 5.

Beatnik 1.3.2

Beatnik is an audio player that handles many of the standard audio formats such as MIDI, WAV, AU, AIFF, and several of the MOD formats. It also plays its own Rich Music File (RMF) format. The version included here works with Netscape Navigator but not Internet Explorer. Check the Headspace Web site to see if the Beatnik ActiveX control has been released.

System requirements: A Power PC running Sound Manager 3.1 or higher and Netscape Navigator 3.01 or higher.

Shareware info: Freeware, but expires in 180 days.

Web site: `http://www.headspace.com`.

Installation: Double-click `Beatnik132`.

Crescendo 2.0

LiveUpdate's Crescendo 2.0 for Macintosh is a browser plug-in MIDI player that is capable of playing MIDIs before they completely download, using streaming technology. You can detach the plug-in from a Web page and float it on your desktop to continue listening to a MIDI while you browse other sites.

System requirements: System 7.1 and higher and QuickTime 2.1 or higher.

Web site: `http://www.liveupdate.com`.

Shareware info: Freeware.

Installation: Double-click `Crescendo20`.

Crescendo is described in Chapter 8.

QuickTime 3

QuickTime is Apple's multimedia player. It acts as both a stand-alone player and a browser plug-in. The PictureViewer component displays still pictures, and the MoviePlayer component plays movies and sounds. It plays audio files in AIFF, AIFC, WAV, AU, MP2, MIDI, and KAR format. It uses the Roland SoundCanvas wavetable for MIDI files.

System requirements: Mac OS 7.1 or higher; requires 16MB RAM for PowerPC or 8MB RAM for 68K machines; 68K-based computers must also support Color QuickDraw.

Shareware info: Freeware.

Web site: http://www.apple.com/quicktime/.

Installation: Double-click QuickTime3.

QuickTime is described in Chapters 3 and 8.

RealPlayer 5.0

This player from RealNetworks plays multimedia streaming presentations that incorporate RealAudio, RealVideo, RealFlash, RealPix, and RealText streams. It installs as a standalone player, a browser plug-in for Netscape Navigator 2.0 and higher and Microsoft Internet Explorer 2.x, and an ActiveX control for Internet Explorer 3.x and higher. RealNetworks' Web site provides links to sites that are broadcasting live or recorded presentations in RealPlayer format.

System requirements: Macintosh System 7.0 or higher, Power PC; the latest release of Sound Manager is recommended.

Web site: http://www.real.com.

Shareware info: Freeware.

Installation: Double-click realplayer_installer.

SndSampler 3.5.2

SndSampler by Alan Glenn and M. Q. Edison is a sound editor that can record and edit sounds in AIFF or System 7 SND format. It can also import WAVs, AUs, Sun, NeXT, and raw PCM audio to AIFF format; and export to WAV, Sun, NeXT, and raw PCM format. Special effects include Reverse, Echo, Reverb, Tremolo, and Chorus.

System requirements: System 7.0 or higher; if your Mac doesn't have 16-bit audio hardware, you must have Sound Manager 3.0 or later installed in order to play 16-bit sounds.

Shareware info: Registration fee $20 U.S., 30-day trial.

Web site: None.

Installation: Double-click `SndSampler352`.

SndSampler is described in Chapters 11 and 12.

SoundApp

This sound player by Norman Franke plays System 7 snd resources and SND files, AU, WAV, AIFF, AIFC, MIDI, MOD, and more. It can convert any of these sound formats to System 7, sound suitcase, AIFF, AU, and a few other formats. It can also change a sound file's audio properties.

System requirements: Mac OS 7.0 or higher and Sound Manager 3.1 or higher; requires QuickTime 2.0 or higher to play QuickTime movies and to convert to and from QuickTime formats.

Shareware info: Freeware.

Web site: None.

Installation: Double-click `SoundApp`.

SoundApp is described in Chapters 2, 3, and 5.

StreamWorks Player 2.04

The StreamWorks Player from Xing Technology Corporation plays multimedia presentations in StreamWorks XSM format as well as audio files in MP3 format. It installs as a plug-in for Netscape Navigator and an ActiveX control for Internet Explorer 3.0 and higher.

Shareware info: StreamWorks is freeware.

Web site: `http://www.xingtech.com`.

Installation: Double-click StreamWorksPlayer204.hq.

StreamWorks is described in Chapter 7.

Index

Numbers

.669 file extension, 55

A

ActiveMovie, 31–32
ActiveX, 172–173
  Crescendo, 180
ADPCM (Adaptive Differential PCM), 11
Agent Audio 1.2, 301–302, 111-114
AIFF (Audio Interchange File Format), 22–24
A-law, 12
amplitude, 3
analog sound, 5
anti-virus programs, 170
AOL (America Online), 117
  add-on programs, 123
  auditoriums and sound, 123
  basic sound events, 118–120
  Buddy List sounds, 120
  CELEBRITY VOICES keyword, 121
  compressed files, 121
  Door theme, 120
  e-mailing sounds, 219–223
  FILESEARCH keyword, 120
  finding sounds, 120–121
  Gallery of Celebrities, 121
  MMS keyword, 120
  newsreaders, 205
  PCSOUND keyword, 120
  playing chat room sounds, 121–122
  PowerTools, 123–126
  reassigning sound events, 126
  SDW theme, 120
  sound events, 118–120
  sound files, 118–126
  Windows systems, 119
Apple menu ⮞ Control Panels ⮞ Monitors & Sound command, 103
Apple Web site, 299, 303–304
  downloading PlainTalk, 106
AppleCD Audio Player, 15
application sound events, 63
ATT (attenuation switch), 39
AU files, 24–25
audio clips sample size, 9
audio codecs
  ADPCM (Adaptive Differential PCM), 11
  A-law, 12
  compression, 10–11
  encoding files, 10–14
  MACE (Macintosh Audio Compression and Expansion), 13
  MPEG (Motion Picture Experts Group), 13–14
  µ-law encoding, 12
  PCM (Pulse Code Modulation), 11
  TrueSpeech, 13

Continued

Continued

IDG BOOKS WORLDWIDE, INC.
END-USER LICENSE AGREEMENT

READ THIS. You should carefully read these terms and conditions before opening the software packet(s) included with this book ("Book"). This is a license agreement ("Agreement") between you and IDG Books Worldwide, Inc. ("IDGB"). By opening the accompanying software packet(s), you acknowledge that you have read and accept the following terms and conditions. If you do not agree and do not want to be bound by such terms and conditions, promptly return the Book and the unopened software packet(s) to the place you obtained them for a full refund.

1. **License Grant.** IDGB grants to you (either an individual or entity) a nonexclusive license to use one copy of the enclosed software program(s) (collectively, the "Software") solely for your own personal or business purposes on a single computer (whether a standard computer or a workstation component of a multiuser network). The Software is in use on a computer when it is loaded into temporary memory (RAM) or installed into permanent memory (hard disk, CD-ROM, or other storage device). IDGB reserves all rights not expressly granted herein.

2. **Ownership.** IDGB is the owner of all right, title, and interest, including copyright, in and to the compilation of the Software recorded on the disk(s) or CD-ROM ("Software Media"). Copyright to the individual programs recorded on the Software Media is owned by the author or other authorized copyright owner of each program. Ownership of the Software and all proprietary rights relating thereto remain with IDGB and its licensers.

3. **Restrictions On Use and Transfer.**

    (a) You may only (i) make one copy of the Software for backup or archival purposes, or (ii) transfer the Software to a single hard disk, provided that you keep the original for backup or archival purposes. You may not (i) rent or lease the Software, (ii) copy or reproduce the Software through a LAN or other network system or through any computer subscriber system or bulletin-board system, or (iii) modify, adapt, or create derivative works based on the Software.

    (b) You may not reverse engineer, decompile, or disassemble the Software. You may transfer the Software and user documentation on a permanent basis, provided that the transferee agrees to accept the terms and conditions of this Agreement and you retain no copies. If the Software is an update or has been updated, any transfer must include the most recent update and all prior versions.

4. **Restrictions On Use of Individual Programs.** You must follow the individual requirements and restrictions detailed for each individual program in the "What's on the CD-ROM" appendix of this Book. These limitations are also contained in the individual license agreements recorded on the Software Media. These limitations may include a requirement that after using the program for a specified period of time, the user must pay a registration fee or discontinue use. By opening the Software packet(s), you will be agreeing to abide by the licenses and restrictions for these individual programs that aredetailed in the "What's on the CD-ROM" appendix and on the Software Media. None of the material on this Software Media or listed in this Book may ever be redistributed, in original or modified form, for commercial purposes.

5. **Limited Warranty.**

   (a) IDGB warrants that the Software and Software Media are free from defects in materials and workmanship under normal use for a period of sixty (60) days from the date of purchase of this Book. If IDGB receives notification within the warranty period of defects in materials or workmanship, IDGB will replace the defective Software Media.

   (b) IDGB AND THE AUTHOR OF THE BOOK DISCLAIM ALL OTHER WARRANTIES, EXPRESS OR IMPLIED, INCLUDING WITHOUT LIMITATION IMPLIED WARRANTIES OF MERCHANTABILITY AND FITNESS FOR A PARTICULAR PUR-POSE, WITH RESPECT TO THE SOFTWARE, THE PROGRAMS, THE SOURCE CODE CONTAINED THEREIN, AND/OR THE TECHNIQUES DESCRIBED IN THIS BOOK. IDGB DOES NOT WARRANT THAT THE FUNCTIONS CONTAINED IN THE SOFT-WARE WILL MEET YOUR REQUIREMENTS OR THAT THE OPER-ATION OF THE SOFTWARE WILL BE ERROR FREE.

   (c) This limited warranty gives you specific legal rights, and you may have other rights that vary from jurisdiction to jurisdiction.

6. **Remedies.**

   (a) IDGB's entire liability and your exclusive remedy for defects in materials and workmanship shall be limited to replacement of the Software Media, which may be returned to IDGB with a copy of your receipt at the following address: Software Media Fulfillment Department, Attn.: *WAVs, MIDIs, & RealAudio*, IDG Books Worldwide, Inc., 7260 Shadeland Station, Ste. 100, Indianapolis, IN 46256, or call 1-800-762-2974. Please

   allow three to four weeks for delivery. This Limited Warranty is void if failure of the Software Media has resulted from accident, abuse, or misapplication. Any replacement Software Media will be warranted for the remainder of the original warranty period or thirty (30) days, whichever is longer.

   (b) In no event shall IDGB or the author be liable for any damages whatsoever (including without limitation damages for loss of business profits, business interruption, loss of business information, or any other pecuniary loss) arising from the use of or inability to use the Book or the Software, even if IDGB has been advised of the possibility of such damages.

   (c) Because some jurisdictions do not allow the exclusion or limitation of liability for consequential or incidental damages, the above limitation or exclusion may not apply to you.

7. **U.S. Government Restricted Rights.** Use, duplication, or disclosure of the Software by the U.S. Government is subject to restrictions stated in paragraph (c)(1)(ii) of the Rights in Technical Data and Computer Software clause of DFARS 252.227-7013, and in subparagraphs (a) through (d) of the Commercial Computer — Restricted Rights clause at FAR 52.227-19, and in similar clauses in the NASA FAR supplement, when applicable.

8. **General.** This Agreement constitutes the entire understanding of the parties and revokes and supersedes all prior agreements, oral or written, between them and may not be modified or amended except in a writing signed by both parties hereto that specifically refers to this Agreement. This Agreement shall take precedence over any other documents that may be in conflict herewith. If any one or more provisions contained in this Agreement are held by any court or tribunal to be invalid, illegal, or otherwise unenforceable, each and every other provision shall remain in full force and effect.

CD-ROM Installation Instructions

Installing software from the CD-ROM is simple.

1. Refer to Appendix A to make sure your system meets the hardware and software requirements. (Also read the shareware information, if any, to make sure that you agree to the terms of the installation.)

2. Insert the disc in your CD-ROM drive.

3. Locate and open the folder containing the program you want to install.

4. Double-click the program icon to start the installation program.

5. Follow the directions displayed by the installation program.